What Others Are Saying a

Africa—the very mention of the name of this vast continent conjures up images of huge, rolling grasslands; hot, dusty deserts; huge herds of wandering wildlife; and exotic—even romantic—red sunsets that fill the wide skies. These sunsets usher in the nighttime sounds unique to this great empty land that is suffering from such extremities that they overwhelm you in simply looking at them and in trying to figure out—"What can we do to help solve these problems?" The sights, smells, and sounds become indelibly engraved in your mind and saturate your subconscious so that once seen and heard, they never can be forgotten.

When you are standing in the midst of tens of thousands of people in the slums that populate the continent's urban centers, you might have a difficult time hearing the Still Small Voice of God that asks you to leave the safety of all you know and hold dear in the West and go bury yourself in this forgotten land—the graveyard of missionaries in years gone by. Yet God still does that; He did it to two such people—Jamie and Lea Peters.

When I was privileged to visit in Burundi with the Peters, it was during the civil war that spread like malaria throughout that region. I was able to witness firsthand the ravages of senseless genocide, the unbridled lust for power, and the rape of the land. I knew then, as I walked and talked with Jamie and Lea, that I had encountered people who definitely were called by God. For them, being in Africa was no passing, romantic fancy. Rather it was a life-and-death response to give themselves without reservation to the unswerving call of being "Jesus with skin on" to the people of the land who had been inoculated with a syncretism of Western-style religion and tribal animism but never really had found the liberating truth in the person of Jesus.

God always takes ordinary men and women who will say "YES, LORD!" He chooses to use them as signal lighthouses to show people who still are in darkness that freedom and wholeness can be found only in Him and in His Eternal, Unchanging Kingdom. God chooses to take such ordinary people and through them do extraordinary things.

In writing this story of their journey in Africa thus far Jamie and Lea have given you an invitation into the most intimate and sacred spaces of their hearts. Take care in reading; do not trample on that which you read—it is holy ground and should be respected as such. Hopefully your reading about this journey will cause you to take up The Call He has given to you, as He has to all believers, and will enable you to walk in tune with Him wherever He plants you in His field.

Dr. Kevin Dyson, President
New Covenant International University and Theological Seminary

I have been in relationship with Jamie and Lea Peters throughout their missionary journey and service. Their journey has been incredible. I have watched them navigate with wisdom, integrity, grace, and dignity through all the unique challenges they have faced as the Lord has favored them to bring quantifiable change into the lives and communities in which they have served. I am sure your life will be affected and inspired as their journey is rehearsed and as you travel with them through the pages of this book. The Peters' singular passion is to win souls and to make disciples by transforming lives through communicating the gospel of the Kingdom in spiritual, educational, and practical ways. So get ready . . . to be inspired, challenged, encouraged, and changed, because their story is genuine and inspirational and their passion is infectious! This book is a must-read for every Christian who has a desire to respond or to know more about world evangelization and about fulfilling the Great Commission.

David Briggs
Missions Director, Trinity Church International
Lake Worth, FL

No Retreat–No Regrets is a must-read for anyone who desires to follow the God Plan for his or her life. Jamie and Lea have not just written this story; they have lived the story. Your faith will rise as step by step you follow their journey. I've known them since 1988 and many times have told them that their faith is spoken of throughout the whole earth. They both are my heroes.

Dale Gentry
Breakout Prayer Network
Fort Worth, TX

For many years I have known Jamie and Lea; their passion for mission never has lessened; it is infectious. This couple is the real deal. The Peters are not theorists; they are practitioners living out in their own lives the challenges of which they speak in serving mission. Billy Graham was quoted as saying, "I preach the gospel at the drop of a hat; if no one drops the hat, I still preach the gospel." This is true of Jamie and Lea with regard to mission. Read this book and you will be challenged.

Norman Barnes
International speaker and founder of Links International, UK

Almost 40 years ago, when I was in Bible school studying for the ministry, a missionary spoke at one of our chapel services and declared these unforgettable words: "If God ever calls you to be a missionary, never stoop to become a President!" Jamie and Lea Peters have ascended to and are traveling the highway of missionary calling in Africa with no thought of turning back. Their journey is amazing because they are amazing; their story will inspire you because they live inspired to reach Africa with the gospel of Jesus Christ. Indeed Amy and I count journeying alongside Jamie and Lea in serving the Master on this beloved continent for the glory of God to be a great privilege.

Don (and Amy) Matheny, senior pastor
Nairobi Lighthouse Church
Nairobi, Kenya

Ever since I met the Peters in 1988, I've had a great respect and admiration for them. In fact I've often said, "When I grow up, I want to be like Jamie and Lea Peters." The word hero is thrown around a lot, but this incredible husband and wife, by their courage, faithfulness, and impact in so many people's lives, truly exemplify the word. Having the privilege of spending much time with them in Africa—from days of war and revival in Burundi to church planting in Tanzania to expanding ministry into Malawi—before my very eyes I have seen many of the amazing stories in this book be lived out. I am ecstatic that they now will be available for the world to experience. To say you will enjoy this book is an understatement. Soak it in, be challenged by it, be encouraged by it, but certainly be CHANGED by it.

Duane (and Kris) White
Founders of Beyond These Shores Missions Network
Lead pastors of The Bridge Church, Denton, TX

Youth, energy, drive, desire . . . in some ways they have surpassed us [senior missionaries]. And that we enjoy seeing. To mention only one way this has happened: my wife and I speak only two languages, our daughter and granddaughters three . . . but this husband and wife who won't slow down speak five and six. May they ever increase and abound in more and more of the vision God has put within them.

Ralph and Shirley Hagemeier
Bible Outreach Ministries
Democratic Republic of Congo

NO RETREAT— NO REGRETS

One Family's No-Exit Strategy While Serving in Africa

JAMIE & LEA PETERS

 CrossHouse

CrossHouse Publishing
P. O. Box 461592
Garland, TX 75046-1592
www.crosshousepublishing.org

ISBN: 978-1-934749-88-3
Library of Congress: 2010932865

Except where otherwise indicated, all Scripture taken from the Holy Bible,
New King James Version, copyright 1979 and 1980
by Thomas Nelson Publishers

Cover design by Dennis Davidson
Illustrations by Roger Hall

To our children—Tom, Mandy, Steve, and Andreya

May you live lives of no retreat so that you have no regrets.
We love you and are proud to be your parents.

Mom and Dad

*For what is our hope, or joy, or crown of rejoicing? Is it not even
you in the presence of our Lord Jesus Christ at His coming?
For you are our glory and joy* (1 Thess. 2:19-20).

Foreword

When writing a foreword for your loved ones, one easily could be biased. However, I personally know the hardships these family members throughout the years have encountered. My wife and I have been intimately involved in standing on God's promises for them—and for us, as parents and grandparents—during some very dangerous and life-threatening times. Despite all the difficulties Jamie and Lea have maintained a strong desire to walk by faith in God's promises as well as to fulfill their commitment to do the will of God. Even when their lives appeared to be in jeopardy, this husband and wife held fast to their assignment from heaven.

Jamie and Lea Peters were serving in Bujumbura, Burundi, when tribal war broke out there and in neighboring Rwanda—warfare that killed hundreds of thousands of people. When news of an impending attack on the city of Bujumbura was received, the American Embassy informed all missionary families to fly out of the country. At first Jamie and Lea considered leaving, but after they sought God's will as they prayed, they both believed they needed to stay. After the last transport plane took off, they were among the last missionary families remaining in the country.

While Jamie and Lea were there, God opened a door for them to obtain an audience with the president of Burundi. Jamie delivered to the president a Word from God, including an encouragement from the Lord for this official to remain steadfast, because God was with him. Much of the Word that was delivered to the president that day has been fulfilled. After many years of war, peace has begun to make its way back to Burundi.

In the midst of pioneering churches on the continent of Africa throughout the last 23 years (as of this writing) and giving apostolic oversight to them, Jamie and Lea have reared three godly children who today are actively involved in ministry. Recently they added a new addition to the family as they adopted a baby girl born in Malawi.

At this writing Jamie, Lea, and family are serving in Lilongwe, Malawi, as they pioneer another work. Truly the signs of an apostle have been wrought by this couple.

No Retreat–No Regrets is an excellent book that will encourage your heart and cause you to rise up and say, "God will do it again."

Pastor Tom Peters, D.Min.
Trinity Church International
Lake Worth, FL

Acknowledgements

S ince we first began serving in Africa in 1987, we have experienced God's protection, guidance, and provision. This largely is because of those who have believed God with us as we see this vision of 1,000 churches established on the continent of Africa. From the shortest prayer whispered from the lips of a child on our behalf to the buildings that have been built and to the large, 40-foot containers full of food relief that have been sent for feeding hungry children, we thank God. Each one is a piece of the puzzle that has neatly been arranged by God to supply the need for the work and ministry to the wonderful people of Africa.

We deeply appreciate our close family, friends, and partners who faithfully have prayed and given to the ministry of Trinity Church International (TCI) in Africa. While TCI in Lake Worth, FL, is our home church and for many years generously has supported the work in Africa, it is not our sole support. We have partnered with many different individuals, churches, and ministries from around the world. For their unfailing love and support we truly are grateful. TCI in Lake Worth, FL, and in particular Pastor Tom and Mary Ann Peters and the church's elders, gave us the room to dream and live the dream God gave to us. For that we especially are thankful.

Our thanks would be incomplete were we not to include our children. God blessed us with wonderful children (Tom, Mandy, Steve, and Andreya) who, not even on one occasion, ever lamented to us the fact that they lived in Africa. In fact, as the older ones now make their transition to the United States to further their education, they have found themselves missing Africa and yearning for the people they have served; they miss their home. We firmly believe that our obedience to live in the will of God has had its effect on our kids. Were we to have disobeyed His call, we do not want to imagine where they would be today.

We thank God for His call and the opportunity to see His call fulfilled. Even though this call has required much of us, especially the separation from our children as they grow up, we are privileged to live at the very front line of what God is doing in the earth. We have learned that a life lived outside the will of God is a life not lived at all.

Jamie and Lea Peters

Contents

Preface

Nothing prepared us for the events that were unfolding before our eyes. Burundi long had teetered and tottered on the brink of utter chaos; presidents had been killed; violence covered the countryside, but the capital city in which we lived somehow had avoided the destruction that the rest of the country had experienced. However, the day arrived when the grip of war seized the very heart of the capital, Bujumbura.

For months we had heard rumors of war descending on the city, but we, like the rest of the population there, had grown accustomed to rumors; we ignored them. Suddenly, when the gunfire, mortar fire, and even rockets began to sound, we wondered what would become of our city—of our people. Where would they go? Who was going to help them?

With the advent of the war we heard the unmistakable sound of hell itself breaking loose and felt the terror of the innocent who were to become the inevitable casualties of senseless violence. Women carrying their children and what meager belongings they had ran through the city streets in an effort to escape. The humble homes of the city's residents were destroyed in moments in which armored vehicles aimed at them, disregarding whether they were empty, and blew them beyond recognition. Thousands, if not tens of thousands, made their way to refugee camps in and around the city—but they did not find refuge. In those days no one was exempt from suffering. Children cried, families were separated, and loved ones simply disappeared, never to be seen or heard from again.

To this scene we opened our eyes in May 1994. For nearly two months during the height of the violence we housed 16 church members together with our own family of five. Sometimes for days at a time telephone lines were cut and electrical installations were targeted. For three months we went without power. An economic embargo was leveled on the country in a meaningless effort to squelch the violence that ultimately would kill more than 300,000 Burundians[1].

During those days of the war, through an intervention of God none of our church members perished. Many, however, did leave the city; others fled to neighboring countries as they hoped to build new lives among more peaceful surroundings.

But God kept us right where He sent us. At times we were tempted to think that we might have mistaken the assignment He had given to us; after all, we had three young children. Under such circumstances how could God ask us to stay? Despite our occasional emotional wavering God did keep us in Bujumbura. What we saw as a result of staying cannot compare to any other scenario in which we otherwise might have found ourselves.

Once we realized the blessing of being at the right place at the right time, we had no other place we rather would have been. Our place of appointment was in Bujumbura, Burundi. No person or circumstance possibly could shake us from it.

Introduction

"Lift your eyes now and look from the place where you are—northward, southward, eastward, and westward; for all the land which you see I give to you and your descendants forever"
(Gen. 13:14b-15).

God had to tell Abraham to *"lift"* his eyes because Abraham, apparently, was not looking far beyond the place in which he had found himself standing. God said *"lift your eyes now and look . . . ."* In 1987 we found ourselves in the same situation as Abraham was. We were concentrating on our lives as we saw them set before us, but God told us to *"lift"* our eyes and to look up from the place in which we were. He then dared us to believe Him for all the *"land"* we saw. When we were shaken from our personal reverie and realized that God indeed had spoken to us and challenged us to look beyond ourselves, we were surprised by the extent of the *"land"* God had shown us. The *"land"* we saw was not found in our home country; the *"land"* we saw was the continent of Africa.

The challenge occurred at a time that seemed inconvenient and irrational. Our first child was only 1-year old; we were finding our "niche", as it were, as adults in the U.S. We had purchased our first home and owned two cars; we had comfortable positions serving on staff at our home church. We were living the American dream. Until the day God breathed a word into our hearts, our eyes were fixed on the place in which we found ourselves. He dared us to *"lift"* our eyes and believe that a continent was ours for the taking.

Less than one year after God called us to Africa, we found ourselves standing in Zaire (now the Democratic Republic of Congo) and wondering what being called to the continent really meant. The romance of the call of God and the mission field seemed far off when we could not even communicate with the people and had to spend countless hours in language study. Yet from time to time we felt that call stir us to persist. The day arrived in which we were able to communicate and quite easily live in this new culture.

Just as we settled into life in Zaire and were feeling comfortable again, God reminded us of His call to the continent; at that time we began planting churches. This began in Bujumbura, Burundi, and has continued throughout many nations in Africa.

How, even after serving on the field since 1987, can that call in our hearts possibly speak louder than it ever has before? We are amazed that, in some way, that call is as fresh as it was the first day we experienced it. It has become an all-consuming desire; we wake in the morning; our hearts beat for the continent. We lie down to sleep at night; our dreams are of Africa. As the years have gone by, the passion we feel for this call seems only to have increased.

What about an "exit strategy" if something goes wrong? What if things do not go well? In other words, what if God fails? That simply is not an option. In the event of failure we have no exit strategy or backup plan. God cannot fail; therefore, we, His children cannot fail. This does not mean we have not struggled or had trials while we navigated down this path. On the contrary we have gone through some very difficult times when things have not gone as planned or when we have been confused and blindly had to obey when our next day—even our next moments—were in question. Each time God was faithful to lead us; at times we did not understand His directions. But ultimately His direction proved to be the best route. However, even in those difficult times in which we could not see where we were going or what we were doing, we had no exit strategy. We had no question of retreat, because retreat was not and is not an option.

May the writings in this book bless and challenge you to look up from the place at which you are to a land He has given to you. If you dare to take God up on His Word and obey Him radically, as Abraham did, God will give you all that your eyes see. You will find, as we did, that a life of no retreat also is a life with no regrets.

Jamie and Lea Peters
Trinity Church International
Africa

Note: We chose to write this book in a back-and-forth format so that the reader can get both of our perspectives. When Lea is sharing her perspective, the reader will see a picture of a lioness at the beginning of the section. When Jamie is sharing his point-of-view, the reader will see a picture of a lion.

Lea   Jamie

Part 1

Asking for Nations

"Ask of Me, and I will give You the nations for Your inheritance,
and the ends of the earth for Your possession"
(Ps. 2:8).

Chapter 1

Everything Began With a Map

"The place where God calls you is the place where your deep gladness and the world's deep hunger meet."
—Frederick Buechner[2]

Why would anyone ever choose to leave family, friends, church, job, country, and culture? Since the beginning of overseas missions this question has plagued many. Even those who answered the call (and set out on the "adventure of a lifetime") wonder what possessed them to deny everything normal for the unfamiliar and unknown. How does the call occur? Why does it seem to overpower all the other interests and endeavors in the lives of those being called? Perhaps as many answers to these questions exist as do missionaries. But a common thread is woven into the fabric of each person who has entered ministry as a short-term or career missionary. It is quickly discovered and undeniable: life as it was before the call is changed forever.

We are very ordinary people. The fact that God called us overseas to full-time ministry continues to amaze us—even long after early 1987 when we answered His call. When we first began our journey, our thoughts were laced with some trepidation. After all, what could we hope to accomplish? Many others on the mission field possessed greater qualifications than we did. But perhaps the desire of our hearts to follow Him was the only qualification we needed. Or maybe God chose us because we *are* ordinary; in so doing, He would be sure to get the glory. Whatever the reason, throughout the years He has proven time and again that He truly is with us to protect, provide, and guide our every step.

This journey has been a true adventure of faith and has more than satisfied any desire we had before we set out on this path. At times it has been fraught with complications, difficulty, and trials—but God has been faithful to keep watch over us. Besides, what life is void of trial and difficulty? Over the years we have reckoned that, if life is going to buffet us, we might as well fight back instead of lying down and giving up.

 In 1972 Jamie's parents (Pastor Tom and Mary Ann Peters) answered the call to be pastor of Trinity Church International (TCI) in Lake Worth, FL. When they arrived, the entire church attendance consisted of four women and four children. (By the grace of God, at this writing the church has grown to a membership of approximately 4,000.) At this church I met Jamie; in the youth group our ordinary backgrounds meshed. Later we married in the church.

God called Mom and Dad to raise up a missions-minded church. Their love for the world proved to be fertile soil for the seed of world missions that the Lord individually had planted in Jamie and me.

> *For you see your calling, brethren, that not many wise according to the flesh, not many mighty, not many noble, are called. But God has chosen the foolish things of the world to put to shame the wise, and God has chosen the weak things of the world to put to shame the things which are mighty; and the base things of the world and the things which are despised God has chosen, and the things which are not, to bring to nothing the things that are, that no flesh should glory in His presence* (1 Cor. 1:26-29).

Everything began in Haiti

On a mission trip to Haiti in 1982 I fell in love with God's heart for the world. From that time on I became an incurable missions romantic. The place to which any group was going did not matter; if it was a mission trip, I wanted to be included. For a time I thought I might be called to serve in Haiti, a very poor island nation in the Caribbean; on several occasions I had visited there. Wisely my father counseled me to wait and not to do anything in haste. His wisdom has been a constant in my life; in retrospect I can see how all those years ago when I was full of youthful zeal, he proved to be right. Reluctantly I agreed that moving to Haiti at that time would have been a hasty decision and trusted that God in the correct time would reveal His plan. While I waited on the Lord to give me clearer direction, I met and married Lea, whose passion for missions work mirrored mine. In my love for the world I no longer felt alone.

During this season of my life (1984-1987) I was serving as a staff pastor at TCI, which eventually led to my position as the missions director. On a wall in my office I hung a map of the world; over it was inscribed Psalm 2:8: "*Ask of Me, and I will give you the nations for your inheritance, and the ends of the earth for your possession.*" Daily I placed my hands on that map; in prayer I called out, one by one, the names of all the nations of the world. Eventually I memorized every one of them. Through praying for the nations I learned this: if anyone persisted in asking God for the world, He would answer that prayer.

What do you want to be when you grow up?

When Jamie and I married, I somehow knew we would serve on the mission field in Africa because during my childhood God had shown me that in some capacity I would serve on the African continent. While I was young teen-ager, I attended a conference in which cards containing the question, "What do you want to be when you grow up?", were distributed to the audience. Without hesitation, as my answer I wrote the word *missionary*. At that time I had no knowledge of how I would get on the field; in fact, the intricacies of entering the field did not even cross my mind. I just knew I was going to be a missionary. That was enough for me! Not only was I convinced I would serve on the field, I also knew that the man I would marry would possess the same or similar call.

The passion Jamie had for the world earned my respect and love. Clearly God had brought the paths of our lives to the same crossroad. Our mutual commitment to world missions linked us together in such a way that later would prove to anchor us as we found our way in life. When we actually became missionaries, I understood why God plants such intense passion in the hearts of those He calls to go overseas: overcoming the great trials faced *on* the field must be superseded by the greater passion *for* the field.

A lunch that opened the door . . .

 In 1985 Ralph and Shirley Hagemeier, at the time missionaries to Africa for more than 20 years, one Sunday morning spoke at TCI. After the service we received the opportunity to take them out to lunch. Our hunger for the field intensified as we listened to them talk about Africa; their passion and love for the people was so evident. Ralph noticed our interest; in what we later learned was his characteristic, to-the-point approach he said that if we wanted to be missionaries but did not know where to start, we were welcome to start with them. That invitation led us seriously to plan a trip to visit the Hagemeiers in Kalemie, Zaire. Earlier that year I had been to Africa on a trip to Kenya with Jamie, his parents, David Briggs (an elder and current missions director at TCI and one of our dearest friends), and another couple in the church. But with little understanding and a large imagination about the hardships of Africa, I did not want to bring our young son, Tom (then under 1-year old), to such a remote place as Kalemie, which seemed to be at the very end of the earth.

Reluctantly I agreed with Jamie that he should go to Kalemie for two months in September and October 1986. He was set to travel there with David Briggs, who only was able to stay one month. I must say that those two months were some of the longest in my life. I cannot count the number of times I regretted staying behind. Since time began, all over the world women have been having babies and caring for them; I should have taken Tom and gone with Jamie.

Time apart

 I was beyond excited to go to Africa, but as the day to leave drew near, my excitement grew dim when reality set in about being apart from my young family. I tried to convince Lea to bring Tom and to travel with me, but she hesitated about being with a baby in such a remote location. I understood her feeling and let her make her own decision; silently we both felt bad for that choice. Although the sorrow of leaving Lea and Tom behind never was far from my thoughts, I was setting off for a new adventure—time in Africa! Sixty-two days of service on the real mission field was right in front of me! My bags were packed with a gift for the Hagemeiers (a large box of Snickers bars), clothes, shoes, and my Bible. At the airport I left Lea and Tom; Lea was in tears. I felt guilty for leaving them but hoped that, at the end of the trip, the sorrow of leaving would be forgotten.

During the time I was away, I preached and/or taught 58 times in 62 days. Looking back I realize that during this time, the Lord began to develop in me the discipline required to prepare for teaching and preaching on a regular basis. Up until that time this was something I did not have the opportunity to do.

Ralph had me teach in the Bible school they established in Kalemie as well as to preach in local churches in the surrounding area. The various activities in which I participated assisted in preparing me for my future service on the mission field. Once, when Ralph, David, and I were driving into the bush on our way to preach, some soldiers stopped us at a checkpoint. Obviously drunk, they harassed us for a few minutes and then let us continue on our way. As we drove away, I was curious and asked Ralph whether he thought they had bullets for their guns. No sooner had those words passed through my mouth than we heard a shot ring out. Ralph began to slow down, but David and I urgently insisted that he "go on! Go on!" Little did I know that those gunshots simply were a foretaste of what our family in the years ahead would experience.

While during this trip I was not a full-time missionary, I had a desire to communicate with the people, so I memorized a Scripture in Swahili and on several occasions quoted it before I preached. The people really enjoyed my attempts to speak with them; I particularly enjoyed the connection I felt when I tried to use their language.

The ease with which I was able to enter this strange, new world amazed me. The only things pulling me back to Florida were my wife and son. I began to pray about whether this was the place God was leading us to serve full-time.

Feeling sorry for myself

 As I observed Jamie's happiness at leaving, I felt impatient and even angry. *How could he be so happy about leaving us?* I understood he was going to the mission field and that I had agreed to the trip, so I did not have much of an allowance for arguing this time (and I *knew* how to argue). But still I was unhappy. The next two months went by slowly. Every evening I was alone at home and missed my husband. Family and friends were sympathetic and made lots of attempts to comfort me, but any attempt at trying to keep my mind off my situation did not work. My thoughts never were far from Jamie and from the African continent.

During those months we exchanged many letters and cards; Jamie even recorded a video for me that he sent back with David. Watching Jamie cry on the video as he told me how much he loved Tom and me did not help my situation. I just wanted him back home.

Eventually October closed; Jamie's plane finally touched down in Miami. This time of separation, firmly entrenched in my heart, confirmed in me: for a man (or a woman) to be alone is, as the Bible teaches in Genesis, *not good*.

Keep doing what you know to do

 The trip soon ended; our family was reunited. In earnest I continued to pray about whether we were to work under the auspices of the Hagemeiers in Zaire. Lea, while not resistant to the idea, was hesitant. Since Tom was born, his health sometimes was challenged; Lea was uncertain about moving as far away as Africa. Honestly, I did not feel a definite "let's do it" and therefore was unable to make a solid decision to go. This frustrated me. Here was our opportunity to become missionaries, but we were not going! *Why did we not have the "all-clear" sign? Why was God not saying anything?* I practically was begging God to allow us to go! He was not saying *yes*; neither was He saying *no*. He was just silent!

Several weeks later, when I was specifically praying about this very issue, I heard the voice of the Holy Spirit tell me, "Keep doing what you know to do until you know to do different." At that point I stopped praying the "do-we-go-or-not-go?" prayers and got back to concentrating on my work at the church, because the last thing I heard God say was to serve there on staff.

Haiti

In December 1986, two months after Jamie's return from Zaire, we were scheduled as a couple to take a missions trip to Haiti. I was pleased that I was not being left behind. During the 10 days we would be away, Tom would alternate staying with both sets of grandparents. I knew his care was in the hands of exemplary people!

Setting off from Miami's airport we landed in the nation's capital, Port-au-Prince. *Chaos* can only mildly describe the experience of passing through this airport; however, Jamie and I had been to this nation before (on trips with the youth of our church) and relatively were unaffected by the confusion, but this trip to Haiti was a new experience for us. This represented the first time for us as husband and wife to lead a mission trip. We were taking a construction team to build a church facility on a small island off the mainland. For some of those under our leadership this was their first time overseas; the confusion at the airport was a sort of baptism into the mission field. While we did our best to help everyone through the initial shock of navigating customs, going through the process of entering a foreign nation (especially a developing one) can be fully understood and appreciated only after one actually has gone through the experience.

The morning after our arrival we took a bus to the shore from which boats regularly departed for the island. Hearing that boats depart *regularly* brings about the assumption that the boats were seaworthy. These handmade, wooden boats, according to local lore, were "very reliable". When we first saw them, we realized that *reliable* was a relative term. In the eyes of the average American what Haitian nationals deem *reliable could* be viewed as potentially disastrous. Even more amazing was the method by which we were to board the "ship".

This shore had no dock. For passengers to board the boat to the island workers used their shoulders to carry the passengers some five or six yards through the water. The sight of Americans (sometimes three or four times the size of the average Haitian national) on the shoulders of these people was more than comical; it was hilarious. Shortly we became the entertainment, as nationals appeared seemingly from nowhere to watch as our team members made their clumsy ways on board.

To arrive at our destination we had to spend four hours of riding under the intense heat of the Caribbean sunshine. Hats, sunglasses, and water did little to ease the discomfort from the extreme temperature. While we may have lamented the heat, in reality we were blessed that we did not have to face stormy seas or other bad conditions, especially considering our mode of transportation! As soon as I was aboard, I immediately noticed the absence of any kind of toilet and understood that, if someone needed to go to the bathroom, he or she would have to do so off the side of the boat. I made a mental note to keep things under control until a worthy facility could be found.

Finally, after several hours of disciplining my bladder, the shoreline entered our view as we spotted our destination. A makeshift dock appeared near the village in which we were to spend the next week.

The truth about toilets

Waiting for us at the dock was a missionary family that served on the island; this was to be our host family. After I disembarked, I tried to help Jamie and the other men as they worked to pitch our tents on the beach, but I was desperate to find a bathroom. Then I noticed our intended facility was a simple hole surrounded on three sides with cement blocks. The fourth side simply was an opening that faced the ocean. My heart sank as I imagined having to use that facility, since I was the only woman staying on the beach in a tent. On our arrival and on occasion throughout our stay the missionary family was kind enough to allow me to use its indoor toilet; I was grateful for those times. Jamie, of course, agreed to be my lookout when the precious indoor facility was not available, but somehow my concern was not assuaged with his attempts to comfort me. The team had another woman on it, but since she was single, she stayed in the missionaries' home with them and therefore had unlimited use of the indoor toilet. I struggled to refrain from exhibiting my jealousy of her privileged position.

Many of my plans during that week surrounded the use of the missionaries' indoor bathroom. My concern over this very issue was justified. One day when the rest of the team and the local missionaries were gone, I found myself having to use the outdoor facility. While I was not particularly excited about the prospect of going to that little cement structure, I mentally prepared myself to be on the lookout, because Jamie had gone with the rest of the team to the work site. So I steeled myself for the task before me. I looked around and up and down the shore. The beach was quiet; not a soul was in sight. This was my perfect opportunity. But just as I calmed down and actually was making use of this three-walled bathroom with the opening that faced the ocean, I looked up and noticed a canoe passing by, not very far from shore, with someone (perhaps a fisherman) staring at me in a very quizzical fashion and waving at me as he went by. Acting as though I was unaffected, in return I simply waved back at him. My humiliation was complete.

The tide began to change

 During the day I went with the team to work on building the church. In the afternoons we held open meetings in a simple lean-to made of palm branches. During three separate sessions Lea taught the women. We both were enjoying the experience.

At this time the Lord began to deal with Lea about serving under the

Hagemeiers. Once again we agreed to pray about moving to Africa. Perhaps God had not spoken to me initially because He had yet to work on Lea's heart. But as our time in Haiti closed, an excitement began to build in us as we felt the stirring of a changing tide. In Haiti we began to believe that God might be sending us to Africa.

The call arrives

 Explaining the passion that gripped our hearts when we began to feel the pull to Africa is difficult. This intensity was more than a romantic desire someday to be missionaries. It became everything we thought and breathed. Nothing else held any appeal to us; nothing else besides getting onto the field mattered.

In January 1987, some weeks after our return from Haiti, we approached Dad about the leading of the Lord; he agreed to pray with us. He was no stranger to our love for the nations of the world. One Sunday (during this season of praying for direction), as Dad was preaching, he took a Scripture from Acts about Philip being called from Samaria (where great revival erupted) to Gaza to preach the gospel to an Ethiopian eunuch:

> *Now an angel of the Lord spoke to Philip, saying, "Arise and go toward the south along the road which goes down from Jerusalem to Gaza." This is desert* (Acts 8:26).

As he read that Scripture and commented on how God took Philip from a citywide crusade to the "backside of the desert", we looked at each other and knew, then and there, that God was confirming in our hearts that He was giving us the "green light" to go. He was taking us, as He had taken Philip, from our own citywide crusade at TCI to a desert. While TCI always has been an oasis of God's presence to us, now we were leaving that oasis and going to what we reckoned to be a place that in comparison was a desert. That morning neither of us heard much more of the message. In our spirits we had already gone to our Gaza.

Preparation

 God settled the issue of calling us. Now we were faced with the practicalities involved in moving our family overseas. The drive God planted in both of our hearts sustained us as we confronted the realities involved with such a drastic change. We had to obtain a passport for Tom, get his and our international vaccination certificates in order, acquire anti-malaria medication, decide what to do with our home, deal with the emotions of leaving our families, find a reliable secretary who would help care for our finances, and send out our monthly newsletters—not to mention raise the support needed to sustain us and our projects overseas.

While TCI was our home church and committed to support us every month, we never asked, wanted, nor expected the congregation totally to sustain us in what God called us to do. TCI never was, is not, and never will be our sole support; that would rob God's blessings from all those the Holy Spirit has prompted to give to our ministry. We receive TCI financial and prayerful assistance just as any other missionary would in relationship with the church.

Our base of regular supporters began to increase as we headed toward the move. In reality we understood that many missionaries had to itinerate (preach from church to church) for months, if not years, to raise their support to a level that would enable them to go onto the field. As word got out, some invitations to preach in churches arrived. While we initially did not have a very large support base, it did grow enough for us to set a date of departure: June 30, 1987.

The Hagemeier base of operations was in Texas. Ralph informed us he was shipping to Kalemie a container which had some extra room. He welcomed us to use it to ship some of our household items. We had a small, two-door Datsun that Jamie purchased before we married; the car was paid off. Knowing we would need a car in Kalemie, Jamie sent word to Ralph and asked whether Ralph's 20-foot container would have room for the Datsun. To our amazement we found plenty of space for the car. Ralph explained that when one packs a container, every available space is used; not an inch is wasted. We simply would pack boxes in and around the car. In the small spaces we used as space-fillers our rolls of toilet paper and other miscellaneous items.

Our church held a going-away shower for us and filled our arms with gifts: pots and pans, a set of plastic dishes for four, cutlery, towels, sheets, and our own toilet paper—which arrived just in time to be packed into the container. Together with a friend, Jamie drove to Texas a truck that was towing the car and our 20 boxes. There they awaited shipment to Zaire.

An adventure to be lived . . .

June 30 loomed ever closer on our horizon. The pressure to finish sorting all the details at home grew increasingly heavy. Renters were found for our home, because we had committed to serve in Kalemie for only one year and on our return would need to have a place to live. The elders at TCI generously gave me a year-long leave of absence from working at the church; this made us very thankful for their understanding. We were going with the knowledge that this year was a year to "test the waters", as it were. Once we completed our year, we were to return to the States to decide whether we, on a long-term basis, would give ourselves to missions service. With our household belongings packed away and put into storage and our luggage closed, we were on our way to start the adventure of our lifetime.

"Life is not a problem to be solved, it is an adventure to be lived."[3]

Goodbye

The morning of our departure I stayed up until 3 a.m. I was preparing for the trip and struggling to get to sleep when I finished working. *Did we have enough clothes for Tom? Did we have enough suitcases for everything we were bringing with us? Would we fit everything in? What were we to expect on our arrival? How would we make such a long plane flight with a toddler in tow?* Sleep, when it finally did arrive, was fitful; I woke up exhausted. Jamie, on the other hand, always has enjoyed his slumber. While he had only a few hours of sleep, during that time he slept very well. In the morning I growled at him. How could he sleep so soundly while I suffered?

With his characteristic joy, he packed the luggage in the car; we were on our way to the airport with the rest of the team that accompanied us to Zaire. Jamie's parents and David Briggs were going with us. On our arrival in Africa we were to meet up with other guests Ralph and Shirley were receiving—Pastor B.B. and Velma Hankins from West Columbia, TX. The trip was scheduled around the Hagemeiers' Bible school's graduation in July. Dad and David, together with Pastor Hankins, were scheduled to speak during a seminar that was to take place the week after graduation services.

The drive to the airport in Miami normally takes about an hour from West Palm Beach. That day that hour's journey seemed to last a whole lot longer. My parents were seeing us off at the airport. They put on brave faces, but we knew that, under the smiles, tears were not far from the surface. Tom, unaware of what was about to happen, played with his grandparents at the departure gate while we watched them struggle somehow to part with their little grandson. The time arrived for us to board; of course families with small children were called first. Tom was not happy to be taken from his *Mummi* and *Pappa* (what he called my parents) and cried loudly as one last time we embraced each other and pulled him from their arms.

So Jesus answered and said, "Assuredly, I say to you, there is no one who has left house or brothers or sisters or father or mother or wife or children or lands, for My sake and the Gospel's, who shall not receive a hundredfold now in this time—houses and brothers and sisters and mothers and children and lands, with persecutions—and in the age to come, eternal life" (Mark 10:29-30).

Busy

 Tom was an extremely active and inquisitive child. As the mother of such a child, most of the time I felt tired as I did my best to keep up with his busy agenda. He seemingly was born asking questions and finding things to do; he never was content to sit still. At all times he needed to do something and be involved with some kind of activity. Not only did he have to be involved with something, he had to have a variety of activities, as he quickly would tire of one and after only a very short time would need to change to something else. Of course he was never content to do things alone; he and I endlessly played with toy cars and looked for strange insects. Explaining to 18-month old Tom the reason for sitting still during a transcontinental flight was out of the question. He wanted to know where everything was, where everyone was sitting, and why we could not land the plane after only 30 minutes. "*Why?*" was the question of the day; when that question had no fitting answer for Tom, all those sitting within a short proximity of him had to bear the consequences of his disappointment!

Our agenda took us through Frankfurt, Germany, in which we had to lay over for several hours before we caught our connecting flight to Nairobi, Kenya. On our arrival we all decided to get something to eat before we took in a few hours of rest at a hotel. Not knowing German we did our best to interpret the menu and prayed that the food of which we were about to partake would be a blessing! Imagine our dismay when the ham and sauerkraut we ordered emerged on our plates in the form of a whole piglet. My stomach turned as others did their best to find the edible parts of the pig. I, on the other hand, picked at my sauerkraut and prayed to return to the hotel room. Tom questioned the humanity of having a baby pig on the plate, "Baby pig, Mommy! Baby pig!" No one had words fit to comfort him. Little did we know or understand that the culture wars were about to begin.

The next leg of our journey brought us through Nairobi, Kenya, in which we were to board a plane that had been chartered to fly our group to Kalemie, Zaire. The flight to Kalemie was set to leave early in the morning, so we settled in a hotel for the night.

Situated in the middle of Nairobi, the Fairview Hotel was our destination for the evening. It was old-fashioned and gave its visitors a small taste of colonial Africa. The Africa we know today is not the Africa that existed during the 1800s and early 1900s, when much of the continent was ruled by mostly colonial European powers. Generally speaking, north, west, and central Africa were colonized by French-speaking nations (Belgium and France). The eastern portions of the continent were colonized by England. A few other countries were colonized by other nations, but the larger part of the continent was under French, Belgian, or British rule. With the colonization of Africa also occurred the "Westernization" of the continent. The colonists brought with them their language, culture, and even architecture and imposed on the African people their way of life. While colonial rule of Africa ended years ago, the remains of that era to this day can be seen and felt.

The Fairview Hotel has a distinct, old-European design to it. As we walked the halls of the old building, we wondered about a bygone era. But our colonial experience at the Fairview did not stop with the quaint furnishings and mealtime etiquette. Later in the evening an unexpected surprise awaited these green missionaries.

Jet lag began to take hold of the entire team. Even Tom began to exhibit signs of sleepiness. So we decided we needed to turn in for the night. Most of the year the evenings in Nairobi are cool; that night was no exception. We laid our heads on our pillows and fell into a deep sleep. Not many hours into our long-awaited slumber we woke to itchy bumps. Supposing mosquitoes were biting us, we sprayed ourselves with mosquito repellant and hoped that sleep would return to us. However, the itching did not stop; our rest was, at best, fitful. When morning did arrive, we were thankful the night was over. Noticing small spots of blood on the sheets on which we had been sleeping, I was horrified when, after inspection, I found angry red welts—three in a row—on my arm. I began to suspect that our itchy night was not because of mosquitoes. Tom and Jamie also were victims to rows of itchy welts on their arms, backs, and legs. *What kinds of bugs were these that could inflict such bites?* Later on I found out that this was our first encounter with the despised *kunguni*, or bedbug. No one else from our group was disturbed with the bedbug assault. I was more than irked that the horrible creatures seemingly had singled us out as the objects of their midnight feast. I had—and still have—an immediate hatred for these intruders. To this day I remain wary of any suspected infestation, which always is met with the deadliest bug spray and manual de-bugging known.

Early that next morning after our night of bedbug warfare we boarded the 20-seat plane and were buckled in. The engines started, the propellers whirled to life, and Tom was enraptured with excitement over this airplane. His happiness was a welcome distraction as we dealt with the emotions of bringing our family to this part of the world. I wondered what was waiting for us on the other side of this last portion of the trip. The year before, Jamie had been to Kalemie and had some idea as to what awaited us, but I was unable even to picture the place in which this plane ride would land and my new life as a missionary would take off. *What kind of place that required us to go through so much just to get there would this be ?*

Concrete in the sand

 The hum of the plane's engines lulled us to sleep during the four hours we spent traveling to our destination. We woke to the pilot's announcing we were flying over Lake Tanganyika, which is the longest lake in the world as well as the world's second-deepest. Interestingly enough, the lake has only one outlet; this outlet is in Kalemie. Because the lake has only one outlet, it is slightly salty. This makes it the home of rare species of fish, which, in better times, were caught and exported for sale abroad. Some of the fish in the lake, notably the Nile Perch, can grow to be quite large. In the market we have seen these fish that were at least four-feet long, if not longer. Their lengths are said occasionally to exceed six feet. We can't verify that, since we never have seen a fish that large from the lake, but we were amused to hear the fishermen in the market tell their tales. All over the world fishermen, while they may be fishing for different kinds of fish, tell the same kinds of stories.

As we approached our destination, our eyes were drawn to the city that slowly entered our view. The pilot explained that he first flies over the city before he lands to alert those expecting us that we were about to land. This, we learned later on, was normal procedure for planes landing in Kalemie.

At last we drew near to the "airport", which was little more than a slab of concrete in the sand. Broken-down tanks and armored vehicles littered the sides of the runway, which, the pilot explained, were the remains of the 1960s uprising. We had heard of the war in the 1960s; it resulted in the deaths of several missionaries in the country, but seeing the actual tanks remaining from that time was shocking. The world outside the United States was not always a friendly place.

As we began to land, we could see soldiers behind a few machine guns pointed directly at the small runway. Because we were on the runway, they were pointing directly at us. As a family, such was our first welcome to Kalemie, Zaire. We reached a stop outside of what was, for lack of a better word, the *terminal*. The building was riddled with bullet holes, cobwebs, and dust. Tom took turns clinging to us as we exited the plane and made our way toward the building.

At the airport Ralph and Shirley, with their daughter, Stephanie, and a few other African colleagues were waiting for us. Smiling, they shook our hands and escorted all of us to the place in which the customs and immigration officials were waiting. Ralph explained to them that all of us were there to attend the Bible-school graduation and subsequent seminar. Unimpressed, the officials asked for everyone's passports. Assuming we would get our passports back after they were stamped, we handed them to Ralph who, on receiving them, informed us we would get our passports back after a couple of days. The stamp the officials used when stamping passports was in town, he explained; a few days would be necessary for everything to be stamped properly. At the passport agency in Miami, FL, we had been told never to allow anyone to take our passports. Obviously those who counseled us never had visited Kalemie.

After being further humbled by passing through customs and thus having all our personal items sorted through one-by-one, we made our way with Stephanie and Shirley to what was to be our home. Ralph, in the meantime, took the customs and immigration officials back to their office in town. They did not have their own transport to or from the airport, so Ralph, as he usually did, gave them a lift. On the way I immediately noticed that the road from the airport was "slightly paved", meaning that only several-hundred feet of the road was paved with concrete. The rest was rough and sandy. Tom, wide-eyed, never let go of the collar of my shirt. While brave, he still was only a little toddler and was unsure of everything new that surrounded him. I enjoyed this display of "clingyness"; if only for a short time, everything else seemed to take a back seat to the precious few minutes I had with my little boy.

That was short-lived. My reverie suddenly was broken when, after some minutes, we arrived at the house. We found waiting for us there some Bible-school students and a woman we later came to know as *Mama Makope*. Nearly giddy with excitement she had heard a little boy soon would be there with the visitors; she was ready to welcome him. As we exited the vehicle, we were enveloped in warm greetings. Tom, frightened by the sudden attention, began to wail and wrapped both arms around my neck. Mama Makope attempted to pull Tom out of my arms, but to her great disappointment Tom clearly indicated he, for the time being, was not going anywhere. I weakly smiled and made an attempt at apologizing but really was relieved that I, at that moment, had someone to hold.

The crowd eventually dissipated as we made our way inside our new home. We were going to live on one side of an old duplex that had been built during the time the Belgians colonized Zaire; the Hagemeiers lived on the other side. We admired the high ceilings and good ventilation. Our front window looked out over the magnificent lake. In the distance we could see the silhouette of the Tanzanian mountains outlining the horizon. *How,* we wondered aloud, *had such a magnificent country fallen to such a state of decay?*

First impressions

 Our first meal in Kalemie was on July 4, 1987; it celebrated the independence of the United States. Arriving for dinner at the Hagemeiers to enjoy a traditional Fourth of July meal of hamburgers and French fries seemed strange.

When Stephanie explained to me that the hamburger buns were not from the local Publix[4] grocery store but rather were made by hand, I began to understand the sacrifice made for that meal. The ketchup we enjoyed had been packed in the same, 20-foot container that, during the trip across the world, traveled and co-mingled our things with the Hagemeiers' belongings. The potatoes from which the French fries were made were not always easy to find in Kalemie; at times finding potatoes large enough to make good fries was difficult.

Most intimidating of all was the fact that the mayonnaise we were so liberally spreading on our hamburger buns was homemade. I did not know mayonnaise could be homemade. Up until that day I assumed all mayonnaise was from a jar on the grocery-store shelf. As I hid my ignorance, I made sure to use only a very small amount of it. Holding my hamburger with a kind of reverence, I found myself in a state of panic. Jamie was enjoying his hamburger, but I began to wonder whether he ever would enjoy any food from our kitchen! *How was I, a mediocre cook at very best, going to manage to prepare food for my family? Where was the Hamburger Helper aisle or the rotisserie chicken we could pick up from the deli? In these circumstances how could we even make sandwiches?* Tears stung the back of my eyes as everyone laughed and enjoyed the moment. But I was not smiling on the inside. I felt waves of intimidation and fear wash over me—and this was just my first day!

This is the mission field!

 I accompanied Ralph to and from the Bible school that was situated only a half mile or so away from our house. During the graduation and seminar I helped him in any way I could.

I was so excited to be on the mission field that I was bewildered by Lea's initial anguish. Yes, our location was remote, but this was the mission field for which we had yearned since we had been married. Even though she was having some difficulty sorting her feelings, I had confidence in her ability to cope; she was not one to fold and give up. The fact that Africa surrounded our every side and that we were serving under the leadership of such heroes as the Hagemeiers was enough to comfort any anxiety I may have experienced. I heard of and had been warned to be on the lookout for culture shock; I do not know that I ever experienced it as manuals and books had described it. The joy I felt in entering the field helped ease any fear that may have been lurking in the background. My initial reaction was one of awe as well as determination to make a mark on the continent for the Kingdom.

Graduation and seminar

 The first days of our stay in Zaire were a flurry of activity surrounding the impending graduation of the Bible-school students. A great fuss was made over the graduation caps and gowns the Hagemeiers painstakingly had brought to Zaire. To watch these church leaders don cap and gown and make their way to receive their diplomas was moving. The Hagemeiers took every measure to make the entire graduation service as special as possible. While we had not yet sown anything into the lives of any students, we were deeply moved as we watched them celebrate that life-changing day. No other school of its kind existed nor exists (even at the time of this writing) in the region. The day was special for the graduates; we were honored to witness the proceedings.

In the days after the graduation we enjoyed the seminar and the building of our relationship with the Hagemeiers and others who were serving with them. One afternoon Stephanie took me for a walk around the area. We both enjoyed the exercise and fellowship. She introduced me to some people and interpreted the conversations she was having; everyone, myself included, loved her easy demeanor. She made sure those we contacted knew who I was and helped me begin to feel at ease around the community. After an hour or so of visiting with people we needed to return to prepare for evening services. As easily as we started our walk, we finished; then and there I began to learn how not just to talk to people but also to develop relationships with those I will encounter in my life. During those days Stephanie helped me a great deal. I am deeply grateful to her for those lessons she inadvertently taught me just by being herself.

Separation

 Graduation and the seminar ended; the time for my parents and the rest of the team to leave was drawing near. The day before he and Mom were set to leave, my father took me for a walk along the lake. I knew he willingly was giving us to the world for the gospel, but I could see he also was struggling with his emotions over it all. We took nearly an hour discussing the importance of following the will of God and being obedient to His call. Dad said he was proud of me and that he and Mom would be praying for us constantly as we lived out our commitment to the Hagemeiers. He told me that next year he and Mom would return with other members of the team. He said after the next graduation and seminar, we all would return together to Florida. Somehow during that day along the lake I believe we both suspected that the outcome of our time in Zaire would be an event that would change the course of our lives forever.

I always had been close with my parents and enjoyed seeing Lea and Tom grow to love them as much. I did not relish the idea of being separated from them. I relied heavily on my father and mother for counsel; this time apart was going to be a stretch! On the day of their departure we all decided things would be better if we did not accompany them out to the airport. Saying goodbye to everyone else back in Florida had been easier because we had Mom and Dad traveling with us. The fact that they were leaving felt almost unreal. The finality of their returning home hit us when the Hagemeiers picked them up; we had no recourse except to say goodbye. Mom cried as I never had seen her cry before; even Dad was having difficulty holding back the tears. Later I learned that Mom cried all the way back to Nairobi; for the duration of the flight her crying brought everyone else on the plane to tears. Tom, not understanding why all the adults were crying, decided to chime in with us.

With the goodbyes finished Lea took one of Tom's hands and I took the other as we walked in the cloud of dust that rose up as their vehicle left. We decided to head toward the lake, at which we would have the best chance of seeing the airplane in flight. After some time the plane entered our view; we pointed it out to Tom. The sight of his little finger pointing earnestly up into the sky at the aircraft that quickly was disappearing in the distance will remain burned in our memories. "Bye-bye, Mom-mom! Bye-bye, Papa! See you soon!" he cried.

What had we done?

Chapter 2

Books, Bridges, and Butchers

" . . . Why did you haul this congregation of God out here into this wilderness to die, people and cattle alike? And why did you take us out of Egypt in the first place, dragging us into this miserable country? No grain, no figs . . . " (Num. 20:5 Message).

We answered the call and found ourselves on the real mission field. The events we passed through brought change and challenged almost every preconceived idea we had about this area of ministry. Somehow, without vocalizing it, we felt a certain disappointment in the fact that the multitudes of people who would benefit from our presence on the field were, at present, nonexistent. Instead of ministering to crowds the only applause we heard as we memorized vocabulary words and struggled to communicate in Swahili was from each other. Our presence did not bring any significant change to anyone but ourselves. This was, we learned some time later, exactly what God wanted us to discover: before we could hope to bring change to anyone in Africa, Africa first had to bring change to us.

Now it happened, on a certain day, that He got into a boat with His disciples. And He said to them, "Let us cross over to the other side of the lake" (Luke 8:22).

To the disciples, getting into a boat with Jesus must have been exciting. They had just witnessed His teaching to *a great multitude* (Luke 8:4) and were riding the wave of popularity when Jesus said the time had arrived for them to *"cross over to the other side of the lake"*. Without any recorded dispute they all went on the boat, with the goal of reaching the opposite shore. As noted in Luke 8 Jesus fell asleep while a great storm tossed the boat to and fro. So fierce was the weather that the boat nearly sank. Terrified, the disciples woke Jesus and told Him they were about to die. How humorous that the disciples, who had witnessed miracles, believed that they needed to report to the Son of God that they were going under. Jesus, responding to their cries (which were not cries of faith), calmed the storm and then rebuked them.

> But He said to them, "Where is your faith?" And they were afraid and marveled, saying to one another, "Who can this be? For He commands even the winds and water, and they obey Him!" (Luke 8:25).

Such was our encounter in transitioning to Africa. In our preparation to get there we experienced His power and witnessed His provision. Yet, when the storm began to blow on our boat as on another continent we traversed the sometimes difficult experiences of life, we felt as though Jesus was asleep and unaware of our predicament. As He did with His Twelve, each time we needed His intervention and cried out to Him (sometimes not in faith), He aided us and calmed the storm. Each time He did so, we could hear His loving rebuke, "Where is your faith?" In the same way Jesus taught His disciples to trust Him and have faith to change, so He began to change us—to teach us to have faith.

A rude awakening

As soon as we said our goodbyes, life began—and began quickly. No one in our new home was ready to help us learn the ins and outs of living on another continent. What was waiting for us was on the dining room table: a book entitled *Simplified Swahili*[5] and two dictionaries (an English/Swahili dictionary and a Swahili/English dictionary). Little did we know that, other than our Bibles (which were most important in our journey), these books were to become next in importance, because language-learning would determine our usefulness and success as missionaries in Africa. Six weeks remained before we were set to fly back to Nairobi, Kenya, and begin our studies at C.P.K. Language School. Ralph explained that throughout the six weeks a good use of our time would be to study Swahili on our own. This way when we actually began our studies, we would have all the basics out of the way. Those basics included greetings, numbers, and days of the week. Eager to please and excited to begin communicating we planned to dive into the books with a vengeance.

On day two, we set out to begin life on our own. With Ralph and Shirley close by and willing to answer any questions (which were many), we decided to spend as much time as possible in the Swahili books.

 Besides language study I discovered that life in Kalemie does not happen by chance; life happens on purpose. At the start of our first day alone after Mom and Dad left, very early in the morning I stumbled to the kitchen with the intention of having a cup of coffee. Water, being a key element in the brewing of coffee, had to be located and purified. The liquid flowing straight from the faucet in Zaire definitely was not something to drink! (As a matter of fact, water in many places in Africa and around the world is not safe to drink; it first must be treated. For it to be consumable water should be boiled for 20 minutes and then passed through a water filter[6]).

On this first morning by ourselves I picked up the water kettle that normally held clean drinking water and found barely enough water to make coffee! This is an inconceivable problem—almost an insult—to someone of Finnish heritage as I was. Every day in Finland children grow up having *kahvi*[7] with their parents, just as I had with my parents. It represented a rite of passage. But here I stood, after all these years, in a kitchen with my coffee consumption in question. Grumbling, I filled the nearest pot full of water and set it on the stove to boil. To make matters even more interesting the stove appeared to be older than I. A very long time was required to bring the water to a boil. (Right then I made a mental note to boil water at least twice per day.) Once the water boiled long enough and cooled some, I poured it into the filter and waited to hear the telltale dripping sound that indicated some drinkable water was on the way. A very long time seemed to pass before the water began to drip; even when it dripped, it was very slow. I decided to ignore the panicked feeling bubbling up in my stomach and, while I waited, spend time reading the Bible.

Jamie, who had been awake nearly for the entire duration of my initial debacle in the kitchen, now was sitting in the living area of our home. He was praying and watching the sun rise as he comfortably sipped the cup of coffee I made him after I spent nearly an hour boiling and filtering it. Returning to make another cup of coffee, I stopped in the middle of my mounting frustration (complicated by my discovering nearly microscopic ants in the sugar) and stood in the kitchen as I listened to him pray. Momentarily I admired his peaceful silhouette in the living room, but then I heard myself say, "Can you believe that we have hardly any drinking water in this house?"

Still praying Jamie looked at me and simply said, "Well, we'd better boil some then." And he went on praying.

His was such a simple answer, but he did not seem to realize that, while we could boil it with our slow-boiling stove, we seemed to have a filter problem. (Frustrated, I found myself making another mental note to ask Shirley what was up with the water filter. I thought, "Too bad it is only 6:30 a.m." I knew I could not ask Shirley any questions because of the early hour.)

After we drank our coffee, Tom woke up and demanded his breakfast. He was a big breakfast-eater. While he did not always enjoy lunch or dinner, breakfast was his main meal of the day. Grouchy and still upset because of the departure of his grandparents the day before, he touched my heart deeply, so I did my best to be cheerful despite my fiasco with coffee and water in the kitchen. Not wanting to hear him complain I looked for and then found his favorite cereal (Cheerios™) that was stashed away in my suitcase and that first morning served him two bowls. His humor much improved, a glimpse of satisfaction fell over me as I thought perhaps we might get through the day. Tom and I went out to the front porch and played with his favorite Matchbox™ cars while I silently made a list of things that needed to be done.

Not long after we sat down together, Mama Makope walked up the front steps and greeted us, "*Habari za asubuhi?*" ("What is the news of the morning?") I just smiled and replied, "Good morning." I hoped this was the appropriate thing to do. She sat down next to me and joined in the fun of playing cars. Tom began to laugh as she made all kinds of noises and funny gestures. This was the first of many mornings we spent playing cars with Mama Makope; Tom and I learned to enjoy this time very much.

Opening the books

 After breakfast the time arrived to get into the language books. Lea had some errands to run and asked me whether I would stay home with Tom. I found this to be my perfect opportunity to begin studying Swahili. Of course I would stay with Tom. Having time with my son—and have the Swahili book to myself—would be wonderful. Since we had only one book and two of us, sharing would present a challenge. This would give me a jump on the studying, because I was intent on learning the language. My drive to study the lessons amazed even me. I was not a language person. For four years Lea had studied Spanish in school. Besides growing up bilingual (her parents were from Finland; at home she grew up speaking Finnish), she had an apparent natural ability to speak in other languages.

I spoke only English and in school had not studied any foreign languages. In middle school I wanted to study a foreign language, so I asked my teacher to add my name to the list of students who that year would study either Spanish or French. After she received my request, she refused and said, "Your English grades are not good enough for you to take another language!" As I sat in my living room and began to study this new form of communication, my teacher's words spoken many years earlier still stung my ears. I decided to prove to myself I could learn to be fluent in speaking another language. That first morning I opened our Swahili book and began on page one of chapter one, "Greetings".

Groceries

 Africa is a traditional place. Women are left to see to their traditional roles as housekeepers, mothers, wives, cooks, and the like. For me these areas never were great strengths; I knew how to cook like the average, American, young wife. If we did not have time to eat at home or did not want to eat there, we would make haste to the nearest fast-food restaurant or to one of our parents' houses! I could cook hamburgers, roast beef, and, on occasion, a stew in a slow cooker. That was the extent of my culinary knowledge base, which was not a base for anything at all in Kalemie.

Our first morning together already had proved I was woefully unprepared for the adventure of the African kitchen. I opened our cabinets and wondered what we could eat for lunch and dinner. I found a few tiny cans of tomato paste (that looked like they held about two ounces each), a bag of rice, carrots the size of golf balls, and a few tiny onions that looked as though they were dice you use to throw across a Monopoly board. People soon would be hungry and in a few hours were going to want to eat. *What was I going to give them?* Shirley was going to town later and offered to give me a lift so I could pick up some groceries. I was most appreciative and gladly accepted.

Having not yet been to "town", I took in the sights as we made our way over the dusty road. To get there we drove from the house, past the Bible school, to a bridge that goes over the Lukuga River, Lake Tanganyika's only outlet. I noticed the current was very strong. I also noticed that the bridge looked as though it could topple at any moment. The day we arrived, when we flew over the city, I saw this bridge from the air as well as—right next to it—the remnants of something that sunk. When I asked the pilot what was under the water, he retorted that it was the previous bridge used by cars but that at some point it had fallen into the river. He continued to tell me that the bridge currently used formerly was a railroad. Suddenly I found myself staring at this bridge and the strong current of water flowing underneath. Shirley, making light conversation, took no notice of the bridge and proceeded to drive over it. I did my level best to push my beating heart back into my chest. I prayed I would not begin to hyperventilate on our way. Later on I was told that pedestrians would, from time to time, fall from the bridge into the Lukuga River, because it was not even secure for people to cross by foot.

As we pulled into town, I heard the blasting sound of electric guitar music wafting from the storefronts. In the U.S., I heard electric guitars on more occasions than I could count. But in Africa electric guitars are played very differently—a kind of plucking at the strings one by one to produce a very distinct, almost acute, sound.

No tall buildings were on what we would call "Main Street." The tallest building was two-stories high. The road (which at some time had been paved) was filled with deep potholes. No large grocery stores could be found. As people were passing to and fro, everyone from Kalemie that day seemed to be in town for something.

Our first stop was at the butcher's shop. A Belgian man who lived in Zaire for a large portion of his life owned a butchery, where people said he sold the best meat in Kalemie. I heard Ralph wistfully comment that sometimes lunch meat could be found at this same store. That day I desperately hoped to find some for my family. *Oh, just to have a simple sandwich!*

As I walked into the butchery, I was taken aback by the strong smell of raw meat and had to cover my mouth momentarily as I gathered my senses. In the rundown display case I observed various animal parts I never had seen displayed in this fashion before: hooves, ears, tongues, and even heads sat in the open; they waited for eager customers to arrive for dinner supplies. Stunned, I watched a tiny woman walk out of the shop with a bucket on her head. What was stunning was not the bucket on her head but what was inside the bucket: a cow's head, complete with horns and a tongue hanging out of the side of its mouth.

Pulling my attention away from the bucket and cow's head I remembered Shirley coaching me on what meat was the best to purchase. She had had me write this down on a small piece of paper. Scrawled onto the page of a small yellow pad was my order: beef filet, ground beef, and lunch meat. I handed the paper to the man behind the counter. Taking my little order in hand he looked at it and said my order would be ready in the afternoon. Trembling, I thought, "What! I have to come BACK over the BRIDGE?" I smiled and swallowed my horror. After all, Shirley was laughing and having conversations with people. How embarrassing I would have been if everyone had known what childish fears were churning in my mind. Crossing the bridge again temporarily was forgotten as we continued shopping.

Next on our list of stops was one owned by a Greek man, George, and his wife, Maria. They were a kind couple. She herself had been in Kalemie only a short while and took pains to assist me in finding some needed supplies for the house. I located strange-smelling bath soap, canned margarine, bleach (to disinfect any fruit or vegetables that were to be eaten raw), and clothes soap (also used for washing dishes, floors, and anything else that needed cleaning).

Shirley and I went on, shop by shop, down the dusty street as we looked for groceries and household supplies. All the food I could find seemed to be those two-ounce cans of tomato paste, rice, sugar[8], flour, oil, tea, and instant coffee. Everything began to blur; I lost count of what I had spent and what I spent it on. Whatever food item I saw, I handed over some unknown amount of money, put the food into the basket I brought from our house, and moved on. I hoped something would find its way to the dinner table.

Alongside the road were for sale some very large tomatoes plus some bananas and pebble-size potatoes—all of which I purchased and threw into my basket. I mixed the fresh food with the other strange groceries I found. Jamie does not like tomatoes, but I bought them anyway. I figured that, if he had no other options for things to eat, he may just have to learn to like them. I pictured a raw tomato on our dinner plates together with uncooked, knobby carrots and tiny potatoes. My heart was sinking faster than a car falling into the Lukuga River. I felt doomed! Far from my mind were the ideas of preaching crusades and touching thousands. I was hoping only that we would eat dinner that night.

We had been gone for more than an hour. Shirley finished her errands; I did all the purchasing I could do. I needed to get back to the house. I had yet to open the Swahili book; the time was well past 10 a.m. On our way home Shirley mentioned that later that day Ralph was going into town and could pick up our meat order. (To this day I do not think she knows how grateful I was for that!) After we packed our purchases into the car, we made our way down the road toward home. I made a great effort to enter into conversation and to ignore the bridge over which we had again to cross to return to the house. Perhaps seeing my concern about that day's lunch Shirley invited us to eat this midday meal at their house; I could find no words befitting my gratitude for her offer. Between the blessings of the lunch date and of not needing to face the bridge later that day, I knew God was keeping a close eye on one of His beloved—me!

Tom was in Mama Makope's arms; at the door he waited for me as we pulled up to the house. At the sight of me he nearly squealed and hugged my neck tightly. While all I wanted to do was to hold him and to tell him about my day in town, the mysterious mix of groceries was waiting to be unpacked, so I put Tom down and had him "help" carry the bags into the kitchen. He busily played with the tiny tomato paste cans as I attempted to tell Jamie, who was buried in Swahili study, about my morning. After all the groceries were put away, I retreated to my room with Tom in tow, collapsed onto the bed, and prayed that lunch would get here quickly.

Figs do not really matter

 Thus, our lives unfolded during the weeks that followed in Kalemie. I spent my days at war with the kitchen and Swahili, while Jamie busied himself conquering Swahili grammar and vocabulary and along with Ralph learning the ropes of missionary life. These first few weeks Jamie and I spent together in Kalemie became a crash course in REALLY getting to know each other. When we moved to Africa, we thought we knew each other well; we had been married three years and during that time had gone through numerous experiences. However, nothing could have prepared us for the pressure that life in Africa had begun to put on our marriage—and on us individually.

In the United States we were an average couple that spent work days apart and evenings involved in some family- or church-related activity. Our lives, while together, were lived very independently from each other. This independence was shattered in Kalemie, in which the simple activity of visiting the market or grocery-shopping required us to cooperate and communicate about the most minute of details—from who would stay with Tom to who would watch the car while the other dashed into the store to search for necessary supplies (because of security concerns, cars should not be left unattended). Occasionally these small details put us at odds with each other; the level of frustration between us at times was tangible.

While we struggled with our own personal growth issues, Tom contracted a case of malaria. We believed we were prepared for any medical problems that could have arisen, but we sorely were mistaken. Malaria, although a very common disease in Africa, can have deadly consequences if it is not treated properly. This was extremely frightening. We faithfully took anti-malarial medications. Not until later did we learn that the medication we had been taking to prevent malaria no longer was effective; the parasite causing the disease had become resistant to that particular drug. Tom, refusing to take any malaria medication by mouth because of its bitter taste, grew increasingly unwell.

Some kind Finnish missionary nurses in Kalemie treated Tom. They decided that, because of his refusal to take medication by mouth, they would have to give him a series of five quinine injections. This was not the preferred method of treatment, they explained, as quinine is a drug that when given by injection can be very painful and can cause abscesses at the injection site. Thankfully the medication together with prayer did the job; Tom responded positively to the treatment.

One morning not long after he recovered, Tom woke up ill again. He had a fever and was feeling poorly. Once again we found ourselves at the home of the Finnish missionary nurses; we sought their advice. The sites of the quinine injections indeed had abscessed; Tom was given a course of antibiotics. While the antibiotics alleviated his general malaise, the abscesses, after a week of treatment, did not get any better. In fact they grew worse. At that point we decided Tom would be better off if we flew to Nairobi two weeks earlier than our scheduled trip to start language school. We needed to seek medical treatment there. A little plane that landed in Kalemie made room for our small family. In short order we made arrangements and found ourselves flying to Kenya.

> . . . *So He led them through the depths, as through the wilderness.*
> (Ps. 106:9).

To parents no trial is more difficult than seeing their child suffer. Tom spent many of the first weeks we lived in Kalemie struggling with one sickness or another. In the United States malaria and abscesses from quinine injections were not even a "rare occurrence"; to the average American they were unheard of. Here we were, feeling as though we were subjecting our son to these foreign dangers and wallowing in the guilt flooding in waves over us. The frustrations of filtering water, grocery shopping, and language study all faded into nonexistence as our concentration was set solely on Tom and his well-being.

Nairobi

Landing in Kenya for the first time without knowing a place in which we would spend the night was daunting. Because we had no telephones or other means of communication in Kalemie, we had no way of making reservations at any guesthouse or hotel. At a guesthouse we did have reservations set for the time we would study Swahili (which was two-weeks away), but we did not have a clue about any place to which we could go after we had arrived unannounced that night. The one person who did profit from our situation was the taxi driver who drove us from the airport. He was kind enough, with payment of course, to drive us to each and every guesthouse he knew. In the end for a few nights we did find a temporary accommodation at the PAOC[9] guesthouse. The room apparently was one that was not used very often; it boasted just enough space for a set of bunk beds and a sink. At that point we were just thankful to have found a room.

Phone home

The missionaries who ran the guesthouse gave us some advice about a place at which we could make phone calls, because their phones were not available for our use. The same day after we landed, we set off on foot to make a phone call at another guesthouse, at which an international line was available. The walk only took 15 minutes, but in a strange city those 15 minutes seemed to be much longer.

Once we finally were able to call home, we immediately felt comforted when we heard our parents' voices on the other end of the line. Although we had been apart from them for less than two months, somehow we felt as though we had been gone much longer. Phone calls to the States were very expensive, especially for new missionaries with a small support base. All too soon our phone calls ended.

Hanging up was difficult. We looked at each other in amazement at the unspoken change taking place. We were beginning to grow up and learn how to trust God on a whole different level than the one we knew when we lived in the U.S. While still attached to family members in the States and loving them all the same, we had begun to depend on each other as we never had done before. In some way this strange feeling had God's handwriting all over it. He gently was prodding us and encouraging us to keep listening to His voice on this new path we were walking. For a moment—just a moment—the heavy emotion of the past few weeks faded as we felt the Lord's presence comfort us. Finally we knew that all was well.

> *"And let it be . . . that you do as the occasion demands; for God is with you"* (1 Sam. 10:7).

When He leads you in His will, God rarely will give you a clear plan or "exit strategy", for if we knew what lay between our starting point and our destination, odds are good that we would not go. Sometimes we make the mistake of thinking that the will of God is a place; however, Jesus did not die for a "place". God's will for our lives always leads us to people, because Jesus sacrificed His life for people. On the way to those people His challenge to us is to understand that He is with us and will give us the grace to *"do as the occasion demands"*, no matter what that may be. If God is with us, what more can we ask? What situation could we possibly face that He would not have the power to sort? As we made our way in the will of God, we could trust only that, as complications arose (and they did on many occasions), the Spirit of God would lead us to make the right choices.

Unprepared

 We found some missionaries who could direct us to a good pediatrician. Dr. Forbes was an older man who was well-liked by his patients. Perhaps this was because of his seemingly endless supply of concern and calm demeanor, which defused even the most panicked parent's fears. His office thankfully was within walking distance from the guesthouse in which we were staying.

The reception area was set in a very child-friendly scheme, with books, toys, and plenty of cushions on which to lie. After we took a few minutes to fill out the obligatory forms, our names were called. I could tell by the look on Lea's face that a thousand emotions and an equal number of questions brimmed under the surface. I hoped Dr. Forbes was ready to meet with the force that was behind the diminutive figure that housed my wife. I knew we would not leave that office until she was satisfied that the doctor had heard what she had to say and that her concerns were assuaged.

Quietly, after he listened to Tom's health history, the doctor examined him very gently. Few physicians had been able to examine Tom without his complaining angrily and loudly, but our respect for Dr. Forbes was earned when he succeeded in giving our son a thorough physical examination without so much as a whisper emanating from Tom's mouth. "What do you suppose you have in there?" Dr. Forbes questioned Tom as he examined his stomach. "Did you have bananas for breakfast?" Giggling, Tom allowed the examination to go on and even entered into conversation with the doctor.

Once he looked at the quinine injection sites, which had abscessed and were our reason for traveling to Nairobi two weeks before planned, he immediately stated, "Those need to be taken care of surgically." Although this news was shocking, he apparently had dealt with such situations before and assured us that, once the abscesses surgically were cut out, Tom would heal quickly.

That morning we left the pediatrician's office with the name of a pediatric surgeon in hand. On foot we slowly made our way to Nairobi Hospital, in which the surgeon's office was situated. Dr. Forbes called ahead of our arrival; this facilitated our seeing the doctor sooner rather than later. His examination of Tom was not as gentle as Dr. Forbes' examination had been nor did Tom take it as easily, but it did bring the doctor to the same conclusion: surgery was necessary and was to take place the next morning.

Surgery

 The procedure Tom was to undergo at the hospital was simple: the abscesses had to be cut out and then tended to for seven to 10 days afterward. As unnerving as this was, we were thankful Tom would not have to stay there overnight. Hospitals in the regions of Africa in which we have served are very different from those to which we are accustomed in the U.S. We have imagined hospitals in the States or Europe in the 1950s or 1960s to be similar to those hospitals that are considered to be of good quality in East/Central Africa. To such a place we brought Tom the morning of his surgery.

We watched as he was placed on a very cold table and held down by several attendants while the anesthesia was administered. In true Tom fashion he did not go to sleep without a fight; his screams echoed down the hospital corridors. Thankfully the medication took effect quickly; he was asleep and wheeled out to the "theater" or operating room. Bewildered by the whole scene and unfamiliar with what was next, we were led into a hallway, in which we sat on a wooden bench and waited for news from the operating room. After what seemed to be a very long time (but actually was far less than an hour), the surgeon arrived to give us a report. All had gone very well; for the next several days we were to report to his office to have the wounds packed and bandaged. The types of abscesses Tom had were, the doctor said, common to those who had malaria that was treated with quinine injections. Then and there we understood that we had better educate ourselves about the prevention and treatment of this disease.

Later Tom woke angry and sore from the procedure. He was upset that we had to wait for permission from the doctor to leave. His "Bobbin" (a favorite stuffed animal) was at the guesthouse; Tom's patience in waiting to hold Bobbin was wearing thin. Somehow we managed to keep our son quiet while we waited for the discharge orders. Seldom have we seen Tom as happy as he was that evening when we returned to Bobbin and the comfort of being together and away from the cold hospital rooms.

As uncomfortable and painful as the surgery was, the change for the better in Tom's overall health was immediate. The morning after the operation Tom woke up hungry, which was something we had not seen for some time. He ate breakfast with fervor and, while he was sore, wanted to go out to play in the yard. Keeping him quiet and as still as possible were good problems to have, we told each other; what relief we felt that day. This was a great change from the day before in which we had awakened to a totally different set of circumstances.

Surprisingly Tom seemed to understand that we had to see the doctor the next morning and uttered only a small whimper as we got into the taxi that would take us there. However, when we entered the examination room, he began to wail loudly—he knew that what was going to happen would hurt. As gently as possible we lifted Tom onto the examination table and helped the doctor hold him down as the wounds were packed and bandaged. That first day we made the mistake of having Lea hold Tom's feet as I held his arms still. As the bandages were removed, Lea nearly fainted as she watched the wounds being packed and bandaged.

"Do not look!" I said in earnest, but she kept watching. Quickly I took control of the situation and changed places with her. After that day she never held Tom's feet again. As gruesome as his undergoing such treatment was, he did heal very quickly. Almost as suddenly as he was wheeled into surgery, he was well.

Language school

 We bounced from pillar to post and went from guesthouse to guesthouse while we waited for language school to begin. Finally the day arrived for us to go to Mayfield Guesthouse, at which we had a room reserved for the three-and-a-half months we would be studying Swahili. The room was the size of a large bedroom and was the very last room at the end of one of the wings of rooms. Tom slept on a cot; we had two twin beds. The mattresses were not new but felt wonderful after two weeks of moving around and not knowing at what place our feet would land.

We quickly acclimated to life at Mayfield: breakfast at 7 a.m. (except on Sunday, when breakfast started later), lunch at 1 p.m., and dinner at 7 p.m. We learned the meal schedule and knew that hamburgers were served on Saturday night; that was not the night to miss a meal at Mayfield. The day we did miss a meal was Friday lunch, in which fish was served. That was and still is not a food either one of us ever has enjoyed.

Staying at the guesthouse for an extended period of time gave us the opportunity to meet many other missionaries—mostly those from East Africa, although the occasional straggler from regions far away sometimes would pass through. The missionaries who ran the guesthouse (Chuck and Bobbie) welcomed us with open arms and helped us as we navigated through life in Nairobi. Often, when Tom would act up during mealtime, as he complained loudly for one reason or another (and we felt the gaze of all the other guests on the backs of our necks), I needed to take Tom out to "educate him". At that time Chuck would applaud as I exited the room, so the education process could take place in the next room without an audience. Their encouragement and the friendly atmosphere at Mayfield made the lengthy language course bearable.

 Without transportation available to us for the first weeks we were in the city, we often would walk to our language classes housed in a building not more than 100 meters (or a little less than 100 yards) from the Fairview Hotel, at which we stayed during our initial trip to Africa in 1985. The first morning of orientation we arrived with Tom in tow. The school had provided an *ayah*[10] (for those parents with small children) who during classes would be responsible for taking care of the children. I was not at all sure about my feelings about this arrangement. Tom had just undergone some difficult times; the thought of allowing anyone other than one of us to care for him unnerved me. However, I had no other solution available to me, so no other choices could be made in the matter. Other parents were submitting their children to the care of the *ayahs*; perhaps this was not such a bad idea. It would give Tom the opportunity to play with other children in his age range. Up to this point Tom spent most of his time with us or with other adults. His 2-year-old vocabulary was more like that of an adult than of a toddler. I even entertained the thought that Tom may enjoy playing with the children rather than listen to the boring conversations of grownups.

During classes I would seat myself by the window on the second floor, on which most of our classes took place, and glue my eyes to the form of Tom's blue sweater as he toddled out in the playground with the children. I'm amazed that I emerged school with a concept of the language, since I spent nearly every minute of our class time making sure that the *ayahs* were taking good care of my son. On more than one occasion Jamie had to nearly hold me down in my seat to prevent me from running out of class and abandoning the whole idea of learning Swahili because I was so torn over leaving Tom for four hours every morning.

As things turned out, studying Swahili on our own in Kalemie for a few weeks before we arrived in Kenya had, as Ralph and Shirley predicted, turned out to be a blessing. We somehow learned enough things that enabled us to enroll in the second-level class instead of enrolling in the beginner's class with those who were just learning greetings and days of the week.

During this time I was the one glued to the books. Lea spent her free hours walking around the guesthouse with Tom and speaking with the workers to get her language practice. But I had to see a word to say it. I decided to arrange for extra tutoring in the afternoons. Initially Lea accompanied me to these lessons, but she felt uncomfortable leaving Tom for any extra time and eventually left me to go on my own while she spent time with Tom. Our individual strengths in language study soon became evident: Lea swiftly was able to hear and understand the language; I was the one who became strong in grammar. We found ourselves in many situations in which something would be said; I would ask my wife what was said and she could tell me. In return she then would ask me what to say in response. In our case, especially when learning languages, two were better than one!

Transportation

Getting around on foot or using public transportation with Tom in tow was no easy task. One afternoon we were in town and got on a bus to return to the guesthouse. The type of bus we were on, locally known as a *Matatu*, usually is filled with passengers. I rarely (if ever) have seen a *Matatu* that was not overloaded. This particular afternoon our *Matatu* drew near to our stop. As it halted,

I was able to push through the mass of people and make my way off the vehicle. Lea, on the other hand, was not nearly as fortunate or strong as I was. The bus began to pull off with her still inside. She shouted; the bus barely slowed down enough for her to get out. Passing by me she mumbled something about "not ever" riding one of "those things" again. I had to restrain myself to keep from laughing out loud, which I knew would be a great error.

In the days ahead when we were off on errands, I would opt to take the bus home, but Lea would insist on walking. The exercise, she insisted, was good for her. She had "no intention" of getting stuck on a *Matatu*; she was committed to her word. I rode the bus because I usually was carrying Tom (the stroller we had brought with us from the States did no good on the uneven roads and pavements of the city). Knowing I could get out of a *Matatu* without a problem, I would ride home and spot Lea walking home as I rode up toward the guesthouse in the bus. I have to admit that the bus was uncomfortable, but it was much easier than was walking all that way with Tom on my shoulders. This was our peace accord in the transportation arena!

Ralph had sent money with us to Nairobi to purchase a vehicle for the mission's use while we were in Nairobi. As we settled in the city, we began scouting for a vehicle that matched Ralph's budget. I was amazed he, knowing our inexperience, would entrust us with such a task. But I was determined to get the very best vehicle we could find. Our home church pitched in some more money with Ralph's; we were able to get a small station-wagon-looking kind of car. The back seat had no seatbelts with which we could buckle Tom, so Lea usually would sit with him in her lap, with both of them buckled into the front seat. Riding to language school that first day in the car was sweet; the kind of car we drove did not matter. We were just thankful no longer to be at the mercy of the weather. Rain or shine, we easily could arrive at class on time.

Life in language school

 The weeks slowly passed as we struggled with Swahili. We had days in which we believed we were making great progress. We also had many other days in which we had the impression that we were going nowhere with the language. To forget studying and find interpreters would have been so easy! Our hope was that one day we could communicate with the people without the help of a translator. This hope kept us fixed to the task of learning to speak Swahili.

Daily lessons full of grammar and vocabulary left little time for much more than our few outings to the giraffe farm and to church meetings on Sunday. We felt as if we were on "information overload". Both of us regretted not having a better grasp of English grammar, because understanding grammar is vital when one learns to speak another language. Terms such as *helping verbs, participles, adverbs, prepositions, adjectives, present tense, conditional tense, future tense, noun classes,* and *agreement* became common topics of conversation between us. Understanding grammar helps translate thoughts from one's own tongue to a foreign language while the person uses the rules he or she learns in class. What a stretch this was becoming!

To further complicate the learning process was the fact that African Bantu languages (such as Swahili) do not construct their sentences at all as we do in English. This unexpected complication required us to translate not only words but grammatical rules as well. We often wondered how long would be required for the language actually to sink in and to begin to make sense to us. The romantic notion of preaching and teaching and affecting millions of lives on the continent had changed. We slowly understood we would pay a price if ever we were to bring any positive change to the places God would call us to go.

Our course at CPK ended in early December; we took our final exams. Both of us passed with decent marks; we were eager to show off the results to the Hagemeiers. During those last weeks in Kenya before our studies ended, we found a house that had become available for us to use. The missionaries renting the place were leaving. The couple offering the house was happy to allow us to use it while my parents arrived for an early Christmas visit before we returned to Kalemie. Another family working with the Hagemeiers was on its way to Kenya for language study as well and would be able to enjoy the use of the house after we departed. For all involved the setting was helpful. The arrival of Mom and Dad in December was more than welcome to us; we spent our days together playing a card game —Rook—we all enjoyed.

Throughout our time in Nairobi Tom struggled with health issues that had plagued him since his infancy. Dr. Forbes ran numerous tests without any conclusive results as to what was causing the symptoms that had beset him for so long. While Mom and Dad were with us, they suggested that Tom and Lea return to the States so Tom could receive a thorough medical check. After time in prayer and discussion we concluded we would be wise to have Tom checked in the U.S. Arrangements were made for them to fly back for several weeks while the medical checks were done; I would fly back alone to Kalemie. While this was to be our first Christmas together overseas, it turned out to be Christmas spent apart on opposite sides of the world.

Wanting to be willing

> . . . *for it is God who works in you both to will and to do for His good pleasure* (Phil. 2:13).

"When we get to the end of our own willing, we can be assured of the fact that God is at work in us to be our willing, our working and our fulfilling".[11] We had begun to arrive at the end of our own desire to do the will of God; emotionally, the struggles went to a depth we never had experienced. In our hearts we were sure we were being obedient to the will of God, but our emotions about all the difficulties we had experienced (especially with Tom's health) weighed on us heavily. During this time we began to learn how to allow God to work out His willing through us—to learn how to will to do His will. John 7:17-18 states, "*If anyone wills to do His will, he shall know concerning the doctrine, whether it is from God or whether I speak on My own authority. He who speaks from himself seeks his own glory; but He who seeks the glory of the One who sent Him is true, and no unrighteousness is in Him.*" In effect, as we ceased to struggle with how God's will fit in with our own wills (or how we thought things should be done or how they should happen) and focused on God's will working through us, the less we agonized with the "how?"s and "why?"s of what was happening. Thus knowing we were not seeking our own glory (our own will) but the glory (the will) of God, we were set in a place in our faith in which we could "fight the good fight of faith"[12] for Tom and gain the victory.

Testing

 Watching Lea and Tom get into the taxi with my parents as they all journeyed to Florida without me was, to say the least, an unexpected bump in our journey. I was bewildered at this turn of events and during those long weeks we were apart felt intensely alone. While we were in language school, we had bought Tom a puppy. I busied myself with acquiring all the proper documentation required to transport the puppy to Zaire. I wanted Tom to have his dog waiting for him when our son arrived home. Nothing was going to make me

69

waver in my determination to do so. Finally all the documents were in order, the travel crate was ready, and the dog was loaded into the MAF plane I chartered months ago for all us to return to Kalemie.

On my return the usual missionary crew was waiting for me at the airport. The group did its best to rally around me in my temporary, solitary state. The customs and immigration officials took great pains to complicate my bringing Tom's dog into Kalemie. After we spent a long time discussing the matter, the decision was made that the next day I would meet with the officials at their office in town. Shirley agreed to go with me to help translate to the officials my side of the story. While all the documents were in order, the officials earnestly looked for a reason to charge us for bringing the dog into the country. At last perhaps they grew weary with my explanations and polite refusal to pay any unofficial fees, so they let us go. But with our departure we heard a warning that, while we did not pay anything at that time, we would pay customs if the dog were to have puppies. I wondered whether they had noticed that the dog was a male.

On most days I was invited to the Hagemeiers for lunch and dinner. This was a great help during those otherwise quiet evenings alone, to which I was not acccustomed at all. Ralph also had scheduled me to teach two classes during my first term back from language school. Staying busy preparing for those classes as well as assisting Ralph with other chores at the Bible school helped me pass the time. While we were apart, I spent hours in prayer for Tom and Lea and determined that the enemy would not have the last word in the matter. Because Kalemie is so remote and communication with the outside world was done mostly via the post arriving from Kenya, during most of the time we were apart I had no knowledge of what was happening with Tom[13].

This was not in our plan

 Landing in South Florida after being away for six months was strange. This was unplanned; I struggled with feelings of failure. *How could this have happened to Tom? How could we have prevented this condition?* Thankfully we did not have much spare time for agonizing as we swiftly made arrangements for Tom to be seen by a physician in Miami (about an hour's drive away). A myriad of tests checked for everything from cystic fibrosis to multiple sclerosis; nothing conclusive was found.

After some weeks of travel between Lake Worth and Miami we held our final consultation with the physician. She kindly explained she had concluded that Tom had been suffering with irritable bowel syndrome, which, at that time, usually was diagnosed through a process of ruling things out. She went on to explain that individuals react differently to the condition and gave us some guidelines to find out exactly what would irritate Tom and what to do to alleviate his discomfort. The condition, she went on to explain, could be aggravated by consuming large quantities of liquids, which Tom did. Whenever he suffered with symptoms, we had been counseled to push liquids to prevent dehydration. Under normal circumstances, the doctor explained, this counsel is the right counsel to follow. However, with someone who has this condition, drinking large amounts of liquids only serves to aggravate the already uncomfortable situation. Unknowingly we had contributed to the onset of symptoms, but we were relieved finally to get some useful information. Once Tom was "in the clear" and we worked on following the doctor's orders for his diet, we made plans to return to Africa.

Undergoing these tests on Tom without the presence of my husband at my side at the very least was unsettling. Not only was Tom's welfare at stake, an early pregnancy also was at risk. While I was at the hospital, I had a blood test taken; this confirmed my suspicions. The year after Tom

71

was born, we already had experienced a miscarriage. But I had set my hopes on this pregnancy working out normally. Unfortunately, the familiar symptoms I felt with the previous miscarriage returned; I lost the pregnancy. Because this happened early on, no complications set in. I was able to go on without incident and recover.

While Christmas and New Year's Day passed, I barely had taken note. We spent time with both families and felt badly for the inevitable "goodbye" that soon was going to take place. Six weeks after we arrived in the States, we boarded yet another plane that would take us back to the continent. Accompanying us on our trip were my father and another Christian brother, A. T. Lowery, who would assist the Hagemeiers in some construction projects under way at the Bible-school compound. I was relieved, not only because Tom was cleared of any serious medical condition but also to have others traveling with us. As tiring as transcontinental flights can be, I almost was comforted to return to what was becoming our "normal" lifestyle.

Nairobi was exactly as we had left it: the roads were full of traffic, pedestrians crossed the streets in their characteristic, disorganized fashion—and I found myself loving every moment! Our chartered flight to Kalemie was set for the next morning. I was intent on showing my father and our other guest the beauty of the Rift Valley that was only an hour's drive from the city. Having Ralph's car available to us while we were in Kenya was convenient. We took the opportunity to drive out of Nairobi and enjoy the scenery the country had to offer.

In Kenya and other nations that previously were colonized by the British, cars drive on the left side of the road, which at first is very disturbing to those of us who have grown up driving on the right side of the road. My father sat in the passenger's seat while I drove; Tom sat in the back with our guest. I could not help but make note of the irony: I was driving while my father nervously sat in the seat next to me. I had flashbacks of years earlier and his teaching me to drive. Despite the nervous tension in the car we arrived at several lookout points at which we were able to admire the valley beneath us. All too soon we had to make our way back to town on the narrow, potholed roads of Kenya. I still can sense my father's relief at our safe arrival to the guesthouse.

Reunion

The day after our courageous scenic tour, we rose early and went to Nairobi's Wilson Airport, at which we were set to board our chartered MAF plane to Kalemie, Zaire. That day, because we had only three adults and one child as passengers, we took a small, single-prop Cessna. Before we boarded, everyone and everything was weighed. No estimating could occur; the weight had to be calculated exactly for the pilot to know whether we could get off the ground! Thankfully none of our luggage had to be left behind. We were able to set off for what swiftly was becoming home.

When we were flying to Kalemie via Nairobi, we usually set down somewhere in Tanzania to refuel the plane. On this trip we stopped at the *Mwanza* airport. I could not help but notice the fighter jets resembling what we thought were "Russian migs" sitting near the small airport terminal. Curious, I asked the MAF pilot about these planes. He replied that during the darkest days of the Cold War, these jets were stationed at the airport but had become useless because of a lack of maintenance. How they ended up there was anyone's guess. The "army planes" we were studying fascinated Tom. Just looking at them I felt vaguely uncomfortable and was glad when the refueling was done and we were ready to go on with our journey.

Waiting for us at the airport in Kalemie were Jamie, Ralph, and Shirley. The delinquent tanks and battered building had shocked me no longer; this was the place at which we were supposed to be. I was glad to be back! Jamie was allowed to meet us on the runway. We did not have enough hugs and kisses to express how happy we were to be back together as a family. Escorted into the now familiar "terminal" building we went through the arduous process of clearing customs. In Kalemie customs consists of three or four men who take to the side you and your luggage, open it, and inspect every article they find (we are not ever sure whether they are the actual officials, because no one wears a uniform or ID). On occasion one may be fortunate enough to have a benevolent customs official go through one's suitcase. A benevolent official does not pull out undergarments and other unmentionables on which all those around can see and comment. In my "other life" (before I moved to Africa), I easily was embarrassed and perhaps excessively private. However, in Kalemie, this part of my character was swiftly being sorted as I was learning how to bear up under all kinds of embarrassments when I went through customs.

 By the time Lea and Tom arrived back in Kalemie, I was finished teaching half a term of classes. For the first time I taught after I returned from language school, Ralph and Shirley graciously gave me an interpreter. But I was warned: after the first term I would be required to teach in Swahili without an interpreter. When Lea returned, she did not have to teach any classes for several weeks because we were so far into the term. I could tell she was happy to wait a few more weeks to brush up on her Swahili, which she was unable to use while she was in the States. We spent many hours talking about what happened with Tom's medical tests. Knowing he was fine and developing normally was a great relief.

During their time with us Lea's father and the other guest worked together for two weeks. Their goal was to scout out the building projects, return to the U.S., and then later in the year return to Kalemie with a full building team to work on the property. While they were in Kalemie, they worked diligently and even were able, with the help of many national workers, to roof a sizeable church. The plans were laid for their subsequent visit. Once again at the small airport we said our goodbyes. Saying good-bye, we quickly learned, was part of our job description. We thanked God for His grace in learning how to flow with this part of our job.

As we look back on our first few months in Africa, we easily see how God was stripping the "figs", or the things and attitudes that do not really matter, from our lives. God never stops removing those "figs". As He prunes us, those whom He loves, He prepares us to produce, not those useless "figs", but fruit that will remain. What is the fruit that remains? People's souls.

> " . . . and every branch that bears fruit He prunes, that it may bear more fruit . . . You did not choose Me, but I chose you and appointed you that you should go and bear fruit, and that your fruit should remain, that whatever you ask the Father in My name He may give you" (John 15:2b, 16).

Chapter 3

Home is Not Home Any Longer

"Do not pray for easy lives. Pray to be stronger men. Do not pray for tasks equal to your powers; pray for powers equal to your tasks."

–Phillips Brooks[14]

E xplaining why we remained in Zaire after all we experienced during our first six months on the field is diffiult if not impossible. When friends and loved ones later asked what pressed us to stay after all we had experienced, we were at a loss for words. How could we explain the will of God? Deep inside we knew we were exactly at the place in which God had ordained us to be; that was all we needed to know. Do not think we never were attacked with thoughts of doubt. We were, but we simply trusted the last word we had heard from God, which was for us to go to Zaire. Stubbornly we hung onto that word.

More challenges

 School ended; we had a couple of weeks off from teaching until the new semester began. Ralph informed us that, for this next term, we were not going to be allowed to use interpreters to teach our classes, because he expected us to teach in Swahili. While we had known this step was inevitable, we still struggled with the "how" of accomplishing such a task! Lea was given one class to teach; I was given two classes.

Almost immediately I rose to the task and in earnest began preparing for the upcoming term. Slowly (at a snail's pace at first, or so things seemed), my classes began to take shape. Each class period lasted one-and-one-half hours and, depending on the class, met once or twice per week.

I thoroughly enjoyed studying not only Swahili (as I prepared for my classes) but also for the class itself. During those times I had the double blessing of learning the language as well as learning the content of the lessons. Additionally, lasting relationships were developed with my students—something I had hoped would happen.

Initially teaching for an hour and a half in Swahili required us to handwrite at least 21 pages of notes from which to read. But as the days and weeks passed, the myriad of note pages gave way to outlines as we dared to stray from reading every word to teaching from our hearts. By the end of the first term our fluency of Swahili resulted from our obedience in accepting the Hagemeiers' directive to learn the language and to the positive encouragement to step out into the waters of faith. We believed God that we could teach in the students' native language.

Time with God

The months passed by. Gradually we found ourselves not just adjusting but more importantly enjoying life as the Lord gave us the strength to grow and fit into our new surroundings. From the time we married, our mornings always had been spent in prayer and Bible reading. When we moved to Africa, this did not change. More than ever we desperately needed time with God. Our lives depended on the spiritual vehicles He gave us daily to face each new day. Sometimes as early as 4:30 in the morning I would wake and call on the Lord, as if to remind Him of how much I needed Him that day. Lea usually awoke to the sound of my praying and got the coffee going. We knew we had to meet each new day by talking with our Father.

Change me

 During those first months on the field I personally learned so much, as God began gently to challenge me to see those areas that were flawed in my character. I could do little for Africa before these areas were addressed, so almost immediately after we arrived, God started working on me! I had, in times past, often been guilty of placing expectations on my husband to satisfy the needs in my life that only God could fulfill. As a young wife I easily expected that in marriage I would have all my spiritual, emotional, and physical needs met. When those expectations were not fulfilled, I was greatly disappointed.

The stresses the mission field places on a couple bring all such unrealistic expectations to light. In Africa I learned that Jamie could not fill the void that was created for God to fill. Once I let Jamie off the hook and began to look to God for myself, my soul was relieved and refreshed in His loving presence. This personal revival for me also brought Jamie and me closer together as a couple. I began to love my husband without expecting anything in return.

Before we lived in Kalemie, I had been more than a little difficult to live with as I wrestled with some deep, personal issues. Much of my young life was spent in struggles over matters of my heart and soul. I felt as though I was a failure when my ability to overcome was not enough to bring me to victory. The disappointment of not being an overcomer often was taken out on those I loved the most; this frustrated me even further.

God brought me to Zaire—to a place of solitude. There I began to undergo a sweeping change that permanently would alter the course of my life. My prayers went from "change him" or "change them" to "change me". God had to bring me to a place in which He and I were alone together. In that seclusion He was able to address those issues that only He knew how to change. For me that place was Kalemie, Zaire.

Family time

 I could not have been happier anywhere else than I was in Kalemie. I had hoped someday to have the joy of actually serving seasoned missionaries such as the Hagemeiers, so living in those days was beyond my dreams! My time was filled with teaching classes, preparing messages to preach on the weekends in various churches of all denominations, and basking in the joy of being on the mission field. In serving Ralph and Shirley I felt complete.

Each day my ability to speak Swahili grew; soon I found myself interpreting for visitors. About a year had passed since our arrival; here I was, defying all the odds my teacher gave me so long ago. Not only had I learned a foreign language, I also was becoming fluent enough to interpret. Measuring the satisfaction I felt at this accomplishment was impossible. All this joy made the struggle we had endured to get this far well worth the effort.

Our family life also was becoming better than it had ever been. Kalemie was not (nor is it today) a big place with lots of things to do, so we had to make up our own social and entertainment calendar. Our "big night out" as a family was going to town to check the mail. We would pop some popcorn Ralph gave us and with Tom would drive to check the mailbox, which usually was empty.[15] In those days we did not have phones—cell or otherwise—which made knowing what was in our bank account back in the U.S. next to impossible. Going weeks and even months without news from home was not unusual. Nevertheless, while we often were disappointed that mail did not make its way to our Zairian post box, on those drives we had a great time together. We had no traffic jams; Tom loved being the center of our attention.

The evenings as well were centered on our family. Lea learned to cope with the kitchen. Nearly every evening while she was working on dinner, Tom and I sat together and played with his favorite Matchbox™ cars. After dinner Lea would join in; sometimes we played late into the evening, as we laughed and enjoyed our time together. Those days were some of the best days of our lives; they passed all too quickly.

Visitors

 Some months passed. Lea's father and mother, Esko and Kaisa, and her younger brother, Matthew, were arriving for a visit. A rather large construction team (put together by our local church in Florida) accompanied them. Kaisa assisted a local clinic and cared for expectant mothers. Esko arrived to help with the construction team working on Bible-school facilities (as planned on his trip a few months earlier).

The large size of the team called for all missionaries, for the duration of their visit, to work together by providing things such as meals, lodging, and transportation. Needless to say, the weeks the team was with us were filled with activity.

Meals were divided by households, since we had several households of missionaries. Each household daily was assigned various tasks to help keep up with the load of serving the visitors. For example meals would be divided by meat, vegetable, and starch. Lea was exceptionally happy when Shirley assigned her to vegetable duty. Preparing a pot of green beans was a snap compared to cooking the main course of the meal. From time to time in those days Lea jokingly said, "Give me vegetable duty any day!" Unfortunately, just as everyone else did, she had to take her turn with the main course. The first time she had "main-course" duty, the whole afternoon she panicked while she prepared the main course of meatballs and gravy. Happily, the meatballs turned out just fine; the rest of us were off the hook as she relaxed for a few days before she took another crack at the main course.

The construction-team members worked fervently. Shortly before they were about to leave, I took a few of them on a short trip to visit a village that was approximately and hour and a half from Kalemie. Among those I was leading on the trip were my parents-in-law; I hoped our excursion would be a positive experience for them. During the time I served in Zaire, I learned that a trip to the bush was no easy task. Spending time ministering in the villages requires preparation; on these trips adequate fuel, spare tires, water, and other various supplies must be brought.

The day of our departure arrived. I left Lea with Tom and Matthew in Kalemie as I headed out with a vehicle full of *Wazungu*[16] (people of European descent) for a village called *Makungu*. The trip to Makungu took longer than usual because of the extremely poor condition of the roads. (I imagine that, as of this writing, the roads are not any better than they were in those days.)

My concern for my in-laws' experience in Makungu was alleviated soon after our arrival. Even during those early days our experience has been that visitors to Africa often would put their noses up to the national fare. In the village our group was treated royally as the national believers prepared for us generous meals of truly African cuisine. One of the staple foods they served us is called *ugali*. *Ugali* simply is cornmeal mixed with boiling water; the mixture is formed into a stiff paste very similar to bread dough. Eating *ugali* neatly is an acquired skill that foreigners rarely achieve to the same degree as the national does. Usually it is served with some kind of sauce and, if possible, meat. A small piece of *ugali* is taken between the fingers and then rolled, scooped in gravy, and eaten. It usually holds its heat very well; often we have burned our fingers while we attempted to eat it as the Africans do.

My father- and mother-in-law both did well with the first hurdle of eating *ugali*. I was amazed at their courage in eating nearly everything that passed in front of them. My father-in-law, however, was the one who was truly astounding when during one particular meal he saved us all. Customarily the *matumbo*[17] (entrails) of the slaughtered meal animal is served to guests; to be served *matumbo* is an honor. Not eating *matumbo* when it is served to you could be considered an insult. During this one meal in question we were served *matumbo*. Those of us present stared at the pot; an awkward silence fell over us. As if to understand that we needed rescuing, my father-in-law took the pot in question and filled his plate with the contents. Apparently he relished every bite of the food and chuckled. He knew he did better with this meal than the rest of us did. This gesture earned him the respect of the entire team and village.

One year

> *And how blessed all those in whom you live, whose lives become roads you travel; they wind through lonesome valleys, come on brooks, discover cool springs and pools brimming with rain! God-traveled, these roads curve up the mountain, and at the last turn—Zion! God in full view!* (Psalm 84:5-6 Message).

 Something special takes place when you do not give up on the will of God. The road, while it seems too difficult at times, really is not unbearable. It is just tough enough to push us to realize our own helplessness, which brings us to use our faith in God to help us do what He has called us to do. On the completion of our first year on the field this is exactly what we experienced. For us the year had been one of "firsts": learning our first new language, living in a foreign country, teaching in a Bible school, and being radically obedient to God's call. These roads we traveled at times truly were lonesome roads, but we never lacked the rain when we needed it. After that year was complete, we were able to recognize that His presence guided us throughout the journey and that He had walked those roads with us.

Graduation services once again were on us; we were set to return to the U.S. with Jamie's parents, who were, for the second time, braving the journey to Kalemie. This included the ride on a small MAF plane. Before they arrived, Ralph called us in and asked whether we would consider staying on for an extra six months, because he and Shirley had planned to take a leave and would appreciate the help in their absence. Neither of us had a question asked between us; of course, we would stay. In fact the extra six months would give us time to put off the inevitable journey home. Leaving Zaire was not an option we really were looking toward. As we contemplated our future, between us passed an unspoken question: *What if, after this term was finished, we never returned to the continent?*

The busy schedule that usually accompanies seminars was set, but we were unruffled by the extra duties. I braved the kitchen as in the U.S. I never dared to do; into Ralph's vehicles Jamie easily siphoned gas and diesel fuel from large metal barrels. Tom, fully recovered from the past year's health scares, bounced around from house to house and bragged that his grandparents were arriving with presents. Jamie's father was one of the speakers for the seminar; a long time had passed since we sat under his preaching. We could not wait to hear him!

Finally their plane landed at the now-familiar airport, whose bullet-riddled exterior and dilapidated runway no longer affected us in the least. Memories of our initial arrival and especially my own reaction to Kalemie suddenly flooded my mind. I chuckled as I pictured what just one year before my facial expressions must have communicated to those around me. Customs and immigrations officials proceeded to hurl their usual demands at the visitors. We both hoped that Mom and Dad would not be too upset by their experience. While we waited behind the barrier, Tom stood as still as a 3-year-old can stand. At last, when the usual grumblings of the officials (about whatever they thought might be in disorder) were complete, we were allowed to take the dusty road back home.[18] While disappointed that we would not accompany them to the States after their trip to Zaire, Mom and Dad were very understanding and supported our decision to stay while the Hagemeiers took their leave.

During the time of the seminar our family evenings were spent laughing together and playing card games. After one evening meal with the Hagemeiers and the whole team of visitors I returned home early with Tom and Jamie's mother to get Tom ready for bed while Jamie and his father stayed behind and talked with the Hagemeiers. While he was a busy little boy, Tom did need his sleep—or was his mother the one who needed him to sleep? In any case, once he had his bath and bedtime story, he easily went to bed. I was thankful, because in those days Tom had been known to refuse going to bed. I headed into the kitchen to clean up the remains of the mess I had made while I prepared dinner and then joined Jamie's mother in the small living area. I enjoyed her company as we waited for Jamie and his father to return.

As a leader and pastor's wife, Jamie's mother is an honorable woman; very few are as honorable as Mary Ann Peters. She is soft-spoken, supports her husband and family, and carries herself with great dignity, which is something I hope I have learned and even to a small degree have demonstrated in my own life. Therefore I listened when she turned the conversation in a more serious direction. Tears sprang to her eyes as she complimented me. She said she had been watching me and had noticed how much in the past year I had grown and learned how to care for my family. She said she was very proud of what the Lord had accomplished in me. I never had received such an encouragement. Its effect on my life has been profound. Such a small word, yet I remember it to this day.

> Thank you, Mom, for the moments you spent with me that day. In Africa I had been keenly aware of my shortcomings as a wife. I did not notice I actually had made some progress, but God did. He made sure someone told me.

The seminar went off without a hitch; however, one morning Jamie woke, just days before the end of the series of meetings, and felt unusually ill with chills, sweating, and fever. Malaria was the undisputed culprit; he immediately began taking what we call the malaria "cure". We did not go to a clinic for treatment, because our experience with Tom indicated that the treatment available in Kalemie was far from sufficient. Shirley had told us when we went to Kenya to ask a pharmacist for the best malaria cure to have on hand in case we would have another malaria encounter. Thankfully we listened to her advice; almost as quickly as it had begun, the nasty bug was eliminated from his system. Just a couple of days later Jamie was well enough to see his parents and the entire team off at the airport. While at this goodbye tears were flowing, they were few in comparison to those of the year before. After all, we would be seeing each other in just six months' time.

Just when we were getting comfortable . . .

 As soon as the team left, Shirley began setting up the teaching schedule for the upcoming school term. Since she and Ralph would be leaving, everything had to be put into order before their departure. Each teacher was given his or her assignment; we were not left out. Since I was given some extra duties to cover while Ralph was out of the country, my teaching schedule remained the same as it had the previous term, which was two classes. We hoped Lea again would be given one class to teach. Shirley, however, had other ideas, because the school had shortage of teachers for that term. When she was handed her assignment, Lea was told she was going to be teaching two classes. While we had made great strides in speaking Swahili, my wife was at her wits' end and felt overwhelmed with the responsibility of teaching two classes and overseeing our home. She asked to meet with Shirley to beg her to be relieved of one of the two classes.

You can do more than you think

 When I entered Shirley's office, tears were welling up in the back of my eyes; a large lump was forming in my throat. I sat down and began to explain to Shirley how I believed I was unable to meet the demand of teaching two classes. My reasoning included my small son, a home, and a husband. Unflinching at my response Shirley began to challenge me and asked me why I thought I was incapable of more than what I was doing. "The reason the Lord brings us to these places," she went on, "is to challenge us to reach for more, to do more, to be more than we had dreamed. Lea," she said, "I see you are capable of so much more. Besides, we need you now to rise to the occasion." And, as if what I already had on my plate was not enough, Shirley told me that one of the national teachers was on a trip out of the country. His return would be delayed several weeks, which meant I in the interim would be teaching a THIRD class as a substitute! All this and my continued responsibilities as a mother and wife almost were overwhelming. At that moment I had a choice to make—to operate in rebellion and refuse to do what I was being asked to do or to trust that the woman before me was in my life for a reason. I knew I trusted her. Of course I would teach the third class, even if it was "apologetics". I left her office not feeling discouraged but rather encouraged. I decided to believe God to do more in my life this coming term; I began to understand what Paul meant in Philippians 4:13: *I can do all things through Christ who strengthens me.* Nothing—not even teaching three classes—was impossible when God was involved.

Seeing Him walk by

And when they saw Him walking on the sea, they supposed it was a ghost, and cried out; for they all saw Him and were troubled. But immediately He talked with them and said to them, "Be of good cheer! It is I; do not be afraid" (Mark 6:49-50).

Jesus' disciples had just returned from witnessing a great miracle; the feeding of the 5,000 preceded this incident on the sea. Jesus had sent His disciples on the boat to go ahead of Him to Bethsaida as He, after sending away the multitudes He had fed, went to spend time in prayer on a mountain. The disciples encountered a great storm. Jesus, true to fashion, noticed their struggle and walked on the water toward them. In verse 48 the Scriptures indicate that Jesus *would have passed them* (the disciples) *by* had they not seen Him. Somehow they must have recognized Him, but at the same time the Bible says that *they were troubled* (verse 50) at the sighting, because they supposed He was something He was not: a ghost.

This pattern of life–going from great victory (such as the disciples did in feeding 5,000) to a trough of distress (like the storm on the sea)–holds true today. Jesus never is surprised by the unsuspected storms we will encounter. Surely, when He sent His people on the boat, He knew the storm would arrive. But His purpose in sending them beforehand on the boat was to get them to the other side. Why He chose to send them on a boat instead of to accompany Him to the mountain is up for debate. However, we do know for sure that, once Jesus entered into the boat with the disciples and they recognized Him for Who He was, they did arrive at their destination.

In many ways our initial experiences (and those that followed in Africa) mirrored those of the disciples. We experienced the great victory of learning the language and growing and maturing in the work of the Lord only to have those victories go almost forgotten as we fell into the troughs of the storms that occurred after great victory. Tempted as we were to forget the victories and concentrate only on the storms, we somehow focused on "getting to the other side" of the inclement weather. Jesus always found His way to our boat, even though, much like His disciples, we often did not recognize His presence until the storm nearly consumed us.

Many theories exist as to why we encounter the storms we do in life. We know that God does not seek to destroy life but to give it (John 10:10).

At the same time, we live in a fallen world in which Satan is at work (2 Cor. 4:3-4). He looks to destroy the people of God—we do not have a free ride guaranteed to us! In fact, once a believer truly lives for God and His will, we have the assurance that trouble will occur.

> *"These things I have spoken to you, that in Me you may have peace. In the world you will have tribulation; but be of good cheer, I have overcome the world"* (John 16:33).

Not only do we have the assurance that trouble will arrive, we have the greater assurance that Jesus already has overcome those troubles for us. What remains for us to do is to allow God's peace to rest in our hearts as we confront those troubles—for we are assured of ultimate victory if we stay in Him.

Hopeful

Taking on extra responsibilities and teaching extra classes was difficult but not impossible. In fact, we found ourselves enjoying the journey and understanding that God was capable of doing whatever was necessary to help us make the trip. Evenings still were set aside for family time; Tom remained the center of our world. We were hoping for another child and later on in the term learned that another baby was on the way. Tentatively hopeful, we took care not to do anything unnecessary, such as driving on the bumpy roads. We made sure that in between classes, Lea got plenty of rest. The fact that this baby was due after our return to the States was an added blessing.

One morning just a few short months into the pregnancy Lea woke with pain in her back. I took matters into my own hands and arranged for someone to teach her classes for that day so she could stay home. At first the pain subsided for a few days but returned with a vengeance. Her condition grew increasingly worse; we reluctantly went to the hospital, which we usually avoided. Entering into the "examination room" we thanked God that we had our own sterile gloves, because no one appeared to have cleaned the room in months, if not years. But we had no choice in the matter and allowed her to be examined. The nurse confirmed that she had not miscarried. All we could do was go home and pray. Later on that night, to our great disappointment and sorrow, we did lose the baby.

Hoping the worst was behind us, I resumed my activities and arranged for Lea's classes to be covered by the other teachers as she recuperated. Thankfully, the teacher whose return was delayed finally did return and was able to teach his class as well as shoulder some of the unexpected teaching burden. Things with Lea seemed to be taking a turn for the better.

Two days after losing the pregnancy, the back pain Lea had been experiencing returned; it was worse than it had been before the miscarriage. This went on for another two or three days and progressed to the point in which we knew medical intervention was necessary. The problem we faced was the difficult task of getting out of Kalemie without a chartered plane. Lea was in no condition to take a boat across the lake to Tanzania or to drive the roads of Zaire; we knew the local hospitals had nothing they could offer her in the area of medical care. The only solution was for God to help us mightily.

One morning nearly one week into this crisis we heard a small plane circle the city. The aircraft, loaded with supplies to deliver to an inland mission, stopped in Kalemie on its way to the interior. The plane was set to return the next day after it delivered its cargo. After we communicated our situation to the pilot, he agreed to collect us the next day as he returned to Nairobi, Kenya. We were not even charged for this flight, which could have set us back several hundred dollars.

Saved

 We took off from Kalemie the next day. Tom and I could do little more than watch as Lea suffered through the flight as she vomited and fought the pain in her back. Finally, late in the evening, we arrived and the next morning were able to see a physician. She was sent to the hospital and underwent surgery. The doctor found that not only had she miscarried, she was suffering from appendicitis and a list of other complications resulting from the miscarriage. The appendix was about to burst, the doctor said matter-of-factly. She did not want to speculate what might have happened had Lea not gone to the hospital when she did. I was surprised by this unexpected news and, as I waited for her to wake from the anesthesia, thanked God my wife was still with me.

What do you mean my appendix?

 My first memory after the operation was the pain I felt as I was transferred from one bed to another. I howled! Whoever was moving me seemed not to care that I had just emerged from surgery. Groggy, I asked the nurse (who was attempting to quiet me down) what had been done to me. She replied, "I think they did many things to you. I know you had your appendix taken out."

My immediate response was, "What? My appendix?" I supposed I had been mistaken for another patient. I then became able to focus on Jamie's face; he agreed with the nurse. He told me they had taken my appendix out and that the next morning he would explain everything.

Before surgery the doctor said she was going to try to fix everything with a simple laparoscope, which would leave me with just a small incision in my belly. She assured me it would heal quickly. What I felt after surgery was not just a small incision. When, the next morning, I became aware of things, I swiftly noted that the incision was about five-inches in length.

The hospital staff explained what had happened to me and speculated that, perhaps, the appendicitis had been the cause of the latest miscarriage. Whatever the cause I was sore and grouchy and desperately wanted this episode to end! Hospitals in Kenya, even the nicest ones, were very basic and reminiscent of hospitals in the States and Europe in decades past. I was fortunate to be in one of the best; however, the care I was given at that time still was very different to what I might have experienced if this occurred in the U.S.

Time constraints

 As Lea recovered in the hospital, I began making inquiries about our return to Kalemie. Our departure to the U.S. was drawing near; in our haste to leave Zaire we had not packed the house or even left Ralph a report on the activities that took place in his absence. MAF flew weekly to Bukavu, a sizeable city on the border of Rwanda, north of Kalemie. From Bukavu we learned that flights occasionally went to Kalemie. Since a family working with the Hagemeiers lived in Bukavu, we decided to fly there as soon as Lea could be released from hospital. From there we hoped to make our way to Kalemie.

Convincing the doctor to release Lea from the hospital so we could return to take care of business in Zaire was another story. While Lea was making good progress, the physician was loath to release her until Lea was at least five days out of surgery. On the fifth morning after the operation nurses entered the room nonchalantly and began cleaning the incision as they had done every day. Without any due process my wife was told to "exhale" while one of the nurses pulled out the drainage tube. This was apparently a painful procedure; Lea's eyes opened doublewide. I did my best to avert my own attention from the gruesome process. Then without further ado, the nurse who so efficiently removed the drainage tube said, "Tomorrow, the doctor will remove the stitches when you see her at her office." As swiftly as we had entered the hospital, we found ourselves out-side the entrance, as we held a bagful of medication Lea had been pre-scribed to take. We hoped the doctor would clear us for travel the next day.

Extra tape

In the morning Jamie packed all three of us into a taxi so we could make our way to the now-familiar doctor's office. My doctor was a very to-the-point individual. She simply said, "This will hurt some", as she clipped the ends of the stitches and pulled them out. Sting it did! Quickly she cleaned the site with disin-fectant and very adeptly taped me up and handed us an extra two rolls of this tape. She said the tape would be necessary in case the site opened. "Keep it taped up for another week" was her advice. Also, to avoid any further complications, she advised me not to lift anything heavy nor for some time engage in any strenuous activity. My mind still wobbled around the need for tape and the "in-case-it-opened-up" scenario, which for a few minutes made the room a bit fuzzy! Our next important question was whether we could fly, to which she answered, "If you must, go ahead."

We were pressed to fly because our return ticket to the U.S. now was-non-refundable. We had to make the flight back to the States, which by this time was just more than two weeks away. Time was not on our side; so much was left undone.

Travel, African style!

Remembering the teacher for whom Lea had to substitute—the one who was delayed in returning to Kalemie because of the difficulties of traveling in Zaire—we prayed for favor, open doors, and flights. Thankfully, we were able to get to Bukavu, Zaire, easily enough with MAF's weekly flight from Nairobi. The family working with the Hagemeiers, Paul and Emily Hoyt and their children, graciously received us at the small Kavumu airport situated 45 minutes from the city. The Hoyts helped us with lodging while we worked to find a way home. Unfortunately, true to Zaire's pattern, we could not find a plane flying to Kalemie. Several days passed without news of any flights, so we decided to charter a small plane with MAF. This was an unexpected expense; together with the recent hospital bill, the flight from Nairobi, and the lodging bills we had incurred while we stayed in Kenya, things were very tight financially. But God was true to His pattern and was faithful to care for us. While things were tight, we still were able to afford the charter and to make our way back to settle things. He not only was our Healer but also our Provider in every part of the unexpected way.

The small plane we chartered had room for five passengers and for a small amount of luggage—just enough for our family and the pilot. We sent word via short-wave radio that we were hoping to fly in and asked whether someone would meet us when we arrived. Not knowing whether the message made its way through, we knew the pilot would fly over the city anyway; this would alert people to arrive at the airport. In any case we trusted that one way or another, word would get out about our arrival.

As we flew south from Bukavu, we encountered some clouds and turbulence. December normally is a rainy time of year; we were not surprised that along the way we encountered some rain. What caused us concern was the fact that, because of the storms, the pilot decided not to circle the city. To avoid being caught in the storm and perhaps having to stay the night in Kalemie, he decided to land the plane and turn around as quickly as possible. This quick landing, while a blessing to him, left us at the airport without a lift home. Under normal circumstances (had Lea not just gone through surgery), this would not have been a problem; we easily could have made the long walk home from the airport.

Initially I suggested that Lea stay with Tom at the airport while I went ahead to get a lift. She resisted my idea; she felt uncomfortable staying alone with Tom and the Zairean soldiers. I sighed and complied with carrying most of the luggage. When he tired, I at the same time carried Tom on my shoulders. To make matters worse, after I walked only a short while, rain began to fall. Then Tom began to shiver; his lips turned blue. I had hoped to find a passerby who would help carry the luggage, but most everyone else (besides us) had the sense to get out of the rain.

Finally, along our way, we arrived at a building that offered some kind of shelter. From there we were able to send word that we arrived. Since we were not far at all from the property, help was there quickly. We soon were at home.

Walking into the house swiftly reminded us of the fact that very soon Kalemie, Zaire, no longer would be our home. Even having gone through as traumatic an experience as we had, the thought of leaving was difficult to accept. As we prepared to re-enter our old surroundings, life as we had learned to live it was ending.

Thankfully we did not have much time left to sorrow over our upcoming departure. Reports had to be written; our few belongings had to be packed and sorted. In less than a week our chartered flight from Nairobi was set to get us on our way back to the U.S. Being busy somehow helped us cope with the inevitable—the time to leave was at hand.

Suddenly as things began, they ended

 Almost as suddenly as our time in Zaire began, it ended. Some tears were shed as we climbed into our seats on the MAF flight to Kenya. More than feeling sorrow, we also seemed to grapple with confusion. We believed this departure was not supposed to happen, as if we were leaving home and going to a strange place! Before we boarded our flight to the U.S., we stayed overnight at the Mayfield Guesthouse, in which we had stayed during the time we studied Swahili. The day had been long; we were glad to arrive just as the dinner bell was ringing. The meal schedule still was the same as it had been when we studied language. We laughed as we correctly predicted what would be served for the evening meal. Our laughter was bittersweet as we thought of having to fly out of Africa the next day and to make our way back to Lake Worth, FL.

We will go

 We arrived home just in time for the year-end holidays. Christmas was memorable; we relished the company of family and friends. I went back to work at the church while Lea worked on setting up the family home. In our absence we had rented out our townhouse and stored our furniture and other household goods. Once we arrived, Lea arranged the house and began using the stove as she showed off her newfound cooking ability. The first meal she prepared for us at our home in Florida after our return was teriyaki steak. As we sat down, we enjoyed our meal in silence. We knew that had we not had our Zaire experience, that evening we would have eaten fast food. Everything we experienced on our return was compared to Africa. Nothing seemed to hold a candle to the continent; no one could offer an adequate explanation for our feelings.

The New Year arrived and went without much recognition on our part. Instead of enjoying the festivities surrounding us we were wondering what was happening in Kalemie during the holidays. *Was Ralph calling a special seminar? Did they find someone to bring a turkey in from Nairobi for them? Was Stephanie planning something special for the kids at the Bible school?* Fireworks, celebrations, and friends, while wonderful, did not fill our empty hearts. The church was exciting, the congregation loved us, and our families loved us, yet inside our hearts we felt emptiness that could not be filled in North America.

One evening as we walked around the perimeter of the church parking lot, once more Lea and I talked of our beloved Africa. During the five years we had been married, although we were young and inexperienced, we did know that, for God to bless us, we had to make all our decisions in unity. Africa was no exception. As much as we loved the mission field, we were careful not to push each other in any direction. That evening on our walk, almost simultaneously, we both said we believed the time had arrived to make the choice to serve as missionaries full time. Otherwise, we concluded, we would miss out on the purpose for which God had brought us together. Our hearts beat for Africa; our spirits yearned for Africa. The time to go home was at hand.

> *Also I heard the voice of the Lord, saying: "Whom shall I send, and who will go for Us?" Then I said, "Here am I! Send me"* (Isaiah 6:8).

(left) Jamie, Lea and Tommy
Peters, 1987

(middle) Tommy on the shore of
Lake Tanganyika, 1987

(right) Desperate for coffee,
Lea cleaned, roasted, and
ground our own coffee with a
locally made mortar and
pestle.

(left) Jamie works diligently to study Swahili.

(above) Jamie with Bible School students,
Kalemie, Zaire, 1987

(right) Bible School
students graduating.
The Hagemeiers
always worked to make
graduation a special
event for the students.

Part 2

A Lifetime Call

*"He who finds his life will lose it, and he who loses his life
for My sake will find it"*
(Mt. 10:39).

Chapter 4

The Call of Our Lifetime

"The missionary church is a praying church. The history of missions is a history of prayer. Everything vital to the success of the world's evangelization hinges on prayer. Are thousands of missionaries and tens of thousands of native workers needed? *'Pray ye therefore the Lord of the harvest, that He send forth laborers into His harvest.'*"

–John R. Mott

The yearning desire of the missionary to part, at time, can conflict with the desires of those left behind. Understandably, people who stay may misinterpret the joy of the departing missionary as a lack of love and appreciation. But this conflict need not hinder those at "home". For those of us going, we must help our loved ones to understand that the departure of the missionary actually is an answer not just to one prayer but to the prayers of the Church, both far and near—prayers for laborers to enter into the Lord's field. Those of us who have gone through the "departing" experience sometimes are bewildered by the reactions of those around us to our answering the call. We think: *Is not every believer destined to serve God? Should not those around us rejoice for us when we find our life's calling?* Without exception every family must learn how to cope with the difficulties that the call places on those going and those staying. This learning curve sometimes can be so steep that navigating it seems impossible. Yet with the grace of God, all things are possible . . . even learning how to live apart from loved ones. Therefore, rejoice when a friend or loved one answers the call to go, because that also answers your prayer to send.

Preparation

After the two of us took that walk in the parking lot, our lives were set to obey the Lord. We spoke with our church elders, who concurred that serving in Africa was the will of the Lord for us. "Do the will of God" was their consensus! The same obstacles we faced before our first departure—finances, support, education, health insurance—loomed over us once again. All were issues with which we must deal before we left. Because of all these concerns, taking our time to return to Africa would have been simpler, but staying in the U.S. much longer simply was not an option for us to consider. Another staff member already had been secured to take our place at church; we set to the task of putting things to go to what we now considered to be our home—Africa!

In early 1989, some months before we were confirmed to leave for Africa, our home church hosted a world-missions conference. We were thrilled to be in Florida for these meetings; many great men and women from all parts of the world were present; we rubbed shoulders with so many of them. Among those ministering at the conference was Wayne Meyers, a well-known missionary from Mexico. As he spoke, our ears strained to hear every bit of wisdom from his wealth of experience. During these meetings he stressed one particular subject: giving up what God asks you to give up to serve Him. Everyone is asked to give up something; not everyone will be asked to give up the same thing. Some, he said, would be called to give up time to serve God in various ministries. Others would be called to give up finances; yet a third group would be called to give up things. Each was to give something up as God directed, because God requires us to give up things that would hinder us from serving Him with a whole heart. The congregation was asked to pray about what God was calling each one to relinquish; at the appropriate moment, a time would arrive to surrender those things as the Lord would lead.

Failure is not an option

 Sitting in our seats at church during that first meeting when Wayne Meyers preached on giving our offerings, we knew something big was about to happen to us. *What did we have to give? While we never lacked, we were far from being well-off—what more could we give to God?* We had given our lives. Our futures were to serve Him. In those meetings the presence of God was unmistakable; we were ready to listen and obey the Lord as He directed us.

Several days passed; as the conference neared its end, both of us heard the voice of God speak about our giving. Neither one was ready to start the conversation, because we knew our thoughts would mark us as radical! During this pivotal time an uneasy and unusual quiet had settled over us. One evening as we left our home to get to the meeting, I finally broke the silence. As we sat at a red light not far from our house, I said, "I think the Lord has spoken to me about what we are supposed to give."

Lea replied, "I think I know what you are talking about." Somewhat surprised, I asked what God had said to her. All the while I knew what her answer would be. Sighing, she said, "Is it about the house?" Smiling, I knew we had arrived at the same conclusion—God was asking for our house. Lea loved our house. While we had not been able to do much more than paint its walls, she loved having a home of her own. Once we decided to return to Africa, one of her first remarks was, "At least when we come back to the U.S. to visit, we will have a house to come back to." I knew what this decision meant to her; I appreciated her all the more for it.

Young and radical may have been the mark we were given, but even more than young and radical, we desired to be marked with obedience. Although in church we gave our house as an offering (it went to the church), in our eyes we gave our house to God. Foregoing our Stateside place of refuge for us meant that we had nothing to return to "just in case . . .." Failure was not an option—we had only God on which to rely. He had to be enough in the event of "just in case".

During those frenzied days of preparation we once again found out we were expecting. Hopeful that this would be the pregnancy to give us our second child, from very early in the pregnancy we made sure I was under the care of a physician. The doctor, after learning my history, was careful to assure me that many women undergo several miscarriages and still are able to carry a baby normally. Even though we had miscarried three times, our physician still held out great hope that this pregnancy would be normal. The last loss had taken place nearly six months prior; otherwise I was healthy. *Do not worry*, was her counsel. So, we left her office feeling hopeful —and on our way out of her door even began arguing about names.

With a new baby on the way and our move back to Zaire imminent, our lives rapidly were changing. Speaking engagements were made with churches that possibly would become part of our support, papers were signed, overseas health insurance was secured, and a quick missions trip to Haiti was set for Jamie. I began to shuffle through our personal belongings. I had to decide what to keep, what to give away, and what was ready for the trash. Tom had great fun going through the items with me. As one by one he brought each to me, he asked, "Do we keep this, Mommy?" Before I had a chance to answer him, he either would take whatever item he had and throw it over his shoulder toward the trash or place it in his "keep" pile. Our son, as young as he was at the time, in his own way understood that our home was not in Florida. Not once did he ask "why" we had to move. He did cry when the time to say goodbye arrived, but never did he resist the idea.

Not long after our preparations began and Jamie was set to go to Haiti, I began to feel unwell. Those all-too-familiar pains and symptoms of miscarriage surfaced. Our doctor counseled me to take life easy and see what course nature would take. Jamie canceled his trip to Haiti. For several days we seemed as though we might be able to overcome and not miscarry. But to our disappointment, some days later we did lose the baby. During this loss things were a bit more complicated; I was admitted to the hospital overnight. No one had an explanation for us as to why this had happened so many times. The doctor suggested that I undergo testing, but we were on our way out of the country. Tickets had been purchased; not only that, we also had to take into consideration what our insurance would say about such procedures. We decided to forego any tests and take our time to pray and see what solution God had for the situation.

God had a word

 To say I was upset at this time was quite the understatement. Any woman who has had a miscarriage understands the physical and emotional costs of the experience. However, I did not have much spare time to feel sorry for myself (which, in retrospect, was good for me). I wanted to lie down and "lick my wounds" and get some sympathy, but that luxury was nowhere to be found. Days after the miscarriage we boarded a plane and set out for Texas, Louisiana, and Arkansas, in which we had set up an itinerary to preach in several churches. Our first stop was in Houston, in which we attended a few sessions of a missions conference hosted by Pastor John Osteen and his church. For the few days we were in town for those meetings, friends hosted us. The last morning we were there I woke up early and spent some time with the Lord. While I prayed, I began to feel burdened for a couple we knew was on the verge of divorce. At the same time I sensed the Lord speak to my heart to say that within a year's time, my prayers would be answered. I was a bit puzzled by what He had spoken to me, but I figured He was speaking about my prayers about this couple. Without further thought I finished my devotional time, got ready, and set out with Jamie and Tom to the meetings. We walked in on the tail end of a message by T.L. Osborn and stayed in the back of the auditorium, because we were going to have to leave the meeting early to make our next engagement.

Pastor Osteen took the microphone after Brother Osborn had finished and began to lead the congregation in prayer. As he prayed, he began to point out individuals in the congregation and give them prophecies, words of wisdom, and words of knowledge[19] as the Lord spoke to him. I was encouraged to see the Lord speak so directly to people; I never suspected in this congregation of several thousand that God would choose to put His hand on our lives. Suddenly, I heard Pastor Osteen say, "You, the blonde-haired young lady in the back." My heart fluttered with excitement, but I reasoned that we were in TEXAS, in which countless, young, blonde women live! He pointed at me and said, "You, yes, you; I am pointing right at you." Everyone stared in my direction to hear what God might say. "God says that He is healing your body right now. Also, that couple you were praying for, God says that He is healing that relationship as well." Nothing else was said; that was all I needed to hear! That day, April 19, 1989, marked a change of course for our faith. We knew that never again would we lose another baby. I did not feel different physically, but I knew God had met me right in the place in which I needed Him to meet me.

Homecoming

 In June we made our way back home to Zaire with great joy and anticipation for the future. We got to Kalemie in time for graduation services; Jamie served as one of the interpreters for the usual post-graduation seminars. We were so happy to be back home. The house in which we had lived in before our departure seven months earlier now was taken with new missionaries, so alternative housing was found for us within the same compound, which was called "Filtisaf". It formerly was used as housing for the Belgians who in colonial times before Zaire gained its independence worked in a nearby factory. When looking at a Filtisaf house, one easily can see the colonial design and outline of a once-beautiful home. Most of them are now eaten with termites and infested with a variety of other insects. On one occasion we actually heard the termites munching away on the door panel that led to our bedroom. Then one morning we woke to find the door panels caving in. We were interested in peeking into the myriad of tunnels made by those almost-microscopic insects. For many weeks this provided Tom with hours of entertainment and a great conversation topic.

Around the time the door panel caved in, one night the termites (which can fly) decided to swarm in our bedroom. This further was complicated by the fact that we had a fan at the foot of our bed. The fan pointed directly at our faces, so we woke to the "ping" sound of the termites hitting the fan and then being catapulted onto our faces. This is the glory of the mission field.

 Ralph and Shirley's extension Bible school in Bukavu was undergoing some change. The couple who had been serving in Bukavu (and who generously had hosted us on our way back from Kenya when Lea had her surgery) was leaving. While Ralph did not ask anyone to volunteer to take their place, we began to feel as if we ought to be the ones to help. On hearing our offer to go, Ralph gave his consent; barely one month after our return to Kalemie we were off to Bukavu.

On our arrival we conveniently moved into the house that was previously occupied by the family working with the Hagemeiers. It was set down nearby Lake Kivu, which borders Rwanda on the opposite side; the scenery was beautiful. We had heard that living near the lake was not safe because at night bandits were known to cross the water and to rob the houses on the lakeshore. So we took care to lock the doors and keep an air horn handy in case we needed to sound an alarm. No driveable vehicle except a Honda motorcycle was available for us to use.[20] All three of us fit quite well on the bike: I drove with Tom sitting in front of me and with Lea holding on as she sat behind me. This was quite a sight and experience.

Lea was not too keen on driving a motorcycle around town, especially in the rain (and rain fell a lot in Bukavu). Tom, on the other hand, thought it was the best way to get around and loved being with his dad on the "Honda bike".

Our duties in Bukavu were to serve the national pastor, who was in charge of the school. Since he often traveled, I filled in for him and also taught classes. Lea took care of office duties and taught classes as well. Soon we began to fit into Bukavu and made friends among our national students and missionary colleagues in the city. Our classes were taught in Swahili, but we had to adjust to using many French words, such as days of the week and counting, because French was used more in Bukavu than it was in Kalemie. Since we already knew Swahili, we began to think about someday learning French, since many countries in central, northern, and western Africa (such as Zaire) are Francophone.

 A few weeks after our move we had a break in classes. At that time Ralph made the generous offer of sending one of his vehicles, a Toyota Hilux truck, to Bukavu for us to use. We were overjoyed at the prospect of having a reliable vehicle on the tough roads. Because most of our household items still were boxed and packed away in Kalemie, Jamie planned to return there quickly to retrieve our belongings, pack them in the back of the truck, and make the three-day drive back to Bukavu.[21] This seemed to be a perfect plan. Jamie, together with the national leader of the school in Bukavu, set off for Kalemie. For the first time in Africa I was left alone to "hold the fort".

Sleeping under a mango tree

 I was thankful for the proposed use of Ralph's truck, yet I was hesitant to leave Tom and Lea alone in Bukavu. The area of town in which we lived was not the most secure area in the city. We already had several small thefts take place at home.

Most notably, on a Sunday morning while we were at church, thieves noticed we were away and stole several bedspreads Lea had washed and set out to dry on the porch (which was surrounded by iron bars). To this day how they managed to pull large blankets through the narrow openings remains a mystery. So leaving my young family behind under these circumstances was far from ideal, but our need for the vehicle was so pressing that we had no other option available to us except for me to travel by plane to Kalemie to retrieve the truck and our belongings and drive back to Bukavu. I was going to make this trip as short as possible.

Not long after we arrived in Kalemie, we loaded up early in the morning and began the trek back to Bukavu. The truck—laden with the dog, boxes, and a cross—was cumbersome to drive over the exceedingly rough roads. Our first night we "camped" under some mango trees that surrounded a village. The vehicle, with its strange-looking cargo and *mzungu* driver, proved to be a good topic of conversation, especially for the children of the village. Everything would have been fine if the mango tree story was the only tale to tell of that journey.

During our travels we arrived at a bridge that had only two metal beams on which the driver was supposed to balance the wheels of the vehicle to travel across. Some thoughtful passersby must have left some pieces of sheet metal lying over the metal beams on the bridge; we used this to cover the beams as we drove to the other side. As I gingerly drove the truck forward, doing my best to ignore the river that flowed underneath the so-called bridge, the brother traveling with me devised a system to place one metal sheet over the beams, which is where I tried to keep the wheels—and weight. Every time we drove across the metal sheet, he would lift it up from behind the vehicle and place it in front of the truck—until we arrived at the other side.

Driving over the bridge was not the only time I needed help with guiding the vehicle. On many occasions my colleague would get out of the truck and expertly guide me, especially as we drove over several mountains.

On one occasion as I was driving around the very outer edges of a cliff, he became very nervous and had me back up and re-navigate the edge. Apparently one of the front wheels of the truck had moved up several feet from the ground. I do not know how many times God saved our lives during that trip.

> *For He shall give His angels charge over you, to keep you in all your ways. In their hands they shall bear you up, lest you dash your foot against a stone* (Ps. 91:11-12).

 Tom and I waited anxiously for Jamie to return from Kalemie. I knew the drive would be challenging and numerous times fought the temptation to give in to worry. Because school was not in session, during this time at least I did not have to contend with getting to and from classes. So my days were spent preparing for the upcoming term as well as doing the housework, which in Africa is more like manual labor than that to which in my American life I had been accustomed.

The "daily dread", as I called it, was the laundry. In those days we had no washing machine; our budget was not one that allowed us to hire much more help than the watchman, who provided some measure of security. So after much trial and error, I devised a semi-successful laundry system. Every morning as early as I could, I got the dirty clothes and hand-washed them in the bathtub. I very quickly learned to color-coordinate the clothes, but I also knew which items of clothing could be combined without ruining everything else. Laundry can be backbreaking and knuckle-baring work, especially when one washes blue jeans and towels. I wanted to avoid as much backbreaking and knuckle-baring as possible.

My method? First, I would let the clothes soak in the tub for about an hour while I attended to the rest of the housework. Once the hour had passed, I would pull away from whatever else I was doing and return to the bathtub to scrub away. Sometimes, especially with the blue jeans, I would repeat the procedure several times before I felt satisfied with the outcome. When the clothes were clean to my standards, I lugged them outside to dry on the line. In those days laundry pins were not easy to find in Bukavu, so the few pins I had were used sparingly. (Very early I learned never to leave laundry and laundry pins unattended on the line.) Not only did I have to contend with the laundry-pin thief, but more dreaded than he was the inevitable rain that fell nearly every day in Bukavu during certain months of the year. At times the rain would fall for days on end. Because we did not have a clothes dryer, I devised yet another clever way to dry the clothes in time and alleviated the chance for them to become smelly. I hung all the clothes inside the living area, plugged in our two fans, and let them rotate the air around the wet clothes. Experience taught me to wash clothes every day to avoid the stinking-clothes problem that arose with the rain. Of course daily I would pray for sunshine. I even had begun to know the time at which the storms would start; they usually rolled in late morning. So if I got the clothes done by eight a.m., they possibly could be dry by the time the rains fell. While I was not successful every time, inwardly I was proud that I rarely had a big backlog of laundry.

To escape the quiet at the house nearly every day Tom and I stepped out for a walk and occasionally would take the time to visit a few other missionary families in town. One family that lived nearby worked with MAF and had a small son the same age as Tom. The boys enjoyed playing together; I enjoyed the moments I spent watching them play. Sometimes we would walk to town to visit another couple that had a TV and VCR. They kindly offered us its use to watch our few children's movies. Tom and I tried not to wear out our welcome by visiting too often, but when the day did arrive that we could go watch a video or two, we both were ready.

One night after Jamie already had been gone for several days and we were expecting him to return at any time, I heard an earnest tapping at my window. Tom was asleep on his mattress next to me in our room, so I rose as quietly as I could and carefully pulled the curtain back just enough to see the watchman's face looking directly at mine. Startled, I whispered, "Pascal, *unataka nini?*" (Pascal, what do you want?)

His response was forceful, "Madame, *niliona mtu kuingia katika lupango.*" (Madame, I saw a person enter into the yard.) He pointed to the lone, small tree some 25-feet away on our property. At that moment I saw another intruder jump over the fence and vainly attempt to hide next to his comrade behind the small tree. In my chest my heart was pounding hard; I could feel my breath against the window. Pascal began to talk loudly and wave his machete. He said, "*Akitukaribia, nitamkata na panga!*" (If he comes near to us, I will cut him with the machete!)

Taking Pascal's cue, I responded loudly, "*Fanya hivi! Umkate na panga!*" (Do that! Cut him with the machete!) For some time we continued our threatening discourse. In retrospect our threats were quite comical. Pascal was shorter than my five-foot, five-inch self; he weighed no more than 100 pounds. Together we were no match for much more than a couple of fifth-graders! Yet we continued to talk "big and bad". Eventually our threats must have wearied them, as we watched the thieves make their way back over the wooden fence. I was thankful that, throughout this two-hour ordeal, by my feet Tom slept undisturbed.

The next morning I decided to leave off the laundry that day and set out after breakfast to watch some videos at our friends' house. On that particular day after the previous night's experience with thieves I was not at all excited about staying home without Jamie. As we made our way into town, I noticed a loaded truck far down the road. Tom asked, "Is that Daddy coming home?" Yes, indeed, it was Jamie; I recognized the cross sticking up out of the back. The year before, Jamie had built the cross in Kalemie; he used it in an evangelistic outreach to the city. Many had trusted the Lord when Jamie had dragged it through the town and preached. I could not forget that beautiful cross!

Tom cried, "Daddy's home!" Smiling, not only because I was glad Jamie was back but also with relief because we would not be alone that night, I climbed into the back seat with Tom; as a family we made the rest of the drive home together. The dog barked in the back of the truck; I stared at the obvious pile of dirty clothes in the seat next to me. Despite my earlier decision to skip the laundry, the clothes did get washed that day.

Unexpected complications

 Tom was an energetic and brave child. He was not one to be left out of anything and strongly resisted anyone saying he either was too young or too small to participate. When we were invited to a village to preach a seminar for a former student of ours, Tom naturally declared that such a difficult trip was not beyond his years. Doing our best to shield him from any unnecessary dangers, we diligently packed enough clean drinking water, snacks, and clothes to last us during the three-day stay in the village.

For the duration of our visit our former student and his wife, who were pastors of the church that received us, kindly arranged our housing. The quarters consisted of a vacant storefront with no windows for ventilation; this made the nights almost unbearable. To sleep we had to open the front door and take turns sitting in the doorway so we would have some ventilation. Insects were in abundance; we were bitten more times than we could count. Nevertheless the seminar was a great success, the church was encouraged, and we made our way back home to Bukavu.

Not long after our excursion Tom took ill with a mysterious fever. This puzzled us, because at the time he was taking an effective anti-malarial medication. To be on the safe side we did have him tested for malaria, but the test returned negative. Local missionary nurses seemed to think he was suffering from a viral infection. Their counsel was to wait for a couple of days and simply treat the symptoms, which they believed most likely would disappear once the virus had run its course. Instead of getting better Tom's fever not only remained but also at times was very high. Several trips to the nurses did little to ease our concern. With the doctors at a nearby mission hospital in Rwanda out on holiday, sound medical advice was difficult to find. We became especially alarmed when Tom woke one morning with a mysterious rash and such sore joints that he almost was unable to walk. The whole experience lasted only a few days, but we felt as though it had lasted an eternity. Every hour Tom's condition seemed to deteriorate.

Finally the MAF missionaries gave us access to their ham radio; we were able to talk directly with a missionary physician (we knew her only as Dr. Elizabeth) who worked in a mission hospital in the interior of the country. After hearing our description of all of Tom's symptoms, she asked us to look on his body for a small, dark scab. Sure enough, between two of his toes was a small, dark scab. She explained that it was probably the site of an insect bite (from a flea, tick, or other blood-sucking insect). She went on to say that the insect that bit him was, most likely, carrying typhus and transferred the disease to Tom. Dr. Elizabeth guessed that Tom probably was bitten at some point during that recent trip to the village, where typhus could be endemic.

Relieved for a diagnosis, we were told to put him on a course of tetracycline, because it was the best antibiotic available in the area for treating typhus. This would clear the infection but could have the undesirable side effect of staining his permanent teeth. Tetracycline was normally not prescribed to children as young as Tom, who was 4 at the time. However, in light of the gravity of his illness, we had no other choice except to give him the medicine. In a few weeks' time Dr. Elizabeth was scheduled to visit Bukavu. She told us that when she got into town, she would examine Tom.

As suddenly as the typhus arrived, it left. Tom quickly recovered. The doctor who diagnosed him over radio transmission finally visited our town. Soon after her arrival Dr. Elizabeth examined Tom. We thanked her for her help as she pronounced Tom healthy and assured us that the residual heart murmur she found would disappear after some months, which to our great relief it did. To God's glory Tom's adult teeth did not suffer any effect from the tetracycline. Today his teeth are unstained and healthy.

Moving

 More complications followed the drama of our first months in Bukavu. Our landlord decided she wanted her house back; this forced us to look for another place to live. Neither one of us was too disappointed in having to seek alternative housing, since in our current place security was negligible at best. However, our budget did not allow for us to spend much for rent, which made our house-hunting efforts interesting. Properties were available in the city—very nice properties with great security and nice gardens. Yet these properties were far out of our reach financially. People find the fact that, in the developing world, the rental prices can be comparable to those in Europe or the States and sometimes can cost even more, which is unbelievable. One major reason for the high prices in these areas is the presence of international aid organizations and diplomats who are willing and are able to pay top-dollar for the best properties. For missionaries this not only makes renting difficult, it also serves to further the great divide between rich and poor. The countries in which we have lived and served have little or no middle class. People are poor or wealthy; the poor depend on the rich employing them for sometimes less than $1 per day. In light of this great difference between rich and poor in Africa, finding the "happy medium" where housing is involved is tough.

One can find many trains of thought in terms of how and where the missionary should live. While ours is not the only opinion in this matter, we always have endeavored to demonstrate balance. Some say the missionary should be abased and not enjoy any Western conveniences; others say the missionary should live at total ease. Perhaps the house itself is not so much the issue. How the missionary's house is used instead of what kind of house it is (whether it be large, small, furnished lavishly or sparsely) may be what is most important. Our home always has been a place in which visitors were welcomed, church offices were situated, and our own children were reared. We have lived wherever God has opened the door for us to live—sometimes those places have been little more than two rooms with a small kitchenette and bathroom. At other times those places have been large and spacious. Early on we learned what Paul meant when he penned Philippians 4:11-13:

> Not that I speak in regard to need, for I have learned in whatever state I am, to be content: I know how to be abased, and I know how to abound. Everywhere and in all things I have learned both to be full and to be hungry, both to abound and to suffer need. I can do all things through Christ who strengthens me.

In the end we finally did locate a newly built house that was furnished. Its location, unfortunately, did not provide any more security than did our previous house. Not one mile from the new house was the main prison for the city; our "view" was of one of the larger slums known as *Kadutu*. While living near the prison was a source of concern, the house did have one particular issue in its favor: it was very near to the Bible school. We easily were able to walk to and from classes, which was a blessing compared to our previous location in which transportation always was an issue. Before we had Ralph's Hilux truck, we would go to school via taxi, foot, or with the motorcycle, which Lea did her best to avoid.

At the time we were there, Bukavu had no reliable medical facilities, so when in September 1989 we again suspected Lea was pregnant, we made the two-hour drive to a mission hospital in nearby Rwanda. Our suspicions were confirmed; the doctor gave us the usual prenatal counsel together with the advice to be cautious and to stay away from as many bumpy roads as possible. All of us, doctor included, chuckled at that particular point; the road leading up to the hospital itself was nothing but potholes. We stared at the small, ultrasound screen, on which we saw the smallest evidence of life, and began to allow ourselves the luxury of feeling joyful and hopeful. Earlier that year God had spoken to us—we knew He could not lie; we would fight for this child.

As we drove home to Bukavu, we stopped just at the border town between Bukavu and Rwanda. The town was called *Cyangugu*, in which some kind missionaries who were well known for allowing missionaries from Bukavu the use of their phone to call family Stateside lived. In those days you couldn't find working phones in the part of Zaire in which we were serving. We made our brief phone calls and then made our way back over the border to Zaire.

Crossing the border in those days was no small matter. At the crossing every paper of which we could and could not think often was requested. We always took great care to have all of our vaccines sorted, all our visas in order, and all our prayers for favor prayed! The law of the land always happened to be what the official who was staffing the desk believed it should be. We do not believe the best testimony for a missionary is to give bribes to officials. Were we to do that, we would mark ourselves forever as those who would give and then never be free from the scourge. Also, giving bribes does not help the local population. If missionaries give bribes, what hope do the nationals have of being free from giving bribes to demanding officials? On many occasions we have heard individuals say that getting anything done without bribes is "impossible". Since 1987 we ourselves have never given a bribe to any official, nor do we plan on starting now. Of course we never can be sure of the various and sundry "fees" that we pay in offices at borders and elsewhere. Our stance always has been to demand a receipt–but we cannot be sure that those receipts we have been given with those official stamps are real, because corruption in these countries is rife. However, we do all we can to avoid playing the bribery game. This stance often frustrated the border officials in Zaire. Eventually they would tire of the game, because we patiently would wait in their offices for our passports to be stamped. Grumbling, the stamp would be issued; after some time, we would be on our way. Sometimes the crossing was quick; at other times we could sit at the border for hours.

In November 1989 classes were well under way when one evening I returned home and felt uncharacteristically ill. My throat was sore; after classes were done for the day, I went straight to bed. The next day Lea talked me into seeing a nearby missionary nurse, who promptly put me on a course of antibiotics and sent me home. However, after several days of antibiotics, the infection did not clear up. She gave me another antibiotic to try. Even after several more days on the new antibiotic my health did not get better. I resisted Lea's prompting to drive across the border to the mission hospital in Rwanda until, after 10 days of suffering, she loaded me, Tom, and our suitcase into Ralph's truck and took charge of the situation.

Kadaffis

 The first order of business was to organize fuel for the truck. We needed a full tank to get to the hospital and back. In Bukavu, fuel was not available at the filling stations that sat delinquent on the side of the road. Rather, men who were known locally as *kadaffis* off the side of the road sold fuel from what usually were plastic jerry cans. These *kadaffis* were well-known by Jamie, since usually he witnessed to them every time he purchased fuel. However, I had little money at my disposal, because we had not changed money since

Jamie had fallen ill. Changing money in a bankless society, such as Zaire, was a challenge. Usually we used a local businessman who accepted our U.S. dollar checks and gave them immediate value. This process generally took some time; since time was of the essence, before we set off for the hospital I went to visit the *kadaffis*. I told them their friend was sick and asked whether they could just fill the truck up; on our return I would pay them back. They obliged my request; they filled the truck to the brim and accepted the receipt of payment of 55,000 Zaires (what the currency was called in those days) that we would pay when we returned.

Once we arrived at the Zaire/Rwanda border, I was determined to get across quickly without the usual, time-consuming banter to which the officials were accustomed. In Zaire when I explained that my husband was sick and needed the attention of the doctors in Rwanda, we encountered no problem whatsoever. When we got to the Rwanda crossing, things were not so easy. When I walked up to the desk at the border, I explained once again that my husband was ill and needed medical attention quickly. I told them he had gone 10 days without much food and was very weak. I asked them whether they could please help me get through the crossing quickly. Without so much as a glance in my direction the man behind the desk began to question me and challenge the validity of my documents and my reason for arriving in the country. The very thought of my documents being out of order infuriated me—I grew increasingly impatient with his line of questioning and asked to see the person "in charge". With his eyes locking with mine he stated, "I am the person in charge." At this very point a man who wore an official-looking uniform walked into the background. On hearing his apparent subordinate declare that he was in charge, the official-looking man became incredulous. Swiftly he walked to the desk and dismissed whoever was attending to me; then he took my documents, stamped the passports, and told me to be on my way. As a gesture of apology he even waived the usual entry fee.

I drove as quickly as I could over the bumpy roads to the hospital. From time to time Jamie would lift his head and ask me whether I knew where I was going. This was a valid question on his part, since on occasion I have been known to get lost, but that day I fortunately was able to stay on the right road. Tom slept most of the way while I did my best to ignore the small twinge that from time to time I felt in my lower back. I prayed that the doctors indeed would be at the hospital. Since Thanksgiving[22] was just two days away, I wondered whether the hospital during the holiday would work only a "skeleton crew".

As we finally made our way up the hill to our destination, I parked the truck and found some of the hospital staff, who immediately took Jamie into the examination room, in which he was given an antibiotic shot. He later was diagnosed with an abscessed tonsil and for several days was given IV antibiotics. If the abscess would not recede on its own quickly, the doctor said he would have to lance it. I felt so badly for Jamie lying in bed with an IV stuck in his arm. He has little tolerance for being sick and now was at the absolute mercy of not one but a whole staff of doctors and nurses. While I was thankful for the efficient medical care he was given, I struggled with worry. Eventually the abscess did recede without having to be lanced; we spent our Thanksgiving at the table of generous missionaries. After just a short time Jamie was taken off the IV; he recovered very quickly. The doctors counseled us to wait to return to Bukavu after the weekend because, since arriving, I had suffered with a lower backache.

On Monday morning we were invited to breakfast at the home of Jamie's doctor, which was the doctor's way of taking care of me as well. While we were there, the doctor noticed I was feeling increasingly unwell. Summarily we were taken to the sonogram room, in which we saw our baby's heartbeat and breathed a great sigh of relief. But the doctor was less optimistic. Despite seeing the heartbeat on the monitor he held out little hope we would keep this pregnancy. "You need to be prepared to miscarry this baby. Come back to the hospital once you have, so we can give you whatever care you may require." These words smothered the joy we felt as we watched the new, small heart beating so strongly. After the examination we politely excused ourselves and slowly began to make our way back home to Bukavu.

> *Who has believed our report? And to whom has the arm of the Lord been revealed?* (Isa. 53:1).

 In our lives circumstances that challenge our systems of belief will arise. At those times we have to make the choice of whether to believe the Word of God. This does not mean, by any stretch of the imagination, that we will not face difficulty and at times apparent defeat, such as we had with the miscarriages we had experienced. However, we had arrived at a point in our lives in which we decided to take the challenge and fight the fight of faith[23]—the time had arrived for us to believe God for what He just a few months earlier had promised us. We had a Word from God; we believed that His report was more conclusive than any other we had received.

I insisted on driving home. Even though I was not yet functioning at 100 percent, I felt well enough to drive. I had enough medicine, rest, and obeying orders—I just wanted to get back home and pick up where we left off. Angered about the news we received, I did my best to encourage Lea as we both stood in faith for our child. She was in total agreement; we confessed life over the child God had promised to us. This baby would *not die, but live, and declare the works of the Lord.*[24] We spent most of the drive home in prayer and speaking life to our children, our future, and ourselves.

For several days after we returned to Bukavu, Lea's condition grew worse. The missionary nurses in town kept tabs on her but were unable to offer much help. One final evening, after Lea for several hours experienced pain as we prayed and declared the Word of God, the pain suddenly stopped. If we ever experienced a tangible moment in which the presence of God was felt, it was that night in Bukavu when we interceded for our child. We went to bed exhausted but woke to "all systems go". From that moment the pregnancy proceeded normally, Lea's belly grew, and the baby kicked as if to announce to everyone that, in the right time, she was going to arrive on the scene.

One month later when we returned to the hospital in Rwanda for Lea's monthly exam, the doctor was amazed she had not miscarried. When he measured the baby on the sonogram, he stated the child had "doubled in size and activity". What else were we to expect when God had promised healing?

Never say never

 As life returned to normal, we resumed our teaching at the Bible school and preaching in local churches every Sunday. All denominations would invite us to preach at their churches; we were able to build strong relationships with many leaders. While we fellowshiped with these pastors and their congregations, we began to feel a change to our call emerging. For as long as I can remember, I had an aversion to becoming a pastor. Lea knew that I "never" wanted to be pastor of a church. I was content serving as a teacher in the Bible school and to be satisfied did not need to add anything else to what we were doing. I knew full well (from having grown up in a pastor's home) what work and sacrifice were involved. I watched my parents as they were diligent in proclaiming the Word to a growing and prospering church. However, as God began to change my heart—and Lea's—we began to pray about planting a local church. This feeling went from being a simple feeling to an all-consuming desire. We had to plant a church.

Amanda

> *All your children shall be taught by the Lord and great shall be the peace of your children* (Isa. 54:13).

Lea's due date swiftly approached. We had so much to do before we left for Nairobi, in which our child was going to be born. We easily could have gone to the hospital in Rwanda for the birth, but Rwanda had no American consulate that would be able to assist us in issuing a birth certificate either in Bukavu or in the small area in which the hospital was located. Because Tom was born several weeks before his due date, we decided to leave some weeks before the baby was due. We also were very excited that Lea's mother was making the long trip to Nairobi to receive her greatly anticipated grandchild and to help us with Tom and the new baby. She arrived just after we did; before the birth we all had some wonderful, uninterrupted time together.

As things turned out, this baby did not want to have anything to do with an early arrival. Obviously she was keeping to her own timetable. Each week, as we visited the obstetrician's office, he would tell us that "by next week" we would have the baby. Yet the next week we were back to hear the same declaration. Finally, after five weeks of waiting, our doctor, Dr. Patel, during the morning visit simply stated, "It is time we gave Mother Nature a helping hand." The decision was made to induce labor. His only question was when we would like to arrive for the induction. Our eyes met as we pondered his statement; perhaps he meant we were to arrive in the next couple of days. But before we could say or think much more, Dr. Patel asked, "How about 1:30 this afternoon?" I was thrilled! The scenario was orchestrated to include both grandmothers—Lea's mother was there for the birth; our baby would be born on my mother's birthday!

By 1:30 p.m. on April 18, 1990, we checked into the hospital; at 3:11 that afternoon Amanda Anne was born. Lea's mother was entertaining Tommy in the hospital corridor when she heard the new baby's first cry. While Amanda did not seem to be very interested in being pushed from the peaceful cocoon for nine months she called *home* and into her new surroundings, we both knew that this birth was the substance of what was declared to us on April 19, 1989, when God truly healed us and within the year gave us our answer.

Chapter 5

Going Without Knowing

Now the Lord had said to Abram: "Get out of your country, from your family and from your father's house, to a land that I will show you" (Gen. 12:1).

In Genesis 12:1 God told Abram to "*Get out . . . to a land that I will show you.*" In subsequent verses he went on to explain what blessings would follow Abram's obedience. The Bible does not clearly tell us what, at the time, Abram's frame of mind was, but humanly speaking surely he must have had some inner conflict. Leaving his father's house, according to the custom of the time, was unusual; this could have meant financial disaster for Abram because of his dependence on his father's wealth. Since Abram's future was secure in his family setting, what caused him to leave and go somewhere he did not know? Have you ever taken a trip with no destination? No plan or map to follow? How Abram began to know the Lord is not thoroughly explained, but he knew Him well enough to understand that He was faithful to keep His Word.

> *So Abram departed as the Lord had spoken to him . . .* (Gen. 12:4a).

During his departure where were Abram's emotions? The Scripture does not record them. What is recorded is his reaction to God's command to go. *So Abram departed . . ..* He simply packed his belongings and family and went on his way. We find no agony—only joy—in obedience. Perhaps this is why missionaries joyfully endure things when they are called to follow the example of the First Missionary:

> *. . . let us lay aside every weight, and the sin which so easily en-*
> *snares us, and let us run with endurance the race that is set before*
> *us, looking unto Jesus the author and finisher of our faith, who*
> *for the joy that was set before Him endured the cross . . .* (Heb.
> 12:1b-2a).

Returning home from Nairobi after Mandy's birth was a joyful occasion. Many of our friends, missionaries and nationals alike, had known of our struggle for her safe delivery and arrived to give their congratulations. The most common "compliment" Mandy received during those days from our Zairian colleagues? "She is so white!" During the first few weeks she was home, her big brother, Tom, really did not know what to make of his little sister, but gradually he fell into the role of big brother and bravely took on the solemn role of little Mandy's protector.

"She is my little sister," Tom would say, "I have to watch her." In line with Tom's character he faced the new challenge with determination. It made him especially happy to have someone around he could "teach everything I know!"

The process of change

 During the months and weeks before Mandy's birth we had begun planning a large pastors' and church leaders' seminar. Invitations were sent out to the various churches that were in relationship with us. Guests would be here for a special time of teaching; all leaders were welcome. My parents, Pastor Tom and Mary Ann Peters, were arriving as guests. David and Melta Briggs, Dale and Jean Gentry, Pastor B.B. and Velma Hankins, and Pastor Chester Clark all would be ministering on this visit. We had no way of knowing how many actually would turn up for the meetings, but we suspected that our hands would be full.

The day finally arrived in which we drove to Bukavu's Kavumu airport to receive our visitors flying in on the MAF flight from Nairobi. At that time Bukavu's airport had an uncanny resemblance to an American chicken coop. The terminal rooms were surrounded with chicken wire that served as a sort of partition between the various areas in the airport. While the airport itself easily could have been called a "fixer-upper", the lush, mountainous scenery all around was breathtaking. In addition, it is close to the only tourist attraction of the region—the mountain gorillas. Even then, we had a tough time understanding how a country so rich in beauty and natural wealth could be oppressed with such an intense level of poverty and injustice.

Airport officials in Zaire did not afford our guests any special treatment. Well over an hour was necessary for the very few passengers on the MAF flight to complete their customs and immigration experience. I somehow made my way through to assist them and serve as their translator, since none of our guests was able to speak any of the languages spoken in the region. (Our ability to speak the language often has served as a means of defusing many complicated situations, and this was no exception.) Eventually everyone's passports were stamped and bags were released; this gave us the green light to head back into town.

My parents were exceptionally excited, because this was their first time to meet their granddaughter. Not a moment was wasted in their getting acquainted. Before long they were besotted with her sweet nature. Making sure Tom was not left out they showered him with love and presents (the universal language of love spoken by children everywhere).

Unfortunately our home was not spacious enough to accommodate everyone, so we made arrangements for our visitors to stay in the best hotel we could find downtown. Bukavu is not a very large city—downtown was just five-minutes away by car. The "five-star" hotel did not live up to its rating. The couches in the reception area looked decades old. When we sat down, dust billowed from the cushions. Lea worried that the setting would be too harsh on our guests. I assured her that all of them were well able to deal with a few days in a dusty hotel. She was right to be concerned for everyone's comfort—five-star accommodations (as was touted by this hotel) is a very relative term when one travels in the developing world!

Participants attended not only from the city but from villages all around. During the days of the meetings local churches arranged accommodations for visiting leaders. Together with the cooperation of local leadership a meal was prepared for all visitors during the entire seminar. The attendance was greater than we had anticipated; we had estimated at least 1,000 pastors and church leaders in attendance. This seminar was the first of its kind. For many years after the event we heard of the positive impact it had on those who were there. Even after we left Bukavu, time and time again we were asked to return. Requests for another seminar continued to pour in. Perhaps one day we will find ourselves there once again—the will of the Lord be done.

Meeting in Kalemie

 The success of the seminar served to energize and encourage all of us to attend the yearly graduation ceremony and subsequent seminar in Kalemie, which took place right after the graduation. In those days Air Burundi offered only one weekly flight from Bujumbura, Burundi, to Kalemie, Zaire. Bujumbura was a four-hour drive from Bukavu; packing all our guests from the seminar into the vehicles was no small feat! Just a few months earlier God had blessed us with a new, four-wheel-drive, Mitsubishi Pajero that held quite a number of people. Besides our vehicle we also made use of Ralph's truck (driven by a missionary colleague, Dan Koehler), which gave us the room to bring the entire team and our family.

Getting to Bujumbura from Bukavu with so many people was a huge undertaking—we crossed not one but three borders. Each time the border officials meticulously inspected the vehicles and luggage. At one particular crossing one of the border officials was going through one of the suitcases and found a large bottle of oregano that was from the U.S. and was being brought to Ralph and Shirley in Kalemie. Initially, perhaps in an effort to scare us, we were accused of carrying marijuana! How, I asked, could this be mistaken for marijuana? Not only is "OREGANO" written in large letters on the bottle, but the bottle also was sealed. "This is seasoning for food such as spaghetti. Have you ever eaten spaghetti?" I asked them.

"Yes," was their answer. So I told them at the time they ate spaghetti, they must have eaten this seasoning! Eventually, they realized their bluff had been called and allowed us to go on our way. Lea said never again would she travel with oregano in a suitcase. To this day she has kept her promise, I believe.

We finally arrived at the Hotel Club du Lac Tanganyika , which would house us for one night before we caught the flight to Bujumbura. The hotel was situated right on the lakeshore, which was a beautiful setting, but the picturesque view hid the true scourge of staying on the lake in a hotel that did not have nets on the windows: mosquitoes. For hours we fought with mosquitoes. When we finally did fall into a fitful sleep, we knew we were at the mercy of the blood-sucking creatures. In the morning all of us were covered with bites, but little Mandy had been victimized the most. On her face, arms, and legs we counted more than 30 bites.

The next morning before our departure we drove to town to pick up our tickets at the Air Burundi office. A short time later with tickets in hand we got into the car to make our way to the hotel to collect everyone. Just as we were driving off, a fight broke out in front of our car; a man pulled out a knife and began to wield it in front of another man who was his obvious opponent. A fierce scuffle ensued; the man with the knife chased the other off. As quickly as it had started, it was over. We just looked at each other, shrugged our shoulders, and went on our way. The crowd that had formed around these men while they were fighting had the same reaction as we did. This was just another day on the continent.

Kalemie

 Ralph, Shirley, Stephanie, and some missionaries (serving with them at the time) were at the airport and waited for us to arrive. Before we landed, we prepared everyone for the customs and immigrations debacle that was certain to take place. True to form the officials proceeded to sift through the suitcases. I chuckled when Lea mumbled that she hoped they would not pull another oregano fiasco. Eventually, after becoming weary of going through the suitcases of so many people, they allowed us to go. We made our way to the Hagemeiers' house, at which lunch had been prepared. Getting to Kalemie from Bukavu took us the same length of time that was required to take two transcontinental flights. While we were not jet-lagged, we were exhausted from the travels.

During the course of the graduation and weeklong seminar afterward, we made time to meet with Ralph, my father, David Briggs, Ralph's pastor (Pastor B.B. Hankins), and Pastor Chester Clark about our growing desire to plant churches. Ralph and Shirley are the most accommodating people one ever could hope to meet. A few years earlier when we had had lunch with them and mentioned our desire to serve in missions, Ralph said, "If you want to come to Africa but do not know where to start, come start with us and work with us until God shows you otherwise."

During this visit Ralph reminded us of his statement and said he was open to whatever the will of God was and would not hold us back. This joint meeting with our leadership from Africa as well as from the States was vital to us; we needed these leaders' covering and blessing. Determined to flow with whatever decision was from them, we were confident that they would speak the Word of the Lord to us. Perhaps we were overly anxious, but in our chests our hearts were beating fast as all the group members began to share what they felt in their hearts about our planting churches. No one felt a "check" in their spirits. Ralph, characteristically, sat back in his chair, slapped his knee, and said, "Well, go do the will of God!"

France

 Knowing that God had put Central Africa on our hearts at that time, we determined that our next step would be to learn French. Many nations in the central and western African regions speak French. We were of the conviction that learning French would be an asset. Stephanie had gone to France to learn the language and was very pleased she had taken the time out to do so. Her experience only furthered our desire to become fluent not only in Swahili but also in French. We learned we had many options available to us for learning the language. Ultimately we chose the same route and we went to France. A friend, Pastor Bert Phagan, put us in contact with a pastor and his wife in Montpellier, France. They were Pastor Patrick and Patricia Berthallon. While we studied the language, they were willing to take us under their wings.

As quickly as we had arrived in Africa, we found ourselves leaving. This step truly was into the unknown. We knew we were going to plant a church. We knew it would be in the central African region. We knew we had to learn French. But that was all we knew. Learning this language was a long process—longer than learning Swahili; we had to plan to be away for no less than six months. Taking this into consideration, we knew we once again also had to visit our supporting churches to communicate the new direction the Lord gave us. A few months were going to be needed to itinerate. This, on top of time in France, most likely would take us away from our beloved Africa for at least one year. The only way we were able to bear this thought was that we knew this was exactly what God required of us—we had nothing else to do but obey the Word of the Lord.

In October 1990 we left our belongings in Bukavu at the Swedish mission in a container on its compound. Our car was parked at another missionary's home; the missionary had agreed in our absence to drive it once a week to keep it running well. Once we returned from France, we would make arrangements to retrieve our belongings.

The process of leaving was bizarre! We spent from October 1990 to January 1991 in the U.S., as we itinerated and celebrated the holidays with our families. In the middle of January we boarded an Air France flight and made our way to Montpellier, France. The day we landed, we were stunned by the cold weather that greeted us. Tom held our hands tightly as he did his best to put on a brave face. Of course French was spoken over the loudspeakers in the airport, but it sounded so complicated. How were we ever going to learn?

Pastor Patrick, who spoke English fluently, greeted us warmly and helped us get to the apartment that had been located for our use. (A member of the church generously offered to rent her two-room apartment on short notice.) The place was pleasant; the church had stocked our refrigerator with some supplies. The apartment had one small bedroom and a sitting room in which Tom would sleep. The one bedroom was just large enough for us to set up Mandy's portable crib next to our bed. Once we set the suitcases down, all of us fell into a deep, jet-lag-induced slumber.

Learning

 The days after our arrival were a flurry of activity as Pastor Patrick took his time to show us the best places to shop for groceries, how to get to church, and how to enroll Tom in *maternelle* (kindergarten) at the local school. We struggled to get our bearings of our new surroundings; rarely have we ever felt as lost as we felt on our arrival in France.

Shortly after our arrival snow began to fall. Tom never had seen snow but quickly learned how to make and throw snowballs at his dad. Our greatest discovery was the bakery not far from our front doorstep—the bread and pastries in France are incomparable to any others we had tasted before or since. Croissants, éclairs, and French baguettes coupled with *café au lait* swiftly became a staple part of our diet in France.

Classes at the local Alliance Française school, at which French was taught and at which we were enrolled to study, were not going to start for several weeks. So, we decided to find an in-home tutor who would help us get going with the preliminaries such as greetings, days of the week, etc. Soon we were put in touch with Jeannine, who was recommended by a nearby Christian mission organization. Jeannine was an interesting person. She was a believer and originally was from Lebanon. During Lebanon's troubled time her family sent her abroad; she was earning her living by giving French classes to foreigners. Her French was flawless; her patience was well beyond the call of duty! Day in and day out for several weeks Jeannine tirelessly taught us. By the time we started at Alliance Francaise, we were placed with the intermediate class. Thank you, Jeannine!

For the first time in his life Tom began attending school. His first morning of school was cold; the night before snow had fallen. By foot the school was not more than 10 minutes away. As we walked, Tom held my hand tightly. His little face was a picture of bravery as he stood before the front gate of the school and said, "Well, this is it!" No one in his class spoke English, but Tom never asked to stay home from school. Without flinching he attended classes every day! His bravery far exceeded my own as each morning I left him to the sound of the teacher's raised voice speaking to the children. On several occasions I approached the head teacher and tried my best to communicate my concern about Tom's teacher yelling so frequently at the children. Eventually I went to the school with an acquaintance, who helped translate for me. At that point I hoped that something could be done to lessen the amount of yelling I heard taking place daily at the school. My concerns went largely unattended; somehow I was left to sort out the tremendous guilt that overshadowed me since Tom had started school. Tom, on the other hand, seemed to take the whole experience in stride; rarely was he the target of the verbal assaults in class. On the occasions he was under the teacher's fire, he seemed to keep it all in perspective. "I'm only here for a little while, Mom", was his way of responding to her tirades. The guilt I battled daily when I left Tom at school in France was a tremendous burden. On that path to and from the school that year I cried many tears.

Our French classes were going quite well. When we started with Alliance Francaise, we did not want to lose the momentum we had gained under Jeannine's tutelage, so every morning from 8 a.m. until noon at school we studied and then spent several hours every afternoon attempting to master the morning's lesson. Consequently we had to find a babysitter for Mandy so I could spend some time studying. A kind woman from church was found; we hired her to watch over Mandy in the mornings. Mandy loved her new sitter; such was her level of commitment to watching our daughter that I had less concern leaving Mandy with the sitter than I did when I left Tom at school!

Time to go home

 The months passed. As summer drew near, we began to feel a stirring in our hearts. The time had almost arrived for us to go back home to Africa. While our concentration had been on learning the language, all the while we had been praying about the place in which God was going to send us to plant our first church. In our hearts and prayers had been three cities: Kinshasa, Zaire; Kigali, Rwanda; and Bujumbura, Burundi. The year before we left Bukavu, we made several trips back and forth and became very familiar with both

Kigali and Bujumbura. Kigali was a beautiful city and Kinshasa somehow was familiar since we had worked in Zaire for several years already, but something about Bujumbura was calling us.

During the summer I made a short trip to Bujumbura while Lea spent a couple of weeks Stateside with the children. When we were reunited in France, we had arrived at the conclusion that Bujumbura was to be our city. We knew where we were going! Our home finally had a name—Bujumbura, Burundi.

This point of the journey brought us face-to-face with a reality up to that point we rarely had encountered up: We were entering into a country without knowing a soul. *How do we work in a country legally? Where do we start? To whom do we talk?* We had no answers to any of these questions. All we knew was that God had given us a clear word to go to Bujumbura. At that time we did not even realize that those questions were just a few of many that in the months that were ahead of us we would ask. However, just knowing we were on track and going to the place God had assigned to us was enough to keep us not only content but nearly exploding with anticipation. We were going to plant a church! For years I said that I "never" would be a pastor, yet now I found myself almost unable to contain the joy I felt at the prospect of seeing a church born.

> If you want to plant something that lasts a season, plant a flower. If you want to plant something that will last a lifetime, plant a tree. But if you want to plant something that will last for eternity, plant a church.
>
> –Pastor Suli, Fiji

Chapter 6

Faith Always Finds a Way

Then behold, men brought on a bed a man who was paralyzed, whom they sought to bring in and lay before Him. And when they could not find how they might bring him in, because of the crowd, they went up on the housetop and let him down with his bed through the tiling into the midst before Jesus. When He saw their faith, He said to him, "Man, your sins are forgiven you" (Luke 5:18-20).

Wen you have a word from God—when you know what His will is and what He has assigned you to do—you better be ready to encounter complications along the way until the completion of your assignment. As surely as God has sent you, Satan is waiting to discourage, disappoint, and work to disengage you from completing your task. Disheartening as this may sound, we have the assurance that God has given us faith as our weapon of choice as we advance against our enemy, Satan. Faith is more than just an internal sentiment or feeling of belief; faith takes form in action. When we have faith, we act on the word God has given us and know that God will meet us at the place at which our faith has brought us. Faith is more than a simple formula that we believers use to receive the fulfillment of our desires; it is our very life's breath:

Behold the proud, his soul is not upright in him; but the just shall live by his faith (Hab. 2:4).

By faith we can find the determination to do whatever needs to be done whenever it needs to be done. By faith we find the way to do the will of God for our lives.

As we made this initial step of faith into Burundi, questions surrounded us. What we had heard from other missionaries in Bukavu (who previously had served in Burundi) was that the country was not, in the natural sense, an especially easy place to work. We heard of the tribal tensions that for generations plagued the nation, of the intense security surrounding the capital city (Bujumbura), of the difficulties many missionaries serving there faced, and of the recent coup staged by the president at the time. *Who were we*, was our unspoken question to one another, *to enter into such a nation to bring change?* Yet, the instruction God had given us in our spirits was clear; we had no choice but to obey and find a way to get into Bujumbura.

> *He encircled him, He instructed him, He kept him as the apple of His eye. As an eagle stirs up its nest, hovers over its young, spreading out its wings, taking them up, carrying them on its wings, so the Lord alone led him . . .* (Deut. 32:10b-12a).

Finding our way to Bujumbura

Our flight from France landed in familiar territory: Nairobi, Kenya. Since we had no connections at our final destination, we decided to remain in Kenya for a month or two while we worked on moving permanently to Burundi. We found temporary accommodations with our missionary friends, David and Jennifer Hatley, who kindly offered us the use of a guest wing that was adjoined to their house. We decided that during our stay in Kenya I would take another short trip to Bujumbura to further research exactly what was required of us to operate legally within the country. We knew this step of the process was critical to the future of the church and its ministry; therefore, we took great pains in understanding this procedure, which was new and foreign to us. In the U.S. and other Western societies we are accustomed to religious freedom and freedom of expression. However, a different reality is present in Africa—one full of administrative red tape and rules that, if we did not obey, could complicate the process or even worse, cause us to be deported from the country.

During my visit to Bujumbura I was able to learn that, to operate legally within the country, we would be required formally to register the church with the government. This meant we would have to form a board, submit the church's constitution together with a variety of other required documents, and wait for the file (composed of all these sundry papers) to pass through a menagerie of offices for approval. The ultimate step was for the file to receive approval from the Ministry of Home Affairs. We realized that, since the process was so intricate, for us to accomplish the registration from outside the country would be impossible; we had to get to Bujumbura to work on the file ourselves. Nothing happens in Africa by accident or simply by waiting for the proper official to do his job. Everything that happens in Africa happens on purpose! For that reason we packed up our few suitcases, took the children, and flew to Bujumbura to begin the process, because no one else could do the work for us.

We landed in Bujumbura, Burundi, on a Tuesday in October 1991. A wave of hot and humid air met us as we exited the plane and took in the beauty of the mountains that surrounded the city. This was our place of assignment; our hearts were pounding with excitement! That excitement was short-lived as we met our first customs official who spoke unintelligible French and little to no Swahili. The official language of Burundi is French; the national language is Kirundi. But to further complicate communication the French language is spoken with a very distinct, Burundian accent. We needed some time to become accustomed to the way the Burundian nationals speak French. During our early days in the country our initial response was to do our best to keep our French as true to the French we

141

had learned in France. However, as time passed, we found ourselves slipping into the Burundian way of speaking French—the people understood us better when we spoke the way they spoke! As we were led through the process of clearing customs and doing our best to understand the strange variation of French that was being spoken to us, we began to notice a great difference between the people we had served in Zaire and those we were meeting at the airport. While clearing customs in Bujumbura is no simple task, it is far less complex than is anything we had experienced during the time we had lived in Kalemie and Bukavu. As suddenly as we had landed, we found ourselves standing on the other side of the airport and looking for a taxi to get us to town.

The hope we had that someone would extend a hand of help was dashed as we realized that no one really cared that we had arrived. We had no welcoming committee and no one waiting for us at the airport. No one was there to help us clear customs or to help us get our luggage (and the obligatory dog we brought for the kids) loaded into a taxi. We had no idea where we were going to stay during our first night we were in the country!

Shaking ourselves into reality we had to find a way to get settled for a few days until we could get our bearings. A copious supply of taxi drivers at the airport were more than willing, for a price, to drive us to town. Loading our bulky cargo into a Burundian taxi could have been comical had we not been so disoriented. We began by asking the taxi driver whether he knew the Johnsons, who were missionary friends of the Hagemeiers. We had met the Johnsons only once very briefly when Ralph had invited Mr. Johnson to speak to the missionaries serving with him in Zaire. We only hoped that we could find them and see whether they knew of a place that for a few days we could put our suitcases.

After much driving and asking what seemed like every passerby we met along the way whether he or she knew who the Johnsons were and where they lived, we drove down a mysterious dirt road that brought us to a stop in front of a small house. On hearing the taxi pull into the driveway, an older couple emerged out the front door and greeted us warmly. These soldiers of faith that stood before us were Carl and Eleanor Johnson, who had served, at that time, at least 40 or 50 years on the continent of Africa. We didn't need long before we realized that we were being received by some of God's best servants in the harvest field.[25]

Carl and Eleanor kindly opened up a small guest apartment in which our family could stay while we looked for a place of our own. The Johnsons even were happy to allow us to arrive with our dog in tow; their hospitality was humbling. We thanked God for His provision for a place to stay. That first evening we pulled in unannounced, dinner still was on the table; Eleanor quickly found provisions to feed all of us, dog included. As tired as we were that first evening in Bujumbura, we found sleeping to be difficult. We were excited that we already had experienced God's faithfulness in leading us to the safety of Carl and Eleanor's home.

Settling in

The next morning after breakfast we set off early with Tom and Mandy in tow; the Johnsons had business in town and were happy to give us a lift. After more than a year of living out of our suitcases, we were eager to get started with house-hunting and were just aching to settle into a house of our own. Questions rose up in our spirits that morning: *Who were we going to ask about renting a house? Where were we supposed to start?* The only idea we derived was to go to a taxi stand we knew in town and to begin asking questions. A couple of years before our move we had passed through Bujumbura; the Lord had led us to a taxi driver at this particular stand we had in mind. We didn't dare hope that the same man would be there to give us advice, but the possibility of his being on the scene was in the back of both of our minds.

As we arrived at the stand, we rejoiced to find this same man who just a couple of years earlier had accepted Christ. He knew of a house for rent.

Some driving around and patience were required, but we ultimately found it. This neat house was less than a 10-minute drive from town and was within our budget. Best of all, it was furnished! A contract was drawn up that day (Wednesday). After we asked Harry Johnson (one of Carl and Eleanor's sons) to look it over for us, we signed our names and made plans to move in on Friday.

During the time we were in France, political tensions had begun to rise in Bukavu. Within that climate our personal belongings and the two-year-old car, while not under direct threat of pillaging, easily could have been stolen. Just before we flew to Bujumbura from Nairobi, Dan and Melinda Koehler and Steve and Debbie Parker—friends of ours in Bukavu—stepped in to load all of our belongings into a truck and drive them and our car down to Bujumbura. With all of the tension in the air, the usual fees for goods entering the country were waived for those leaving Zaire because of the unstable situation. This was a great miracle for us: our belongings were transported into the country; we were not required to pay duty on the car, which could have gone into the thousands, if not tens of thousands, of dollars. Normally only residents in Burundi can bring cars into the country; yet here we were acting as though we were residents when we had only temporary tourist visas stamped in our passports. Each and every step we took seemed to be pre-ordained!

The first day after we arrived in the country, we found our car and other belongings packed in a room not far from the house we were renting—in less than a week, our house was secured and set up.

More miracles

 One of the greatest challenges a missionary faces overseas is transferring money from the home country to the place of service. Six weeks normally is necessary for a U.S. bank check to clear its funds overseas; we did not have enough money to last that long while we waited for a bank to follow this normal procedure. We had to find a way to get our checks cashed without the long waiting period that normally was required. I went into a bank in town and presented my dilemma to the people there. As I was discussing the matter with a bank official, Harry Johnson walked in. Harry, unbeknownst to me, already had an account with this bank. He was able to speak on my behalf. Because of his intervention not only from that time on were our U.S. checks cashed on the spot, but we also were able to open a bank account. Under normal circumstances a non-resident could not open a bank account, but God provided another seemingly small miracle from heaven's stockpile of miracles! In those days we began to think we were taking all of God's miracles for ourselves; we did not know that all of these reminders of God's leading would serve to strengthen us in some very difficult days ahead.

Getting started

Waking up the first morning in our own house was almost a surreal experience. Less than one week earlier we had been in Nairobi; almost overnight God had settled our family members into our own home. Tom enjoyed pulling out his toys that had been in storage during our time in France. Mandy now was free to toddle around in the safety of our home. And the dog was able to run around the yard. While issues such as connecting the stove and washing machine were yet to be done (and would take some extra time to get done), we managed to feed ourselves and get the clothes washed[26]—we were just thrilled to finally be home!

As thrilling as being home was, we knew that the main issue we faced now was at hand: registering the church. Everything seemed to be hinged on that registration. We were unable to request resident permits (known in some other countries as *work permits*), which would allow us to stay in the country and work long-term, without having first registered the church. Our ability to remain in the country was contingent on the church's approval. While we legally were in the country with our tourist visas, they were valid only for three months, after which we would be required to visit the main immigration offices in town to request an extension. We heard that the longest possible time one could remain in the country under tourist visas was six months; we had a lot of work to do and only a small window of time open to us.

Eager to take part in some kind of church activity we thought about having prayer meetings in our home. But before we started anything, we thought we should ask the Johnsons whether doing something as small as a prayer meeting or Bible study in our home would be appropriate, considering we were not yet officially registered. Harry and his wife, Ruthie, urged us not to undertake any such activity because, in Bujumbura, certain "street leaders" (known as *chef de la rue*) and other individuals actually would spy on people. Home meetings or any other unapproved meeting could be considered a political move and were frowned on. We were newcomers in town and surely were being watched. Any false move could result in trouble: fines, imprisonment, or expulsion from the country. We decided to put our plans on hold and find another outlet to allay our need to be involved in the life of a church.

This hunger led us to participate with the English-speaking community's weekly fellowship that met every Sunday evening. While we didn't have an official pastor of the gathering, it was led by a British couple, Graham and Sarah White, who were well-loved by the community. At this fellowship we met other English-speaking missionaries, Christian NGO[27] workers, other Christians from other nations, and national Burundians. At least 10 different nationalities participated in the fellowship. Bujumbura is a small city; at that time, the city's population was approximately 350,000. The English-speaking fellowship was quite small; it numbered no more than 70 or 80, but it was closely knit. The support we experienced from this group was extraordinary; while not everyone understood how God had led us to the country, we felt loved and received.

Unrest

Bujumbura itself is only about 20 minutes away by car from the Congolese (then Zairian) border. Just on the other side of the border is the place in which Uvira is situated. This is the place in which in times past we had ministered. One of the churches in Uvira in which we had previously ministered had heard we had moved to Bujumbura and after we had settled in Burundi invited us to preach there on a Sunday morning. Lea wasn't too interested in crossing the border with the children for only a day; she decided to stay behind while I crossed over to Uvira. We all drove together to the border, where she and the kids left me; later that afternoon we planned to meet at the home of a nearby border official (who crossed the border at the same time as I crossed) for her to pick me up after the meetings had finished. Nothing was unusual about my time in Uvira that day. I preached in Swahili, prayed for people to be saved, over a meal spent time with the local leaders, and when everything was finished, headed back to meet up with Lea and the children.

I was confused by the commotion that met me at the border. People were running to and fro. In the middle of this someone said the border was being closed because of trouble in Bujumbura. In the distance I then heard what sounded as though it was firecrackers going off. At some point during all of this confusion I ran across the same official with whom I entered the country that morning. He had received special permission to cross over; I jumped into his entourage. I believe we were the last ones allowed to cross before the border was shut down. I found Lea and the children anxiously waiting for me. Lea asked, "Did you hear the gunfire?"

Looking at Mandy and Tom playing in the yard I answered only, "Let's get home."

As we drove into town, we observed a strong military presence all around the city. The road that leads into Bujumbura from Uvira meets at a central roundabout; this roundabout, surrounded by well-armed soldiers, was congested with traffic as people who were caught in town that afternoon scrambled to get home. We saw Eleanor Johnson driving their vehicle; she had with her a couple of her grandchildren. She shouted to us, "Can we go to your house? The road to our place is closed!" The danger of the situation was beginning to sink in.

"Of course; follow us home!" I responded. Our convoy of two vehicles drove to our house, closed the gate, and waited for the unknown.

Eleanor explained that soldiers and other unspecified fighters were shooting at each other on the road that led to their home. Her son, Harry, who lived on the same compound as his parents, barely had arrived home safely and somehow had gotten the message to her not to return home with the children. We turned on the television and hoped that something would be announced on TV, but the local station was silent. The children, forbidden from going outside because the distant gunfire we heard when in Uvira now was getting closer, made their way to play in Tom's and Mandy's rooms while the women prepared something to eat. From time to time we would listen to the gunfire, try to estimate where it originated, and determine how far away it was from our location.

Nightfall approached, the city went dark, and the fighting escalated. To this day we can't say for sure how close the fighting got to our house, but we do know it was so loud that we nearly made everyone lie down on the floor. Tom, trying to sleep, became so afraid he vomited in his bed; we held our children close to us and did our best to calm them. All we could do was pray and trust in God's promise:

> *"Because he has set his love on Me, therefore I will deliver him; I will set him on high, because he has known My name. He shall call on Me, and I will answer him; I will be with him in trouble;*

I will deliver him and honor him. With long life I will satisfy him, and show him My salvation" (Ps. 91:14-16).

Never had a night seemed as long to us as had that first night of fighting in Bujumbura. All these years later the sounds of gunfire and explosions that night remain fresh in our memories; we still marvel at the grace of God Who sustained us. Several times that evening we silently exchanged glances between the two of us that said, "What have we gotten ourselves into? Why are we here in such a place?"

The next day Harry called and said Eleanor and the kids safely could join them at home. While in the distance gunfire still could be heard, things were quiet enough for them to travel home. Several days passed before things settled down enough for people to begin moving about. Slowly the markets opened; life eventually returned to what it was before that violent exchange. No one really knew who was fighting who, since several different opposition groups were involved, but for months afterward the underlying tension in the city remained high.

Life goes on

 While for a few weeks our attention was taken away from registering the church because of the unrest, it was taken away only briefly. As soon as things were quiet enough, we worked on what we could to get the file in order and submitted it to the government for approval. Time was ticking; we were beginning the second month of our three-month tourist visas. One of the first issues at hand was making sure the church's constitution, which had been translated into French, corresponded well with Burundian law. After we made the necessary adjustments to the document, we began to compile all of the other documents required of us personally; as we were part of the board and also foreigners, we had quite a long list of things that needed to be submitted: birth certificates, marriage certificate, proof of education, CV's (Curriculum Vitae—a summary of our education and life experiences), and other letters and attestations. Once these all were in order, what remained was to form an official board, appoint the board members, have a board meeting, and together with a cover letter and minutes to the initial board meeting submit the official application for registration.

A legal what?

 Up until that time in Burundi (1991-92) the country had an unofficial yet official law stating that no foreigner could be the chairman or Burundi's equivalent, the legal representative, of any church organization. Because we knew no one well enough to entrust such a responsibility, we began to press for me to be our legal representative. At seemingly every turn, when we pressed for information in this regard, we were told that a foreigner could not possibly hold such an office. Around and around we went; the legal representative in countries such as Burundi held ultimate power; if the wrong person were to take control, the results could be disastrous. We knew of many instances in which the "power" of being legal representative turned churches from being living agents of the power of God into political entities that were known for their division and strife. We were adamant in our commitment to keep any churches we ever planted from going down that route. When we were probed about our convictions—why we were intent on my being the legal representative, we would reply that initially my being allowed to stand in that position was vital. In time, as people proved themselves to be faithful, of course we would be happy for them to stand in such positions, but time would be required before we knew people well enough to make such a step.

Not long after we celebrated the New Year in 1992, I received word that the attorney general wanted to meet with me at his office. I made my way to the now-familiar government offices and wondered why he possibly could want to meet with me. After I was ushered into his office and we went through the obligatory greetings, he informed me that the laws of the land had changed. These new laws would help us, because these new laws clearly were to say that a foreigner could, indeed, be the legal representative of a church organization. He told me to make the necessary changes to our constitution to correspond with these new laws, so our file could be sent for consideration for registration. I made haste in getting the corrections to the constitution done. Meanwhile we formed a board and had our first meeting. Almost coincidentally, Ralph and Shirley were visiting in town when the time arrived for us to have our first board meeting. We asked them to be founding members; they generously agreed to help us in this regard. Letters were written; the final file was put together and scrutinized one more time; and at last in early 1992 the papers were submitted. All we had left to do at this point was to wait!

Burning on, trying not to burn out

Being confident of this very thing, that He who has begun a good work in you will complete it . . . (Phil. 1:6).

 We spent the first part of 1992 studying yet another language—Kirundi —to add to our repertoire of languages. French had been, until that time, the most difficult language we had studied. Kirundi is a very complex language; its verb tenses, noun classes, and tonality proved to make it much more difficult to learn than French is. Fresh in our memories were the hours we spent attempting to master the perfect pronunciation for the French "r", with our French teacher saying, "rrrrrrr" and our desperate attempts to mimic her perfect "r". Not one year later we once again were the victims of language school and wondered whether we ever would escape the classroom!

Days turned into weeks; gradually those weeks were turning into months. Immigration officials initially had mercy on us when we went in to renew our three-month tourist visas. They accepted our explanation that we were waiting for our church to be registered so we could request two-year work permits. Each time we requested an extension, they stamped another month into our passports. As we continued waiting and praying, we pushed the uncertainty of our situation to the back of our thoughts. On occasion churches from the outskirts of town would invite us to minister; we were glad to take time out and preach for these people; it kept our minds off the long wait! Remembering the advice we received about doing nothing until the registration occurred was difficult. At times we felt useless, as if the heavens were shut over us, with no words from the Lord. During those times we reminded ourselves of the way God had led us to the country and without our blinking an eye provided for everything we needed!

It was almost over before it began

 At the English fellowship during this time we made numerous friends who agreed with us in prayer. One person, Chrissie Chapman from the U.K., became an especially close friend. She would attend these meetings and tote a dose of reality for all of us. Nothing was false about Chrissie's demeanor; she was entirely sincere in her pursuit for the Lord and His work, but at the same time she was able to defuse our despair with words of faith and encouragement.

One evening we invited Chrissie, Mark and Sylvie (a young French couple we had met at the English fellowship), and their son, Tony, for dinner at our house. During the visit Jamie suddenly felt unwell. He said his stomach was upset, so everyone, except Chrissie, went home to allow Jamie time to rest. Yet, rest did not occur; within a half hour, Jamie's stomach pain grew nearly intolerable. My spirit suddenly sprang to attention; for the first time in my life I felt a demonic attack being hurled at my family. I knew the enemy worked against all of God's people, but never had I sensed it as personally as I did that night. This was a personal vendetta the enemy had against us; he was bound and determined to get us out of the picture. Shaken, I looked at Chrissie for guidance; she, being a nurse, knew a Russian doctor, Dr. Yuri, whom she quickly called for advice. In a very short period of time Dr. Yuri showed up at our door. With him he brought two other doctors to help assess Jamie's condition. Some friends, David Ndarahutse (a local pastor) and Graham White (leader of the English fellowship), also visited our house and offered their assistance. Chrissie, perhaps sensing my need for help, took control and guided the doctors to Jamie. Since I did not know what else to do, I stood by and began to pray in the Holy Spirit.

The doctors took only a few moments to arrive at a consensus; Dr. Yuri gave me the news: Jamie apparently had some kind of inflammation in his pancreas and needed to be hospitalized. His condition needed to be stabilized and his pain controlled. In a panic I stammered, "How did he get an inflammation in his pancreas? Where can we go?"

Chrissie stepped in and reminded us of a Methodist mission hospital that was about a two-and-a-half-hour drive from Bujumbura. A good doctor there, Dr. Frank Ogden, was someone she knew personally. A time or two we had met Dr. Ogden briefly. I felt momentarily relieved because the hospital was a place in which Jamie could get some help. However, the children couldn't go with us. Without further thought I jumped into our Pajero and quickly drove to Mark and Sylvie's house. I hoped they would be willing to stay at our house and take care of the kids during this crisis. I don't remember how fast I drove that night over the dirt roads, but it was fast. Mark and Sylvie kindly accepted the responsibility of watching Tom and Mandy for us while I stayed with Jamie at the hospital. I wasn't gone for long; as I drove back into our driveway, Dr. Yuri and Graham were helping Jamie into Graham's van, which Graham had generously offered us to use in transporting Jamie to the hospital. Jamie lay in the vehicle on a mattress; he was moaning quietly and attempting to pray as we got on our way.

The road leading to the hospital wound through the mountains of Burundi; I imagined the ride during the day under other circumstances would have been pleasant. Not much conversation was directed toward me; I knew the possible outlook was grim when I overheard Dr. Yuri and Chrissie whispering about "possible medical evacuation", "unusual case", and "surgical intervention." From the start I purposed in my heart not to fear; I steadied myself and turned my attention away from my feelings (which were fearful) and toward the Lord. Still reeling in my spirit from the revelation God had given me that this was a demonic attack, I felt compelled to fast for Jamie. For years I had known the Lord and from my father-in-law and pastor, Tom Peters, had learned about fasting. I remembered Dad teaching us from Isaiah 58 about fasting and decided to take God's word as my promise for Jamie:

> Is this not the fast that I have chosen: to loose the bonds of wickedness, to undo the heavy burdens, to let the oppressed go free, and that you break every yoke? Is it not to share your bread with the hungry, and that you bring to your house the poor who are cast out; when you see the naked, that you cover him, and not hide yourself from your own flesh? Then your light shall break forth like the morning, your healing shall spring forth speedily, and your righteousness shall go before you; the glory of the Lord shall be your rear guard. Then you shall call, and the Lord will answer; you shall cry, and He will say, "Here I am." (Isa. 58:6-9).

We had arrived in Burundi; we had obeyed the voice of God. We were in the nation to plant a church. By preaching the gospel to them we hoped to reach out to those who were lost; now Satan was threatening to put a stop to the work of God. No, this attack was not just meant to stop Jamie and me in our tracks. This attack had a broader purpose: to keep the church that God had purposed to be birthed in Bujumbura from being born. Understanding this I decided I wasn't about to allow that to happen. As I listened to Jamie groan with pain whenever the van hit the slightest bump or jerked ever so slightly, in the van I began to pray.

This fast was meant not only for Jamie's healing but also for the healing of Burundi that would occur through the planting of our church. This understanding propelled me to heights of strength in the Lord I never thought possible before this experience. While Jamie for many days was in agony, I remained convinced that I had no choice but to stand strong and to insist that God bring his healing speedily. In the interim I made several trips back and forth from Bujumbura. I checked on the children, thanked Mark and Sylvie for their help, and took care of any other business that needed my attention. All the while I continued in my determination to fast until the moment I felt the spiritual attack lift off my husband.

Dr. Ogden was a spiritual man. After a few days he called for the elders of his church to visit and anoint Jamie with oil and pray for him. Not only were people locally praying for Jamie, the night Jamie fell ill I had made contact with our home church in Florida. I had called Dad to let him know what was happening so he and Mom could agree with us in prayer. Every day or so I would call Florida and give them updates on Jamie's condition. Initially we saw little change. Dr. Ogden had been able to stabilize him, but his pain continued. Blood samples were taken and sent to a laboratory that confirmed what Dr. Yuri had concluded the first night Jamie fell ill: he had pancreatitis, an inflammation of the pancreas. This was highly unusual; the condition usually was found in someone who drank large quantities of alcohol—and Jamie did not drink alcohol. The morning the conclusive diagnosis was in, about five days after Jamie initially had fallen ill, the doctor along with his wife sat me down in their dining room and told me that I needed to begin preparing for a medical evacuation. The next day they would drive Jamie back to Bujumbura, have an ultrasound done at the main hospital in town to give the doctor a better idea of the condition of the pancreas, and then prepare to have Jamie airlifted to the U.S. via Europe.

My head was spinning, I went to Jamie's room and sat with him. After explaining everything that Dr. Ogden told me, we prayed together. I set off to Bujumbura with Chrissie, who was with me at the time. Chrissie and I discussed the situation and decided that Chrissie would travel to the U.S. with us since Jamie needed medical supervision during the trip.

As we made our way down the winding road, I looked up and noticed some storm clouds giving way to blue skies. Throughout this time God had been close to me, but until that day as I drove down the road, I had not heard any distinct direction. I heard the Lord say that this storm, just as those storm clouds in the sky were vanishing, was giving way. I didn't understand how all this was possible, since everything was stacked against us. Jamie was suffering with a serious condition that needed care that was not available in the country. Whatever God was going to do, it had to be miraculous.

On arriving in Bujumbura I called Jamie's father and let him know the prognosis. He counseled me to make airline reservations. Our home church, TCI, was behind me as I made arrangements; their prayers were carrying us throughout this time. Hastily I made my way to the airline office in town and found out the airline had space available on the Friday flight to Europe but not on the connecting flight between Europe and Miami. Once we arrived in Europe, we would have to fly on standby. Not only would we have to fly on standby, but we also would have to arrange for Chrissie's ticket, the three seats Jamie would take up (he would have been on a stretcher the whole time laid across three seats), my seat, and the children's seats. The entire bill went over $16,000—much more than I ever had seen in my lifetime!

To allow for a medical evacuation I was required to arrange all the documentation for his medications to be administered properly, take with me notarized statements from his doctor attesting to his condition, and finally, indicate the license-plate number of the ambulance that would be picking him up at the airport in Miami when we arrived. With my patience wearing thin I simply took note of all of these requirements and made the reservations. After I arranged for the flights, I then had to be sure the house was closed, decide what to do with our belongings, and figure out where to keep the car. At that time the frustration I felt was indescribable. That afternoon as I pulled into the driveway, I told the Lord out loud, "If I have to leave Africa like this, I never will come back. You have to do something; it is too much for me." With that I greeted Tom and Mandy and spent the evening with them. The children had missed their father and understood that he was very unwell; I needed to tend to them. In so doing I found comfort for myself.

The next morning Dr. Ogden arranged to transport Jamie to the city and at the main hospital have him scanned. I was at the hospital on time—early in fact—and sat on a curb as I waited for them to arrive. Hours seemed to go by before they finally pulled into the parking lot. I wasn't allowed in the room in which they scanned Jamie, but once he emerged, I greeted him and asked how he felt. He seemed a bit brighter and said, "I thought I was beginning to feel better yesterday; I'm even better today than I was yesterday." I smiled, but our reverie was short-lived as Dr. Ogden arrived and told us the pancreas still was inflamed and that we needed to proceed with the planned evacuation.

I did my best to keep my hands from trembling as Dr. Ogden asked me to meet them at a house in town in which Jamie was staying (the house was used for house guests and missionaries). I also was asked to courier a vial of Jamie's blood to a laboratory in town to recheck the levels of various elements in his blood. This test, he explained, would tell us whether his condition was worsening, stabilizing, or even improving. Once I finished taking the vials to the lab, I passed by the guesthouse to visit with Jamie before I moved on to see what the airlines had been able to secure for us since my visit the day before.

I was almost impatient as I exited the hospital; my hands trembled and my heart raced. As I pulled out of the parking lot, I collided with a bicyclist who was carrying various bits of beef. His cargo went careening all over the car and street. Thankfully he was unhurt but was upset that his business would suffer. Instinctively, I asked him how much the accident cost him. He looked at me quizzically and said, "10,000 francs." Without hesitation, I found 10,000 francs[28] in my wallet (I was carrying money to pay for Jamie's lab work), handed it to him, and asked whether I could be on my way. He waved his hand; off I went. I don't suppose he had ever had such an easy negotiation; I simply was thankful no one was hurt.

Nothing happens quickly when labs and medical work in Burundi are concerned; I waited for nearly two hours as the lab received the vials I was carrying. After that I had to go through yet another process to pay for the tests. Everything seemed to be a blur around me as my mind was set in only one direction encompassing three major issues—Jamie, his health, and the possible end to our future in Africa.

Several hours passed between the time I left my husband and the time in which I finally was able to meet him at the guesthouse. After I pulled in and walked to the house, I was met by one of the most beautiful things I ever have seen: Jamie sitting up in bed, drinking an orange soda, and eating a banana. My eyes must have asked my questions for me. Jamie said, "I felt so much better, so I asked for something to eat." For more than a week my husband had been unable to eat. I marveled at the sudden change in his condition. Dr. Ogden said he was going to give him other things to eat but that Jamie seemed to be making a turn. For a while we sat together; that heavy oppression that had hung over me for the past days just lifted. I went home, called the States, and informed Jamie's father of the situation. I said I believed that keeping the airline reservations was unnecessary and that God had other things to do with all that money besides our wasting it on airline tickets; he heartily agreed. I then canceled the plane reservations, drove home, hugged the children, had a meal, and retired for a long nap. I don't know how long I slept that day, but I woke to the phone ringing—Jamie was calling! He said he was hot at the guesthouse and wanted a fan! How nice to hear him talking! "Of course," I said, "I'll be right over with a fan." Imagine my happiness when I drove up to the house and met my husband standing in the driveway—IV removed—waiting for me to arrive.

Back to work

 I was irritated to have been out of commission for nearly two weeks and was eager to get back to business! Lea understandably hovered over me after Dr. Ogden released me to return home, but I grew impatient with being treated like a sick man. God had touched me; life had to go on! Dr. Ogden gave the "all-clear" for me to begin resuming regular activities after the blood tests Lea had dropped off at the lab showed that all levels in my blood were returning to normal. Until the time we received that news, the doctors were uncertain about my condition, despite the fact that the pain had subsided. The doctor even had suggested that the need to return to the U.S. for further treatment might have been necessary were the tests to reveal that the inflammation had not subsided considerably. The day those results arrived, we thanked God for His proving to the medical world that He indeed had healed the condition.

Before I fell ill, I had planned to minister at a weekend seminar for a church situated an hour or so away from Bujumbura. The doctor gave me the go-ahead; for the first time in many weeks I was off to preach. Ministering helped me feel as if I was returning to our main reason for being in Africa—but my heart and thoughts weren't far from the church's file that still was waiting for approval at the Ministry of Home Affairs. We knew God delivered us for a reason—Trinity Church International in Bujumbura had a Divine call to bring healing to the nation.

> *"Sing and rejoice, O daughter of Zion! For behold, I am coming and I will dwell in your midst, says the Lord. Many nations shall be joined to the Lord in that day, and they shall become My people. And I will dwell in your midst. Then you will know that the Lord of hosts has sent Me to you"* (Zech. 2:10-11).

Chapter 7

The Trial of Faith

"But delays are for the trial of faith, not for its discouragement. Often we have had to wait for our best and dearest gifts. When they came we looked up to our Lord in adoration, 'Lord, this was worth waiting for.' So it will be again. He has done so much for us. Will He not also do this that we ask Him today?"

–Amy Carmichael

God is good. He cannot withhold answers from His children's prayers. In fact, whenever we pray, He has the answer to our prayers already prepared! While the prayers have not yet been uttered from our lips, the Father is setting things in motion to get His answer to us. On more than one occasion many of us have been guilty of giving up on God and His answers just before the answer ARRIVES–if we could just hold on to the Word God has given us, we will see His faithfulness with our own eyes. When God calls us specifically to a task, He surely will make a way for us to fulfill that calling.

The first indicator of being in the middle of God's will should be the trouble encountered in working to accomplish that will of God. These troubles, while designed by the enemy to discourage and dissuade us, are used by God to strengthen our faith and to point us in the direction we are to go. This is what we found to be true in Burundi–we had learned and grown during the desperate days we waited for the church's approval. Now, after standing through all those fiery trials, we were ready for a miracle; it was all or nothing!

Back to Kalemie

 We had been in Bujumbura for more than six months; each time we entered immigration for an extension to be stamped in our passports, we prayed the officials would not notice how many extensions actually were there. Every time we called or visited the home affairs office to check on the church's file for registration, we were given the same response: no answer yet; just wait. The miraculous healing God had given to us gave us the added assurance that we were on track—but as the weeks passed and no news arrived from any office, we sorely were tempted to be discouraged.

The Hagemeiers' graduation services for the Bible school in Kalemie were on the horizon; we decided to fly down and meet up with our friends to celebrate with them. We believed the trip, after all the difficulty we had experienced since we lived in Bujumbura, would be a welcome distraction. To travel I had to get clearance from my doctor; after another round of tests showed that my condition was perfect, I was given the "go-ahead" to make the trip. While in Kalemie we made plans to take a trip to the interior with some other missionaries working with Ralph and Shirley. These were Don and Lisa Carol as well as two national colleagues who had been students once upon a time but now were teachers at the school. Tom and Mandy stayed behind with some of our friends as we set off for a 10-day adventure, which we hoped would help us forget some of the trials we had left behind in Bujumbura.

Spending our time in Zaire's[29] interior ministering in village churches proved to be exactly what we needed. As missionaries we were accustomed to working diligently and sending out reports and newsletters of what God was doing; living in Bujumbura had not (up to that point) given us much to report to our supporters besides trials and difficulties. We had no news to give and no ministry activities to report; often we were tempted to fall into the pit of discouragement. Living on the support of others who partner with you in the mission God has given you is humbling and is, at the same time, a great responsibility. During those months of waiting for the registration we struggled with feelings of uselessness; sometimes we questioned God's call on our lives. We and our future ministry seemed to be on the line with this registration. At that time having the opportunity once again to serve the people in Zaire was a most welcome respite, even if this meant that we traveled the rough interior of the country.

Early one morning soon after the graduation and seminar were over, we set off. Our hearts were rapt with anticipation for the many meetings that had been arranged for us. After 12 hours of driving the dusty, rough, and nearly nonexistent roads, we pulled into a village and hoped to find accommodations. This village actually was quite large and, at one time in history, apparently was a vibrant place. The skeletal remains of storefronts and other businesses lined the small street that led to the village's center. A kind of "guesthouse" was rumored to be found near the remains of a train station. Gingerly we scoped out the situation, found the "guesthouse", and decided it was as good a place as any to rest for the night. After we had experienced 12 hours of bouncing and driving down roads, our bodies ached from head to toe, dust settled in places we did not know dust could settle; muscles ached in places we didn't know we had muscles. Such was our state at the end of our first day of driving—and nine more days like that still were ahead!

Sharing our room

 The bed in our room was not very big. Whenever we traveled in the U.S. and had the choice, we always would opt for at least a queen-sized bed. The bed in that "guesthouse" barely would fit one American; however, Jamie and I somehow managed to lie down together as a cloud of deep sleep began to descend over us. On the edges of my consciousness I opened my eyes and looked at the wall, which only was inches from my face. Initially I thought my weariness had affected my eyesight. The wall seemed to be moving and alive. I rubbed my eyes and looked again; yes, the wall was alive—with bedbugs! Amazed, I took a moment to study these creatures. I had seen bedbugs before and even had been bitten by the creatures, but I never had seen so many of them in one place. Every little crevice in the wall was filled with bedbugs. My senses suddenly returned to me and sleep, as much as I yearned for it, no longer was possible in such infested conditions. I rocketed out of the bed faster than what seemed humanly possible; Jamie, who already had drifted off to sleep, jumped in reaction to my terror. "What's wrong? What are you doing?" Everyone in the village must have heard my horrified reply.

"Bedbugs! They're all over!" My husband suddenly was as quick on his feet as an Olympic sprinter. With my heart pounding, pupils dilated, and sweat beginning to fall down my temples, I realized I was doomed to stay in this room for the night. *How was I supposed to sleep? How was I to relax when I knew that I was nothing but prey to these insects?* We soon realized that, not only were the bugs in the wall, they also were fixed into the bed's wooden frame—too many to count. We pulled the mattress off the bed, covered it with bug spray, examined it with a flashlight, set it on the floor, and sprayed the floor around the perimeter of the mattress before we lay down. Rest, as tired as we were that night, did not occur easily. When the rooster crowed just before dawn, I already had been awake for hours. Twelve hours in a vehicle didn't seem so bad in comparison to spending the night surrounded by bedbugs.

Meetings

During those days we held many meetings in many different villages, prayed for more people than we could count, and braved more insects than we can recall before or since. In one village we spent several days and held many services. The people were extremely gracious and offered what seemed to us to be the best little mud house in the village for our accommodation. Each day we were served the best cuisine they had to offer, which usually was rice with a small, chewy chicken (that had the consistency of a tire), a tomato-based sauce that was made mostly of palm oil, and occasionally some fruit. We knew chicken was a meal usually reserved for special occasions; here we were eating it every day.[30] Their offerings of love truly were humbling, yet we found receiving as precious a commodity as chicken to be difficult. One evening in particular I felt the need to minister to the people about the Holy Spirit. This was not a topic I necessarily had set out to minister, but I believed it was the right direction to follow. Things began as usual in the brush arbor that had been prepared for these meetings, which included singing, dancing, and great joy. Dust swirled over our heads as the people praised the Lord; we could not help but join in with them. The response to the message was overwhelming, as after I preached the message everyone in the gathering appeared to want to be prayed for and to receive the infilling of the Holy Spirit. When everything was all said and done, in that dusty meeting place more than 80 people were filled with the Holy Spirit. Whether we had carpet on the floor, airconditioning, or any other convenience did not matter to us—nothing compared to seeing so many people filled with the Holy Spirit. It was a good place to be.

The morning after the service our team pulled out of the village. Although we still were basking in the joy of the previous night's meeting, we knew our days were numbered. The time had arrived for us to start heading back to Kalemie. In our absence the kids had been staying with other missionaries; we were feeling anxious to see them again. This was the first time since we had been in Africa that we had left them; we felt pressed to be by their sides. On our route we had one village left in which to minister before we were to be reunited with our youngsters.

Spiders

The last stop we had set on our itinerary was a resting point in which lorries rested before they made the final journey to Kalemie (a port city), where their goods could be sent by boat to Tanzania or other parts of Zaire that bordered Lake Tanganyika. Because the village was a resting point and the people who manned these lorries (big trucks used for transporting goods) were a strange sort, the village was littered from the lorries and their cargo. While rats ran across the street into random piles of trash, everyone seemed to ignore their presence, so we endeavored to do the same. One of the best rooms in the village was given to us for the night; after we entered the room, we gratefully set our bags down. Momentarily after he put the bags on the floor, Jamie stepped outside; happy to have a few moments of quiet, I sat on the bed. The room, while small, was a blessing. I was surprised with how clean it appeared to be despite the general condition of the village.

Feeling tired after the long journey I decided to lie down on the bed and allowed myself to feel a bit pampered for the first time in more than a week. Once again, just before that blessed sleep for which I was yearning arrived, I opened my eyes. Curled up not six inches from my face was a dead spider. This was not any usual spider; it was the biggest spider I'd ever seen. In Africa insects, spiders, rodents, and the like are super-sized. The creatures with which on the field we have had to deal rarely have been small in size or number. So weary was I from the journey that I barely was able to manage a small yelp and bat the horrid, fist-sized corpse off the bed. That night I slept fitfully as I held the flashlight and turned it on and off to see what I did or did not hear crawling above. My imagination did not give me rest, but I was jealous of Jamie, who, in his usual manner found his way to blissful slumber.

Back to Bujumbura

 After the long separation we were thrilled once again to be with Tom and Mandy. Tom was full of stories and questions about our travels; he was upset that we had not taken him with us on the journey but wanted to hear the "bug stories" over and over. He soon forgave us; we were back to playing cars and talking about going home and sleeping in our own house. Mandy, barely 2-years old at the time, was happy just to cuddle and have her parents back with her. After our children, our thoughts were not far from the church file in Bujumbura. The MAF plane we had chartered to get us from Kalemie back home to Burundi arrived not long after we returned from our time in the "bush". As difficult as our previous months in Burundi had been, I felt energized by our time in Zaire; once again I was ready to fight the good fight. Full of faith and anticipation for the best we climbed aboard the little MAF plane that carried us out of Kalemie.

A telephone call

 Visitors (my parents along with Tom and Sandy Chappell, a couple in our church who are elders) were scheduled to visit us in August 1992, just weeks after our return from Zaire. We were looking forward to this visit more than any other; we felt a little "battle-weary" and greatly anticipated having time with friends and family. Lea, who by that time was becoming quite accomplished in the kitchen, before their arrival planned meals and cleaned the house from top to bottom. We were so encouraged to see our guests step off the plane; God had sent some encouragement our way in the form of friends and loved ones. He always is faithful to strengthen us when we need it.

Tom was ready to see what presents had been brought for him; his grandparents were happy to oblige him. Mandy, following the lead of her big brother, looked for her presents as well and quickly learned to love the joy and busy-ness that arrived when the grandparents were visiting.

That first afternoon after their arrival, among all the chaos of opening suitcases and finding presents, the telephone rang. Lea answered; with eyes wide open, she motioned for me to take the telephone. She said, "It is the Ministry of Home Affairs." Silence fell over all of us as I took the phone.

"Hello?"

A person on the other end said, "Is this Reverend Peters of Trinity Church International?"

"Yes, it is," I replied. The news that followed seemed surreal. "Trinity Church International has been approved for registration in Burundi. You can come to our office and collect your certificate."

I responded, "Thank you, yes, thank you. We will be down to collect it shortly!"

The nine months of prayer, persistence, and trouble melted away in that moment in which God, with a simple phone call, answered our prayers.

Having Mom, Dad, and the Chappells with us when the phone call arrived that announced the approval of the church registration was an unexpected blessing. The remainder of our time with our guests was sweet, as we spent hours and days brainstorming the imminent church plant.

A church is born

We didn't know the first thing about church planting. I had been reared in a pastor's home but never had planted a church. All we knew was that we were supposed to plant a church; what that really meant was yet to be seen. Before we were permitted to work in the country, we had to sort out our visas. Quickly we gathered all the necessary documents and submitted our request for our two-year resident visas that would give us the right to work as missionaries with TCI, because it now was a recognized church in the country. We no longer had to be concerned about our immigration status; we would be allowed to work, to serve, to have a future.

In a matter of weeks after we had our resident visas approved, we began to look for a place in which to hold meetings. Bujumbura is not a very big city; therefore, we did not have a great selection of places to rent in which our new church could meet. What we did find was a building in the inner city in an area known as *Bwiza*. Bwiza was known for its rough population. The building we rented for the church to use was set right in the middle of the roughest area of that part of town. We didn't care for what Bwiza was known, nor did we care that when we opened the doors of the church, the smell of homemade banana beer assaulted our sense of smell. We considered Bwiza to be the best location in town; we felt sorry for all the others who didn't have the chance we had to start a church there. For several days before our first Sunday service we went from house to house and invited people to join us for a week of special meetings that would begin on Sunday of the following week.

On November 1, 1992, for our first Sunday we had 35 people in attendance; most of them were children. I led songs, took the offering, preached, and prayed for people. Lea managed our two children as well as all the children from the surrounding area. During that first week Ralph was in town; he graciously accepted the offer to preach a couple of services for us. The start was a rough one, but we were taken away with the joy of planting a church. Every evening that week we held services; every night the crowd grew every night. On the second Sunday a brother named Wilondja Kingombe was in attendance; we had heard he was a musician. He graciously offered to help us lead in worship; we were pleasantly surprised by his talent with music and song. His life definitely had been anointed for praise and worship—we welcomed this young man and trusted that God was leading us.

More to learn

 The first few months of meetings in Bwiza were filled with new experiences. I never had been a senior pastor. I had grown up in a senior pastor's home, but I quickly found out that growing up in the pastor's home was not the same as being the pastor. Often I found myself understanding my father on a deeper level than I had experienced when I was growing up at home. I began to understand the conflict he must have felt in rearing a young family while at the same time working to rear a young church. For us we had new converts to be counseled, visits to be made, and sermons to prepare, as well as the never-ending headaches of trying to do these things in Africa where the power goes off randomly or unexpected holidays occur that cause everything to close. These types of issues made all business needing to be done one day left undone until the next day. All the while I had responsibilities at home, with Tommy wanting to throw the ball and Mandy just learning to walk and talk. Finding that fine line of giving my attention when and where it was needed kept me on my knees. I understand now, Dad; I understand!

Lea never had taught children's church before, never had been responsible for a women's ministry, never had been a senior pastor's wife, and felt overwhelmed by the sudden weight of responsibility. She did her best to equip the children's church, find materials for teaching the kids, hold prayer meetings for the women, and learn what being a senior pastor's wife meant. On several occasions she remarked how "nice it would be" to have had some kind of manual on what to expect or how to be a senior pastor's wife. Added into the mix was being a senior pastor's wife in Africa, in which she had to learn to navigate the curves and bumps that the different languages and cultures threw her way. Women in the developing world—Africa in particular—often are not seen as much more than property. They enter into marriage often by means of nothing more than a business deal and the exchange of money and/or property. This understandably instills a deep sense of worthlessness within the women and is a difficult barrier through which to break. Only by the grace of God did Lea begin to find her way.

Church planting 101

 I'm not sure how to describe *church planting*. Brother Wilondja, who had become our praise-and-worship leader, did not play with sheet music. Everything he played, he played by ear. Such things go with planting a church. You have to have a keen ear to what the Holy Spirit is saying—the "music" He is playing—so you can know how to proceed with what messages to preach, where to hold your meetings, and what methods to use while you evangelize—you have to be able to hear what He is saying. In essence, everything must be done by ear—by being sensitive to every word He says along the way.

Each church plant, we have found, has been different. In planting a church many things remain constant—prayer, worship, fellowship, preaching, evangelism, giving, and faith principles. They all are constants. However, in each place their implementation takes on different forms. Not only do we need to implement principles, but also (first and foremost) we need to win souls and then train people to become soul-winners. In a cross-cultural setting, this can be surprisingly tricky. On one hand people are happy that missionaries are there to serve in their field; but at the same time an unspoken tension sometimes exists toward missionaries and from time to time is reciprocated from missionaries toward nationals. In times past and even occasionally in the present missionaries have gone to nations and initiated ministries with the distinct flavor of their own cultures, with no consideration to their host cultures. This is not done with bad intentions; it simply is what occurs naturally to those individuals. All of us feel most comfortable within our own cultures in which we received the gospel and as we minister to others, inadvertently can project that culture onto them. The result of this can be church services that often look as though they are Western transplants rather than African church plants. The differences in culture and custom often present so great a challenge to people on both sides (the missionary and the national) that meaningful relationships go unmade; thus, the long-term survival of the outreach is in doubt. Because of the instability we find in the world today, we have learned that missionaries must work in the present and keep the future of the work in mind. We can be sure that at every level Satan will attack God's work. The situations foreigners face in their host countries at a moment's notice can change when governments may decide they no longer want foreign influence in the country. Visas easily can be revoked; civil unrest can force expatriates from the country. So many unforeseen and unexpected complications can and surely will arise; this makes the missionary always work with the future in view. Through the relationships Jesus built with His first 12 disciples He changed the world, not through implementing great services (although great services did take place when Jesus walked the earth). Relationships, we have found, take time and great effort.

This especially is true in a field such as Africa, in which Satan has undermined the development of deep relationships between Africans and missionaries. Oftentimes new missionaries will find that the nationals, while happy to receive them, are wary of their intentions. *Are these here to implement yet another Western church or ministry? What are their intentions? Are they simply here to make money off the poverty of the African, or are they genuinely sincere?* Our African brothers and sisters are very conscious of these issues and will take their time to watch a ministry before they become faithful. Our new little church plant in Bujumbura was no exception—we had to go through many deep waters to prove ourselves as sincere. Thankfully God didn't let us know everything we were about to experience. We simply played it by ear.

Good news

 Not many months after TCI Bujumbura was born, we found out we were expecting our third child. Lea's growing middle reflected the growth we were experiencing as a church. In a matter of three or four months we had nearly 100 people, were holding early morning prayer sessions, and saw a church choir beginning to form.

This pregnancy proved that the healing God had given us some years before truly had taken hold. Gone were the complications of years past. At the Peters household the name wars began once again, as all four of us eagerly looked forward to the day our new baby would make his or her debut into the world.

Hospital outreach

We believe in a holistic gospel message. In other words we believe God wants to demonstrate His love to the people of the world in ways that address their respective situations. In Western countries this would not take on the same form as it would in a developing nation such as Burundi. Through the women of the church news had reached us about the plight of patients in the government hospital called *Prince Regent*. Since patient care at the hospital did not include providing meals, the women of the church proposed that our church cook meals for the patients. We were able to pay for this outreach by taking 10 percent of the church's income and purchasing the food we cooked for the sick in the hospital. During their stay at the hospital many of the sick did not have the means to have food brought to them; while we were unable to address every need, the people greatly appreciated the little bit we did. Every Saturday for many years our church cooked food and brought it to the patients at Prince Regent Hospital. Many trusted the Lord and joined the church. This was our first small step into the world of outreach. In the days ahead this experience would serve as a stepping stone to a much larger outreach.

Politics

The exciting first days of our church plant often were over-shadowed by the politics of Burundi. Burundi's current president, who had taken power in the late 1980s in a coup, had begun the transition to a democratic form of government and declared that in summer 1993 (the time our baby was to be born) Burundi would have free and fair elections. An unspoken tension was present in the city; everyone wondered how the elections would proceed and whether peace would prevail. During those days the memories of past wars as recent as the 1970s, the coup in the '80s, as well as the unrest in November '91 were not far from anyone's thoughts.

Travel

Nearly two years since our last visit to the States had gone by; our baby was to be born during the time we planned a trip back to the U.S. With the political situation in the country we were not too happy about being away from the church. We also realized that Burundi, at the time, was a place of great uncertainty. Our lives' schedules simply could not revolve around what might happen because in those days something always was on the verge of happening in Burundi. We had little choice in the matter of traveling. Not only was the baby to be born, but we also had to visit our supporting churches, which we had not visited for some time. So our trip was scheduled; we were to be gone for almost three months. Wilondja, who by then was a leader in the church, together with a few other leaders in the church, were scheduled to preach and oversee whatever responsibilities were necessary at the time. We waited as long as Lea's doctor would allow and then boarded the Sabena flight that flew straight from Bujumbura to Brussels, the first leg of our return flight stateside.

African tie-dye

Landing in West Palm Beach after a long period of time away was very daunting for Lea in particular. The children simply were happy to see family, but my wife was horrified to return in her condition. As we walked down the concourse after the plane landed, she lamented over her hair, clothes, and obviously extreme pregnant state. I told her repeatedly that she was fine—beautiful in fact—but her humor did not improve with my attempts to encourage her. She was on the verge of tears as she lamented over her appearance in West Palm Beach, a very wealthy place in contrast to the conditions we had just traveled from in Burundi. In comparison to everyone else she felt out of place as she looked down at the only dress she had left that fit her—the dress that she wore on the trip over—an African, tie-dyed dress.

Stephen

When we learned our baby was a boy, we finally had settled on a name. *Stephen* was a strong name; we believed our new son would be a strong servant of the Lord. On July 9, 1993, after I woke to a contraction at 6 a.m., Stephen was born. He entered this world quickly, 30 minutes after our arrival at the hospital—almost as if to say by doing so that we had to get back home sooner rather than later. The hospital staff visited our room and were amazed that the baby had been born so quickly and that both of us were sitting up and watching the morning news together. Tom rejoiced that he didn't have another sister; Mandy similarly was excited when she understood that she was the only girl in the family, which set her apart from the boys. Remembering the difficulties and children we lost to miscarriage in the past made Stephen's birth sweet—when God does a healing work, He does it perfectly.

Home

During our brief time in the U.S. we visited as many churches as possible. Once Stephen was 6-weeks old, we made the long trek back to Burundi. We found ourselves calling Africa *home*; while we loved the U.S., our family, our church, and friends, we were increasingly ill at ease when off the continent. The will of God, we found, is not so much a destination as it is being in a state of obedience to His call—whatever that may be and wherever that may take you. We did not enjoy the troubles or difficulties that were present in Africa, but we just found obeying easier than not doing so.

Stephen, as well as the older kids, made the trip very well. As we walked on the now-familiar tarmac of the Bujumbura airport after we landed, we were astonished at what we saw: a handful of people from our church waiting to receive us. Tears stung the backs of our eyes as we remembered not so long ago when we were alone at the airport with no one to receive us. That no longer was the case. We found that our natural and spiritual families were growing—God was working. Together with our new son a church had been born.

Attempted coup

In our absence the presidential election had taken place in Burundi. A new president was elected and installed; the country apparently had made a turn toward democracy. After he lost the elction, the president at the time stepped down and handed power over to the new president, President Ndadaye. This apparent peaceful transition of power gave everyone hope that Burundi indeed would become a democratic nation. On the surface life went on quietly. Those of us living in Bujumbura slowly allowed ourselves to settle in to what appeared to be peace.

One morning early in October 1993 we woke to the sound of large explosions and gunfire. We wondered what possibly could make such noise and noticed that the light fixtures on the house shook; such was the violence of the explosions.

Although we heard the noise in the city, the time had arrived for early morning prayer at the church! Lea faintly protested my getting into the car to make my way to the church for prayer. She knew that arguing made no difference; I knew people would be trying to get to church for prayer; I needed to be there to encourage them. However, my determination to get to prayer made no difference to the military personnel I found lining the streets near our house. When they saw me making my way down the street, they simply gestured for me to turn around and go home—which I promptly obeyed. I drove back into the driveway and together with Ralph and Dan (who were visiting from Zaire) looked out the front gate. Military vehicles were driving by; soldiers were giving the "thumbs-up" signal. This did not sit well with us; we remained clueless as to what was going on—we only knew that it was not good.

Telephones were cut off; we could not access news on the TV or radio. The city seemed to have been plunged into darkness. For several days this uncertainty hovered over the city; we stayed indoors and waited for news. As suddenly as the phones, TV's, and radios went off, they returned. The news was out: President Ndadaye had been assassinated in a failed coup attempt. The explosions we had heard and felt at our house were the rounds of gunfire from armored vehicles firing at the presidential palace, which was at least two miles from our house. The vice president had taken over and had attempted to restore calm to the country. After several days the mutilated body of President Ndadaye was recovered. Before his death he apparently had been tortured; this understandably caused outrage among the people. Burundi had entered the door of civil unrest that ultimately would cause the deaths of hundreds of thousands of the country's population.

Chapter 8

Retreat is Not an Option

"No wound? No scar?
Yet, as the Master shall the servant be,
And pierced are the feet that follow Me;
But thine are whole: Can he have followed far
Who has nor wound nor scar?"

–Amy Carmichael

Have you ever been in a room in which the power has been cut off? This can be especially frightening if it happens after dark. While growing up in Florida, I remember when a hurricane passed over and cut the power off in the middle of the night. As the wind howled outside, I cowered away in a corner; I was afraid of the unknown. Feeding into that fear, I could hear tree branches breaking in the wind as they struck the windows and doors of the house. *Was our roof going to blow off? Were we going to have to move? Was our house going to be destroyed?*

Up until the storm blew over and the next morning the sun shone, we had no way of knowing what damage actually had taken place. In the light of day we saw that uprooted trees and debris littered the entire area around our home.

Do not rejoice over me, my enemy; when I fall I will arise; when I sit in darkness, the Lord will be a light to me (Mic. 7:8).

War

Not long after the restoration of telephones, TV's and radios, the borders were opened and Ralph and Dan made their way back to Zaire.[31] Businesses re-opened and children went back to school in the capital, Bujumbura. After some weeks passed by, reports of fighting and atrocities taking place in the countryside spread quickly through the city. (Burundi is a small country, about the size of the U.S. state of Maryland, with a very dense population of nine million.) The violence in the country caused a massive movement of internally displaced people; consequently, the resulting damage to the democratic process seemed irretrievable. We heard rumors of schools being burned with students inside, with no one taking the blame for such carnage, but it nonetheless took place. Tens of thousands of people settled in camps along the countryside—many more seeking shelter and safety made their way to Bujumbura. The light of the country suddenly seemed to have been turned off and surrounded by death and darkness. We wondered whether the light ever would be back on again.

Regional conflict

The region in Africa where Burundi, Rwanda, Zaire, and their bordering countries are located is known as the "Great Lakes Region." The Great Lakes Region has seen much conflict and tension in its history. As recently as the 1960s missionaries were killed in Zaire. Then, in the 1970s Burundi suffered through some years of civil unrest brought about by the same ethnic tensions of its unrest in the 1990s. These renewed tensions were nothing new to the people of the region. Explaining how the populations of these countries knew that the trouble brewing under the surface from generations past would resurface, even in our day and time, is difficult.

Many who have heard us recount these events are surprised to learn that the conflict in Burundi preceded that of its neighbor, Rwanda. The actions surrounding the death of President Ndadaye set the stage for a complex political situation that had no apparent solution. Not only did Burundi lose her first democratically-elected president in 1993, but the vice president, who took President Ndadaye's place on his assassination, also was killed. He was in the plane with Rwanda's president when it was shot down in 1994.

During the 100 days of slaughter that took place in Rwanda, in which approximately one million lost their lives in an ethnically-based killing spree, Burundi struggled through an increasingly violent and intricate set of events. A third president for Burundi was set in place from the same political party, but he was so fearful for his life that for many months he took refuge in the U.S. ambassador's residence. Occasionally during those months, when the American ambassador was entertaining his houseguest, he would visit with the missionaries. A bit of humor entered into our conversation with him one day when we asked him how his houseguest was getting along. Chuckling, his quick reply was, "He's watched all my movies!"

As the violence in Rwanda reached a climactic moment, it spilled over into the already volatile situation present in bordering Zaire. Rebel and army groups targeted for elimination certain ethnic groups in the country. Zaire is a very large country, which supplied those fleeing the wars in Rwanda and Burundi ample space and population to hide. The fighting spread as far as Kalemie, in which the Hagemeiers' Bible school was pillaged and bombed from the air and in which even one of the students was hacked to death and buried on the school property. While many fled Kalemie, the Hagemeiers stood firm and believed God for His resolution to the violence. With the help of their supporters and even the U.N., they were able to work with widows and the internally displaced. They provided much-needed food relief and spiritual counsel. Their determination and faith inspired us to keep on the same track in Bujumbura. Their daughter, Stephanie[32] (together with her adopted daughters, Vickie and Mathy), also stayed with her parents; they all faithfully served the people of Kalemie.[33] Knowing they faced pressures similar to our own because they had children with them, we felt encouraged to stay on track with our decision to remain in the country. We had no inclination to leave Burundi—besides, where else could we go?

A growing church

 While war gripped the interior of the country, for nearly two years Bujumbura escaped falling into the conflict. During that time our church grew rapidly to several hundred people. The little building in which we met could barely hold the crowd; the congregation was spilling out the doors. While the structure itself was too small to hold all the people, we had ample space on the property to build a simple shelter to help us accommodate the increasingly large numbers of people joining the church. During those days Don and Sarah Reed, who had served with the Hagemeiers, spent some time with us in Bujumbura. Don, who is a proficient builder, constructed the shelter for us. It was a simple building made of poles set in concrete and had a tin roof. We covered the "floor" with stones. Benches were fashioned by a local carpenter; services continued—yet we could not forget the unrest that grew ever closer to the capital.

Rumors began to circulate of rebel strongholds in the mountains surrounding the city. Sometimes their guns would sound and remind us all of their presence as well as of their imminent invasion of the city. Even with tension tightening its grip on the city, when we began to use the shelter Don built for us, the church exploded with growth. In a very short time on a Sunday morning we were having 500 people attend.

Doing our best to ignore the unraveling of Burundi's political situation, we pressed forward with the church; we were convinced that the key to any situation in any country was prayer. My father often has said, "You'll either pray by choice or pray by crisis." I knew the important role that prayer played not only in an individual's personal spiritual growth but also in the growth of the church. From the beginning we held early morning prayer sessions and even during those tense times continued to do so. The people of the church were incredible and every morning from 6 to 7 rallied together for prayer. In the mornings we easily could have 50 to 60 people show up for prayer.

Our services were held in two languages: Swahili and Kirundi. Although Burundi's official language is French, the national language is Kirundi. While many have a working knowledge of French, most do not have a very great fluency in the language. In the city of Bujumbura a great deal of Swahili was spoken; therefore to cater to everyone we decided to have both languages going in every service and even during early morning prayer. Many in the church were fluent in both languages, so finding interpreters for either language rarely was difficult. I loved preaching in Swahili and had a great time ministering the Word to the congregation.

One Sunday morning as we were introducing visitors, a smart-looking young couple stood up when I asked for visitors to stand so we could welcome them. I noticed that throughout the service, the wife appeared to be translating for her husband. Occasionally she would pause as if she were herself straining to understand what was being said. After the service we shook their hands, learned their names (Emmanuel and Jackie Nkunku), and welcomed them to return. This couple had a young daughter, Axelle, who was just about a year younger than Mandy. The two girls immediately gravitated toward each other and in a matter of weeks became fast friends. This family was from Kinshasa in Congo and was working with NGO's in Burundi. Jackie understood a bit of the Swahili we spoke but was not entirely fluent, so when she translated, she often became flustered. Because they also were fluent in English (as well as French and Lingala), on Sunday mornings Lea began to translate the message in English for Emmanuel. However, after just a few weeks Emmanuel decided that, since he and his family decided to become members of TCI, he had to learn Swahili himself and determined on Sundays to go without English translation to push himself to learn the language. Their commitment to the church was almost immediate. We praised God for committed members at a time in which they sorely were needed.

Feeding the children

 As the church grew, so did the city's population of internally displaced Burundians. In a period of just a few months after the onset of the war Bujumbura's population of 350, 000 increased by many thousands. Close to the church in a neighboring residential area called *Buyenzi* was the place in which two groups of displaced people settled—one in a school and the other in a government building. More than 1,000 children under the age of 12 in both camps were going without food. Word reached us about the suffering of these children who had gone days without food, water, or shelter. After a time of prayer with Jamie and the other church leaders, I called for the women of the church to join together and pray about reaching out to those who were suffering so near to our congregation. We unanimously decided that, while we had few resources, we would do what we could, which meant we would cook porridge for the children and feed as many of them spiritually and physically as we could; we would start with the youngest ones.

Hastily the women began rummaging through their homes and gave what they could toward the outreach. Some had wooden spoons, others had sugar, and yet others had charcoal for cooking. I had several large, cooking pots that years earlier my parents sent to me in a container that had been shipped to us when we lived in Bukavu. They were unused and just sitting in my cupboards, because they simply were too large to cook meals in at home. Until the day we began to cook for the needy children, I often had wondered what use I would have had for such large pots God knew that day would arrive; He had sent and prepared us for the time in which we would be called to feed them.

We had little extra financial support to purchase food for the children; however, we knew we had to do what we could to alleviate some of their suffering. A locally-produced porridge available in Bujumbura was called *Musalac*. This was made of corn, soy, and wheat. We simply added powdered milk, sugar, salt, and a little vegetable oil to make a very high-energy food for them. However, we had only enough extra money to purchase a two-week supply; we were not sure what God was expecting us to do after that supply finished.

Word quickly got out among the missionary and expatriate community about our outreach to the children. One afternoon after we fed the children, we drove up to the house and found the garage full of donated Musalac, sugar, powdered milk, salt, and vegetable oil. It was more than we could have imagined! Another individual donated several large (50-liter) cooking pots; on went the outreach that we began to call the *Musalac Ministry*. So great was the local support that we expanded the outreach to another camp on another side of the city; that camp was called *Kanyosha*. This additional site brought to almost 1,500 the total number of children we daily were feeding.

In and out of season

 As the situation in the city remained calm and the population in the camps began to settle, we started a routine of bringing children's church lessons as an addition to praying for them as we fed them. So great was the reaction of the children and the adults in the camps that many not only were saved but also joined the church and remain with us to this very day. Feeding the children was a wonderful outreach—but we knew that, without giving them the gospel, we only were treating a surface wound. The real need of the children went far beyond the physical; they needed to have their spiritual needs addressed. This could be done only with the Word. We had an encounter with the brevity and fragile nature of life and knew we had no idea what dangers the children and their families in the camps were facing. During those days the possibility that the city could be overrun was great. The children we were feeding would flee far from our influence. This was a life-or-death matter. We had little time to deliberate whether we were going to preach.

> *Preach the word! Be ready in season and out of season . . .*
> (2 Tim. 4:2).

Sudden terror

 All of Bujumbura had grown relatively accustomed to the constant tension in the city and surrounding region. During the war the grapevine of gossip worked like a well-oiled machine. Every morning a new rumor seemed to circulate. One day rumor was that "they" were about to launch an attack on the city. On another day the rumor was that "they" were about to hit other regions. On and on went the rumors. We began to ignore these rumors and realized that God would grace us to do whatever we needed to do whenever we needed to do it. In the event our food supply was cut off by war, we did, however, keep in our pantry a fairly large stock of non-perishable food.

One Thursday afternoon in May 1995 the usual gunfire to which we were accustomed in the hills seemed to draw nearer. Because in the previous months we heard so much gunfire and the like, we simply ignored the "music" (as we called it) and went on with our normal activities. Later on that same day, as Lea and Stephen (who was barely 2-years old) were visiting some friends up on a hill that overlooked the city, the gunfire became so loud, we no longer could ignore it. From our friends' back porch Lea glanced over the landscape, looked in the direction of the church, and saw smoke rising from the area. Because at that time we did not live far from the church and Mandy went to a preschool just next door to our house, Lea loaded Steve in the car and quickly drove home to collect Mandy. As parents were arriving in a panic to collect their children, the school had scores of cars around it. Steve stayed in the house with a friend as Lea dashed next door to get our daughter. A military officer whose child went to school with Mandy told Lea to get inside her house because "they" were coming to raze the city.

I had been out that morning running errands and arrived home just as panic began to hit. Cars were dashing to and fro as people hurried to their homes or places of safety. When I did manage to get back to the house just moments after Lea had collected Mandy, Lea gave me the report she had heard from the officer. Instinct kicked in; I dashed to collect Tom from school. About the same time one of the short-term missionaries serving with us, Sandy Nelson, drove into our driveway with several church members in his car. Sandy and his wife, Debra, and their three young sons only recently had arrived in the country. We advised him to return to his family with those in his car and that we would be in touch via our long-distance radios[34], if necessary. He hurried home; by that evening, we had several church members at our place as well. Meanwhile, we attempted to make a phone call to alert the church in Florida to pray. As we got on the line with my father's secretary and briefly explained the situation, the line went dead. Before our conversation was cut short, we were able to relay enough information about the situation to apprise them somewhat of the state of affairs in Bujumbura. Emmanuel and Jackie also had opened their home to a number of church members seeking refuge. We were not sure how long the violence would last or would keep us housebound, so we stayed on our knees, closed the front gate, and waited—for what, we did not know.

The distant gunfire, which resembled popping corn, grew increasingly louder and no longer sounded as though it was the familiar noise from before. We tried to sleep, but sleeping that night nearly was impossible. We glanced out the windows, saw red tracer bullets going over the roof, and heard the deep booming of mortar fire in the hills not far from our house. Throughout the night and for many nights thereafter the fighting went on.

We have been asked how, during those times, we stayed in the country with our children. Certainly on some occasions we hoped God would re-lease us—especially during escalations in the violence. However, we had a commitment to do the will of God. As long as we knew we were in His will, we determined that we would stay.

> *"You shall not be afraid of the terror by night, nor of the arrow that flies by day, nor of the pestilence that walks in darkness, nor of the destruction that lays waste at noonday. A thousand may fall at your side, and then thousand at your right hand; but it shall not come near you. Only with your eyes shall you look, and see the reward of the wicked"* (Ps. 91:5-8).

Refugees

 The next morning the fighting in town eased; we were able to get some news from church members who made their way to our home to seek refuge. Some arrived with only the clothes they had on their backs and told us tales of armored vehicles moving in during the night and blowing up homes in the slums near the church. By the end of the afternoon our house was full with 16 "refugees" we had taken in as we waited to see what the outcome would be in Bujumbura. Thankfully we had stocked the pantry with enough food for all of us for at least a week, but we did not dare think about "what if" the food ran out. That simply was not an option.

We quickly saw that our situation of living together with our people was going to last for more than one or two nights. Our sleeping arrangements seemed to work: the men slept on the floor in the living room, the women and their children took one of the kids' bedrooms, and our family took up the other two bedrooms. For weeks we sat and listened as gunfire brought the city to its knees. However, not everything that happened during those weeks with our houseguests was bad. As we grew accustomed to the "music" of gunfire, we sat together and told stories. Sometimes the stories would bring us to tears. They often were tears of joy but also tears of pain.

At certain times during the day some shops in town would open for business; some stalls in the market would open to sell food. Even though gunfire often could be heard in the background, we gradually learned our limits of movement. I found a small shop that sold some fresh fruit and vegetables that I squirreled away. Our main staples for weeks were beans, peas, and rice, or the local food—*ugali*. As time passed, I found eating beans every day to be impossible; the side-effects of eating beans for so long were intolerable. Great quantities of food were cooked every evening. I would take my fruit and vegetables, sneak into the kitchen when everyone was eating beans and *ugali*, and make a bowl of salad. Then I would tiptoe into my bedroom and feel wicked for skipping the bowl of beans.

The *ugali* we made at home was prepared with corn meal. Our houseguests, however, enjoyed *ugali* made with cassava flour. This particular type of *ugali* (made with cassava flour) has a strong smell to the American nose. To the chagrin of my houseguests I banned it from being cooked in my kitchen. Even if it was not banned, I told them that we did not have any cassava flour with which to make *ugali*. That simple statement was enough. One morning, not many days after our involuntary confinement, while the gunfire was quiet, I saw one of our guests make his way out the front gate. I asked him, "What are you going to get out there?"

He said, "Cassava flour!" Shouts of joy emerged from all our visitors when, a few hours later, this young man returned with a plastic bag containing five kilos (about 12 pounds) of cassava flour.

So many things need to be taken into consideration when one houses 16 people in a three-bedroom, one-and-a-half bathroom house. Quickly I had to derive a schedule, because I soon saw that everyone was content for me to do all the washing up, laundry, housecleaning, and mending. The final straw was broken one evening when, after dinner, we all were sitting down to eat peanuts. These peanuts had been shelled but still were coated with the thin, dark brown skin. Our family had grown accustomed to eating the peanuts with the skin, but some of our guests decidedly were against such an approach. During our evening's conversation several of our friends took the peanuts, rubbed the skin off, and dumped the little pieces all over the floor. At that moment I needed great deal of effort to hold my tongue, but by God's grace I kept quiet and made a plan to change the existing arrangement. I decided that doing this with a great deal of style instead of losing my cool would be best. Since most of our houseguests were young men (in the African culture women usually wait on men hand-and-foot), one day I set aside a few hours to give them lessons in housekeeping and cooking; after those lessons things proceeded smoothly at the house for the duration of what turned out to be our six-week-long confinement together.

Mass exodus

 For the first couple of days after the initial onset of fighting in our part of town we remained indoors. On Saturday morning, two days after the fighting began, things were quiet enough for us to get an idea of what had happened and what was happening to the city. We had scheduled an all-night prayer meeting for Friday night but because of the situation in the city postponed prayer until the next morning. On Saturday morning we loaded ourselves into the car and cautiously made our way toward the church. An armored vehicle blocked the road we normally turned on to get to the building, so we found an alternate way through some back roads. Once we did drive near to the church, we saw another armored vehicle stationed there; soldiers were standing guard on the road next to our building. On hearing our explanation that we had a prayer service to attend, the soldiers allowed us to pull in and assess the situation.

What we saw that day was surreal; we could not believe our eyes. The church's watchman had stayed for the duration of the fighting and told stories of how to escape the violence he hid under the platform. Fortunately the building and adjoining shelter escaped serious damage, although several of the benches had bullet holes in them, as did the wall of the permanent building. We began collecting handfuls of empty ammunition casings, which we later found out were Russian in origin.

A few church members beside ourselves and those who traveled with us in the car from our home did show up and join us for prayer and for recounting stories of gunfire, death, and great sorrow. Looking out and down one of the streets adjacent to us, we saw images that, until then, we had seen only on major news stations covering wars: women and children carrying their belongings, fleeing down the streets, and being stopped by armed men who searched them, pushed them, and even took some of their things. Smoke rose from the still-burning rubble of Bwiza's homes. The sound of intermittent gunfire still could be heard in the distance. For a little while we wondered whether this was the end of our dream in Burundi.

A line in the sand

 A great anger rose inside of me as I drove through the streets of our city. *How could this have happened? What gave Satan the right to touch the country in which God had sent us to serve?* For a moment we were dazed by what we had seen. However, by

God's grace we were able to shake off our bewilderment and hear the voice of the Lord. After prayer we did not hear God say, "Time for you to go." In fact His silence on the matter seemed to be His way of directing us to stay. Years ago I learned to stay true to the Lord's last command and not change course until He gave new orders. God was not surprised by the turn of events in Burundi. We realized that precisely for this reason we had been sent to the country at that specific time. This clear direction gave us the grace to stay, even though no one would have blamed us if we had left.

After prayer on Saturday I went home and received a message from the Lord for the congregation. We had no idea how many actually would show for services on Sunday, but I prepared what God had placed in my heart:

> So he answered, "Do not fear, for those who are with us are more than those who are with them." And Elisha prayed, and said, "Lord, I pray, open his eyes that he may see." Then the Lord opened the eyes of the young man and he saw. And behold, the mountain was full of horses and chariots of fire all around Elisha (2 Kings 6:16-17).

Sunday morning arrived and our family—together with our 16 new family members—made our way to church. The gunfire still was rattling on the outskirts of the city; most of the area surrounding the church (that just days before had been buzzing with life and business) suddenly had become empty and silent. I preached that morning as I had not preached before. I encouraged the church members to open their spiritual eyes and recognize that this situation had more to it than meets the natural eye—that we had more with us than against us. That first Sunday after the war arrived in Bujumbura, we announced to the community, the world, the devil, and his cohorts that we were not going. He was not going to kick us out. If we were going to be the only ones left in our church on a Sunday morning—so be it. I was spurred to say so because our attendance that morning had gone from more than 500 the previous Sunday to 56. After the service an older man encouraged me by saying that when he heard that we were not going anywhere, he was not going either. This man, Papa Marcel (who later became one of our church's pastors), while not wealthy, had family in many different nations and easily could have left Burundi, but he was together with us. He was staying. A remnant of us—a stubborn remnant—existed; that remnant was not going to let Burundi down. She was our nation; we were going to fight for her on our knees. If we did not wage spiritual warfare for her, who would?

Reality check

 Such bold declarations are both exciting and intimidating. Reality hit us when, as we arrived home, the mortars, machine guns, and grenades resumed their usual activity. Looking at our children we were desperate to hear from God each and every day to make sure we were following His leading and not our own supposition. At the time the violence was as close to us as next door. One evening not long after the initial onset of the violence in our part of the city we turned the lights off in the house and sat silently while we waited for the noise to pass. Gunshots were fired next door to the building in which Mandy went to school. The second floor of the building was unfinished; through our windows, we noticed the shadow of someone trying to hide from whoever was chasing him. At some point during that night someone pointed a flashlight into our yard; apparently this was done in an effort to find this person who was hiding next door. We prayed fervently that our house would not be touched. On that night it was passed over—and on many nights thereafter.

Scattered sheep

> *"My sheep wandered through all the mountains, and on every high hill; yes, My flock was scattered over the whole face of the earth, and no one was seeking or searching for them"* (Ezek. 34:6).

 As the people of Bujumbura grew accustomed to the nearly daily barrage of gunfire, one by one members of our new extended family moved out to their own homes or to the homes of family members who lived in less-volatile areas of the city. Meanwhile, we pressed forward with early morning prayer sessions, Sunday services, and feeding in the camps and hospital. When possible we did our best to maintain a semblance of normal living.

During those days we saw arise youth gangs who from time to time tried to further complicate life for the city's population by calling *ville morte* (dead city). Whenever these youth gangs declared a *ville morte*, no one was supposed to leave home. Schools, businesses, and even the market (on which people depended to shop for their daily food) all were closed. Should anyone have dared to leave the house at such a time, that person risked an attack by the youth gangs.

During those first days when a *ville morte* was called, Lea tried to convince me to stay home. She struggled to maintain her calm about everything while I grew increasingly impatient with these hooligans who thought they had the right to tell the entire city what it could and could not do. I had no patience for these lawless youths and every morning stubbornly made my way to prayer. If I expected others to be at church for prayer, I should be there with them to lead the way! I attempted to understand Lea's struggle, but at the same time I would not allow fear to be my dictator.

Each and every time Jamie left the house to go to early morning prayer in those *ville morte* days, I felt the thumping of my heart in my chest. Under normal circumstances (remembering "normal" was nearly impossible), in the morning I often went to prayer with the children and Jamie. While the guns were firing and the youth gangs were running in the streets, I did not believe that bringing the children out during a *ville morte* would be a wise decision. The children did not complain about my decision to keep them home, because they enjoyed the days off from school as much as children in the U.S. would enjoy a day off from school because of inclement weather. I struggled to put on a brave face when my heart leapt with every gunshot and explosion I heard; we heard many of them. What kind of parents were we—not only for bringing our children to Africa but for allowing them to grow up in these circumstances?

 Our lives settled into a strange routine of listening—listening and gauging how close to our part of the city the "music" was. We worked diligently to rebuild the church. During the violence many of our members fled; we had little knowledge of the places to which they went. News did reach us that many who had fled Bujumbura had ended up in Uvira, Zaire, which was just a short distance from Bujumbura. In the violence a large number of our church leaders and even two of our staff pastors had fled. We were very concerned about their welfare on the other side of the border. We knew that Zaire itself was a potential disaster waiting to happen; those who had fled may just have leapt from the proverbial frying pan into the fire.

We easily could have brushed aside our knowledge of the potential danger for those who had fled to Zaire. In fact common sense could have told us not to do anything. However, these were our people. They had scattered because of the war; as their pastors we had an obligation to do what we could to help them—to find them. Early one morning I got into our Pajero and made the drive to Uvira, Zaire, to look for our people. Because of the unstable situation in the country the border between the two countries would close early in the evening, so I had to leave early enough in the morning to return before the border closed. This was not a difficult decision for me to make; I needed to look for our people. Yet I saw behind the brave face Lea put on as I said goodbye to her that morning that her decision to let me go was not one she made easily.

Uvira

 I made the trip safely across the confusing Burundi/Zaire border. Uvira itself, without added refugees, was a dirty, run-down, and heavily populated city. The conditions were harrowing: people seemingly were everywhere; everyone was looking for something to eat. Hoping I would find some of our people, I slowly drove down the main road. I was quite accustomed to Uvira because of the time we had served in Zaire with the Hagemeiers. (We made several trips to this very city to preach in several different churches.) I scoured the landscape and stopped the vehicle to ask where the people from Bujumbura were. I made my way down the winding road on which I had been directed and that someone would meet me there—wherever "there" might be.

The conditions in which I found people living in Uvira were extreme. No sanitation was available; the city had no running water; little food was to be found. People somehow were scraping bits and pieces of food together and eating what they could find. Children, trying to find some way to amuse themselves, played with what bits of trash were lying around. Little boys wrapped plastic bags together tightly to make soccer balls for themselves.

In the midst of this confusion I tried to find anyone who looked familiar to me—anyone from our church who wanted to return to Bujumbura.

I knew this part of Zaire was volatile and could, at any moment, erupt in violence much worse than what we had experienced in Bujumbura. I left word with everyone I encountered to let our people know that their pastor had been looking for them. I did manage to find one brother who joined me and returned to Bujumbura. After a long day of driving and looking I reluctantly turned the vehicle around and made my way back to the border to arrive home before the border between the two countries closed. While I drove into Burundi, a part of my heart remained with the part of our congregation that was left in Zaire.

> "What man of you, having a hundred sheep, if he loses one of them, does not leave the ninety-nine in the wilderness, and go after the one which is lost until he finds it? And when he has found it, he lays it on his shoulders, rejoicing" (Luke 15:4-5).

Chapter 9

A Land Called Ephraim

And the name of the second he called Ephraim (fruitfulness): "For God has caused me to be fruitful in the land of my affliction" (Gen. 41:52).

At times when we heard the Burundi orchestra playing its music, both of us struggled with the temptation to fear. We did grow weary of standing time and time again, but we could do nothing else but stand. Each time we prayed for direction, God's answer was the same: stay the course. Often people would ask what gave us the determination to stay the course; all we could say was that we simply had no option but to do the will of God. Maybe to others who were looking in from the outside we appeared to be just plain stubborn (and stubbornness did play a role in our decision to stay in Burundi). But more than being stubborn we were determined to see the Bujumbura church plant become strong and stable. Were we to leave under such circumstances, the church definitely would have wavered and possibly even collapsed.

Mercy

The angel of the Lord encamps all around those who fear Him, and delivers them (Psalm 34:7).

Over the years perhaps one of the most valuable qualities we have shared as a couple has been our agreement to obey God, to do His will, and to leave our own wills out of it. On only few occasions have we struggled with this commitment. During the time we were in Burundi our determination to follow God's plan for our lives was tested time and again. After some months of living under the seemingly endless attack on Bujumbura, I grew weary of the battle. While my determination wavered, Jamie's remained steadfast. I found obedience to be increasingly difficult—especially to have the children in Bujumbura, which had turned into a war zone.

War is strange. No straightforward rules govern its movement. Generally when a country is enveloped in civil unrest or war, as Burundi for so many years was, the violence is not continuous in one part of the city or country; it moves from place to place. Gunfire, grenades, mortars, and even rockets being fired (as we had seen shot into the mountains not far from our house) generally occur in a random pattern and may or may not take place on any given day in the area in which people live. This uncertainty is what bred so much fear in the city during the times we experienced civil unrest; this ambiguity is what made daily living so difficult. Simple decisions, such as whether to send the children to school on a given day, often became major prayer topics. We could not possibly know whether the violence would erupt near the school, church, market, or even our home. Leaving the children at school or alone at home was difficult beyond description; finding people to whom we could confide such feelings nearly was impossible. Everyone in the city seemed desperately to be holding on to the hope that normal life one day would return to our once-beautiful country.

My frustration and weariness with the situation often spilled over onto Jamie. I wanted to be as steadfast as he was, but in the face of war my determination had faltered. Many times I felt a physical pressure mounting within my chest as I struggled to maintain control of the turmoil brewing just under the surface. Each day when I left the house to work in the camps with the children (whose situations were much worse than my own), I struggled with feelings of incompetence as I stared into their hungry faces. Who was I to complain when, at the very least, every night I slept in a house and in a bed, not to mention the fact that I had never seen my loved ones killed in civil war? As we taught them and fed them, I had to find a way to work through the conflicted feelings waging war inside my heart.

One evening, after I tucked our children in for the night, I cleaned the kitchen, cleared my desk of some necessary paperwork, and fell into bed; I hoped we would have a quiet night of uninterrupted sleep. We had experienced a particularly grueling week as we worked in the camps. Because no cooking facilities existed there, early each morning I transported the cooked food and feeding teams and supervised the feeding and teaching activities. We nearly had run out of food that week, so I scrambled to write letters to several NGO's for emergency assistance. In our state of things in Bujumbura, food prices fluctuated wildly. From one day to the next we had difficulty accurately estimating what food prices would be. Stress levels often ran high, as they did that week. By the time I collapsed into the bed after I tucked my children in, my energy and joy were spent. The night was quiet—unusual but welcome.

Suddenly, in the midnight hours, I was awakened by what seemed to be singing—not any kind of singing I had heard before. I could not understand any of the words, nor was the melody anything familiar to me. I felt unusually calm and seemed to recognize that the singing was praise to God. Our bedroom was set at the end of a hallway, which had a door that led into our living room. I got up from the bed and somehow was able to observe myself as I walked down the short hallway to the door that led into the living room. As I got closer, the singing grew louder. When I opened the living-room door, I was met by a cool breeze, which surprised me as it brushed across my face. The room was filled with light that was shining outside and radiating through our curtains. I remember wondering how such a wonderful breeze could be flowing in the room with all the windows shut. My attention was inexplicably drawn to the curtains; I saw silhouettes of very tall, almost massive beings standing shoulder to shoulder outside the glass. I immediately understood they were angels. At that moment I not only saw them through the windows; I also saw them all around the perimeter of our house. Their arms were raised and out-stretched to heaven; I wanted to get closer. Just as I got to the curtain to draw it back, I felt a Presence in the room with me; this made me fall to my knees. As I knelt, I felt some kind of material as soft as silk brush the right side of my face and arm. At that moment I knew I was not alone. Great peace filled my heart; all the pressure and heaviness that for so long had plagued me simply disappeared. The great mercy of God to answer me so profoundly was overwhelming. I realized then that God's mercy to-ward me that night went far beyond anything I deserved. From that day to this I am not afraid about the "what-if" scenarios of life. Serving God and being in His will is the safest place on earth.

"You are immortal until your work is finished"
—Jim Elliot[35]

Every home . . . for Jesus

 Since the initial planting of the church we had been evangel-izing the area, Bwiza, in which the church was situated. The war often made our evangelizing difficult, but I knew the gospel was the only help for our area, for our country, and for the rest of the world. Our church was situated in a densely populated slum. We estimated that at least 10,000 people lived in and around this area. The strategy we derived was, by visiting every individual household, to reach every home in Bwiza for Jesus. This was a complicated approach, because each house or property held not just one but several families. One main house was the one in which the landlord usually lived with his/her family; surrounding that home were four or five smaller residences of one or two rooms; these shared a common toilet and, if they were fortunate, a separate bathing area. Most of these homes were built with mud bricks; they were very basic and were in extremely poor condition. Open sewage ran in crudely dug channels outside the houses, rats were a common scourge the population faced, and basic services (such as garbage removal) were not available to these people. Very few of the homes had electricity; even fewer of them had their own water source. Because of the dense population and unsanitary conditions disease was everywhere. When we were out witnessing to the people, we often were asked to pray for the sick.

One afternoon I went out with a team of church members for evangelism while Lea stayed at home with the children. As usual I had a mixed group of people with me, which meant that people from both tribes were represented among our team. This was so vitally important to the success of our outreach because, if we appeared to be taking sides, we easily could have become targets of violence. Our goal was to preach the gospel to any and all we encountered—young, old, armed, and unarmed. Jesus loved them all; they all needed to know about Him!

After prayer we hit the streets and started going from house to house to preach Jesus. Not long after we set out, we happened on a house, introduced ourselves to the occupants, and began to share the gospel. We did not get too far into our conversation when the people indicated they were not interested and that we needed to leave. As we turned and headed back to the street, a group of young men stopped us on our way. I recognized them as the same young men who visited me at the church recently; they asked for money because they said they were hungry. We did not, and do not, usually hand out money to people in need. Instead we would and do purchase food items or offer other similar help for people, because we know that handing out money may lead to misuse, such as purchasing alcohol instead of food. When I told these young men that I would not give them money but I would buy them food instead, they became angry and left. So, standing out on the road that day in front of this house, I realized these young guys had a problem with me and were up to no good.

"Come; let's go talk about this inside that house!" said one of the youths while he was pointing to the house we had just exited.

The Lord in His faithfulness gave me an answer, and I told him, "No, we cannot go back into that house, because they asked us to leave. If we go back in, they would think that we have not honored their request." So went the conversation back and forth until I motioned to my team that we needed to go. At that moment one of these youths grabbed one of our team members by his belt, would not let him go, and threatened to take him inside the house.

"Let's leave, Pastor!" whispered one of my other church members, an older woman. I knew we could not leave this brother behind. He was not of the same tribe as those youth; I was sure that if we left him there, we very possibly would not ever see him alive again. I insisted we wait for our brother; they reluctantly let him go.

Our team walked away from the confrontation unscathed, but even as we were leaving, one of these young men continued to follow us down the street. He shouted insults at us while he held a beer bottle in one hand and a knife in the other. We returned to the church afterward and gave our report of God's protection to the other teams that had gone out evangelizing that day. Despite the difficulties we faced, we were able to visit, or at the very least, leave a gospel tract at nearly every home in the area.

> *"Because he has set his love on Me, therefore I will deliver him; I will set him on high, because he has known My name"* (Ps. 91:14).

Starting over

 We set ourselves to the task of once again building the church. We believed we also were building an entirely new congregation between those faithful ones who had stayed and the new ones God was adding to the fold. Despite the conditions that surrounded us, we never canceled a Sunday morning service.

The people, ourselves included, needed something to remain consistent in their lives. Keeping the church's activities going as usual provided a lifeline of normalcy for everyone.

As the violence in the city slowly abated and the grip on its neck somewhat was loosened, our church's attendance began to climb ever so slowly. The determination of our little congregation was inspiring; as a result, we experienced a move of God unlike anything we had seen before the war. A strong Pentecostal message always was preached, but what we experienced after the violence in Bujumbura can only be called a *visitation*. After Lea's vision of angels at our home, she, along with Jackie (Emmanuel's wife) began to see angels in our services; as I was preaching both had similar visions and saw angels ministering to the congregation. African church services are longer than what is experienced in an average Western church. On a normal Sunday generally we stayed in church between two and two-and-a-half hours. In those days, after the war began and the Spirit began to move among us, often we were in church all day long. The presence of God almost was tangible; no one, children included, wanted to go home. We did not want to miss anything God was going to say or do during a service.

Nothing kept the people from going to church. On the numerous occasions that gunfire returned to our part of the city, we all still met for church and prayer.

We also used to have Saturday evening services. Before the service would start, we met for about 30 minutes of prayer. Those prayer times were full of power; those who attended pre-service prayer had hearts of lions. One Saturday evening during pre-service prayer, the guns began to fire. Before we went to church, we had heard them firing and were not deterred. As we began to pray, the "music" grew louder and seemed to crescendo near the church. Suddenly, a grenade exploded within close proximity; dirt and small bits of concrete from the explosion were blown through the windows and onto the shoulders of one of the praying ladies. As Lea, praying, walked by her, she and the church member both looked at the dirt on her shoulder. Chuckling, both ladies kept praying as Lea gently swept it off her shoulder and walked off, continuing in prayer.

Life, not death

> *I shall not die, but live, and declare the works of the Lord* (Ps. 118:17).

 Prayer has always played a vital role in our personal and church lives. As the war unfolded before us in Burundi (as well as engulfing neighboring Rwanda and Zaire), we knew the call to prayer was urgent. We sensed we had to pray strategically for the safety of our people. God directed us to print out copies of Psalm 118:17 (as well as other Scriptures) and have the congregation in their prayers confess it daily.

Testimonies of God's protection began to flood our offices after we handed out the copies of the Scriptures. A young woman in the church related a story to us that, had we not lived in Bujumbura and knew of the situation, we would have found difficult to believe. At one time during the war, land mines were being laid in the streets and even in footpaths. Oftentimes, when we heard explosions early in the morning, we knew someone had inadvertently found a land mine. This young woman, passing next to a bus stop one morning on her way to morning prayer, was startled when a bus, as it was pulling away, drove over a land mine planted in the street. The bus was destroyed beyond repair; several passengers on the bus were killed, but this young woman, while shocked by what she saw, was unharmed.

On another occasion, Papa Marcel, who faithfully stood by us throughout the crisis, kneeled by his bed with his Bible and his printed-out copy of the Scriptures in hand. (Despite the fact that so many of his friends had fled, Papa Marcel had declared his determination to stay in Bujumbura.) At the moment he was in prayer, a group of young men passed by his house and threw a grenade directly at his home; the grenade exploded over the room in which Papa Marcel was praying. While the damage to that part of the house in which he was praying was considerable, Papa Marcel emerged from the incident unharmed, except for a small piece of shrapnel that embedded itself in his finger. To this day he declares that wound, which left his finger bent, reminds him of the protection of the Lord. When he emerged alive from the front door of his house, the young men who threw the grenade declared, *Mungu wako ni Mungu wa kweli!* ("Your God is the true God!"). One of those young men in the group later gave his life to the Lord.

When we moved to Bujumbura, we did not set out to be in a situation such as the one in which we found ourselves. Yet we believe God sent us there for "*such a time*" as we found ourselves in. Were things perfect, easy, and ideal, our presence would not have been necessary. God had a work to do in the country; He established the church to bear the burden of praying when the *time of trouble* hit.

> "*He shall call on Me, and I will answer him; I will be with him in trouble; I will deliver him and honor him. With long life I will satisfy him, and show him My salvation*" (Psalms 91:15, 16).

Burning barricades

During a period of relative calm my parents took a quick trip to Burundi. Lea, the children, and I made our way to the airport to meet them. The usual boxes full of presents for the children made their way through customs; the party began the moment the grandparents walked in the front door. Stephen, barely 3-years old at the time, following his older brother's and sister's lead, searched the suitcases and boxes for goodies. We are very thankful to Mom and Dad for always supporting us and never pressuring us to leave—even when external circumstances almost screamed that the time had arrived for us to go. Their prayerful counsel gave us the courage to make difficult decisions a bit easier. Under these circumstances most parents would not have had the strength to tell their kids to do the will of God, but they always did; for that, we are grateful.

Dad always has been a man of prayer. Whenever he visited us on the field, he would join me at early morning prayer. Even though the situation at this time was tenuous at best, his first morning in Bujumbura Dad hopped into the car, with the gunfire sounding in the distance, and was ready for morning prayer. Our house was just a few minutes' drive from the church building, but that first morning when I was driving to prayer with Dad, our drive seemed much longer than usual. Another *ville morte* had been declared; we were defying "their" orders to stay home. As we drove down the main road that turned off to the church, I noticed a man running after us with a stone in his hands. I understood that he was about to throw the stone at us because we were out during "their" declared *ville morte*. Almost simultaneously a military vehicle entered our view; at that moment he threw the stone down and ran. I believe God sent that military vehicle at that time to intervene on our behalf.

After we managed to pass by the man with the stone, we happened on a burning barricade made of tires. From a distance we saw the flames; as we drew closer, Dad asked me, "Are we going to go through that?"

As I drove, I replied, "I think I can snake my way through."

The burning tires filled most of the street, but I was sure that, if I drove carefully, I could weave around the flames and arrive at church in one piece. We did manage to navigate around those burning tires (whose flames were so hot, they could be felt through the car windows) and joined the rest of the church members at prayer that morning. Later at home that day Dad said that morning he had been thinking about telling me, "Son, we could stay home and pray this morning." However, when he got to prayer and saw all the people waiting on us, he understood why we had to go to church.

My parents' understanding of the importance of maintaining a steady presence during those difficult days was priceless. In retrospect I am sure their understanding not only was because of their being "in tune" with the Holy Spirit but also was because of their own experience as church leaders. In establishing TCI in Florida they had gone through their own trials and understood the value of consistency in the face of adversity when one is planting a church. Allowing their children and grandchildren to go through war without begging them to leave must have taken grace that not many parents and grandparents have had.

An IV we'll never forget

 Rarely did we have a time in which we stopped feeding the hungry children. God gave us the grace to continue even during the most difficult times. The provision of the Lord also was supernatural. We had not planned on running a large feeding outreach to children; it just happened. We informed people of what we were doing; the donations began to arrive. Local NGO's supplied us with such items as food, blankets, soap, medical care, and plastic sheeting to build schoolrooms in the camps for the children. European and U.S. supporters such as Tear Fund and Joyce Meyers Ministries began to give significantly toward the feeding. What we lacked was endless energy and personnel. I watched as Lea ran herself ragged working the feeding outreach. She often was the only one in the camps together with our church's feeding teams that brought regular assistance to the displaced (internal refugees). My wife worked to balance her roles very well, but after many months of working in the camps, the work was taking its toll, I noticed.

One Friday Lea mentioned that she was tired and had a sore throat. Spending the better part of the afternoon in bed, she arose later, proclaimed she felt better, and went on to make us dinner. During the night her temperature went over 104° F. The next morning we took her to the doctor, who told me she had malaria. She complained that her throat was sore, but the doctor said, "Your throat is not sore; you have malaria."

By Sunday morning the malaria cure had not made any difference in her condition. In fact she grew worse and was not able to go to church. I was not accustomed to Lea being unwell or missing church. I had to preach, but my mind was not far from the house. After service I found her in bed and feeling very unwell; I instantly went to find Dr. Yuri, who treated me when I was sick. He arrived immediately to offer his assistance.

The doctor set up an intravenous line of quinine to combat the malaria and gave my wife several injections of various medications to combat the fever and other symptoms. Lea had become somewhat dehydrated with the fevers; thus the start of an IV was difficult. To get the IV stable enough for the medication to flow freely, he secured her arm with a wooden spoon we found in the kitchen and hung the IV on the curtain railing in the bedroom. She should have been in a hospital, he explained, but the care in the hospitals in Bujumbura was no better than what he, together with our nurse friend, Chrissie, could do by visiting her several times daily.

After two days of quinine IV's Lea's condition had not improved. In fact her throat became so sore that she barely could speak; in addition, her neck began to swell. She also mentioned that her chest from time to time would hurt. When the doctor visited her that morning, she insisted he look at her throat. When he did, his eyes widened in disbelief. Spread across her throat was a grayish white film that almost had threatened her breathing. He carefully took a specimen for analysis at a laboratory. Since the malaria had cleared, obviously another infection was at work in her throat. A regime of penicillin was ordered: five days of penicillin injections followed by a long course of oral antibiotics. Slowly her condition began to improve; after more than a week of injections, IV's, and antibiotics, Lea's voice returned.

I kept on calling about the lab results; 10 days after the infection began, they were ready. When I went to pick up the results and presented them to the doctor, I could not believe what I was hearing: Lea's infection was caused by a case of diphtheria.

She obviously contracted the diphtheria while she worked in the camps. No regular medical care or childhood vaccination of the children occurred in the camps; many needlessly died of measles, mumps, and simple illnesses that easily could have been cured with proper treatment. As healthy as Lea normally was, we could not imagine what such a sickness did to the young children. Allowing her vaccine to lapse was unavoidable because we had not traveled to the U.S. for some time; the U.S. was the place in which we usually took care of updating all of our vaccines. Ever since this episode Lea and I have been particularly attentive to our vaccinations.

From the slums to the palace—the Odeon Palace

The church grew and continued to flow in the supernatural after the onset of the violence, but for months after the conflict Bwiza was nearly empty. Rubble from the houses that had been destroyed by armored vehicles at the height of the fighting remained in the streets. The few cars that dared navigate the area simply made their own paths around the destruction. Because Bwiza had become so dangerous, our church had difficulty growing beyond a certain point. A few months later we found ourselves at a plateau of 200 members on Sunday mornings. When we asked our people why some had trouble getting to church, we were told that many were afraid to travel to Bwiza because their tribe of people was not wanted in the area. This statement and others such as this one pushed us to think about moving the church out of Bwiza. While we had grown to love the area and the thought of leaving it deeply saddened us, we believed we had no choice in the matter. Our stance always had been one to welcome every tribe of people into our church. From the pulpit I had often said to the church that the day our church had only one tribe represented in it would be the day we closed the doors. All people of all backgrounds, tribes, and denominations were welcome; we had to act to preserve our integrity.

A theater called the "Odeon Palace" situated in the center of town caught our eye. Initially, we thought our offer to rent the facility would be rejected because we could not afford to pay a great deal of money. However, the situation in the country worked on our behalf. The Odeon Palace was meant to be a theater, but in those days, very few productions were taking place, and the owner needed a steady source of income. We were able to rent nearly the entire facility for a fraction of what it would have cost to rent it had the situation in Burundi been stable.

The Odeon (as we called it) is well known to nearly everyone in the whole area. It sits at what can only be described as the crossroads of the country: next to the main entrance of the Novotel, a landmark hotel in the city. Most importantly, it was in an area of town that was accessible to everyone of every tribe. On hearing the news of our imminent move to the Odeon, our congregation in Bwiza shouted. We all had dreams of "one day" being in a great facility, and it happened that our little church, which had its quaint beginnings in the slums of Bwiza, was on its way to the Odeon Palace.

Bold as a lion

 On our first Sunday in the Odeon, the large, 800-seat auditorium, swallowed our congregation of 200, which changed from a regular congregation of believers to a group of spiritually mighty men and women. Before we moved to the Odeon, I had preached a message from Proverbs 28:1, which says:

The wicked flee when no one pursues, but the righteous are bold as a lion.

During the season of war this message became a kind of motto for our church. When trouble arises, many Christians are ready to walk away from the promise of God. But I encouraged our people to not back down from the enemy, not take the difficulty lying down, and to take a stand for God! In concluding the message, I taught our people to roar at the devil, "*Rooooaaaar!*" They all chimed in; each made his or her own kind of roar. Every day that we woke to the reality of strife and confusion in Burundi, we kept on roaring. Our people were living through war, walking to prayer meetings and services when guns were firing, and feeding the children in the displaced camps. Nothing could stop us. We had become a pride of lions; those empty seats in the Odeon simply were another challenge to us. Those seats, we declared on our first Sunday together, were not going to stay empty for much longer. Our city, Bujumbura, belonged to Jesus; we were about to take it for His glory.

A passion for the city

 God had given us a word to stay in Bujumbura. He had de-posited a determination in our hearts to stay the course and not to leave our people. This did not mean that we did not struggle emotionally; we most certainly did. But that word from God is what gave us the strength to stand for our city. One day I was reading from 1 Chronicles 11; I happened onto the story of David's mighty men. What amazed me (and still amazes me) about the story of his men was the fact that they did not start out as mighty men. When David's men first came to him, they were *in distress . . . in debt and . . . discontented* (1 Sam. 22:2). In that chapter the Bible says that David *became captain over them*. These men, in their original state, were much like our people before

213

the war. They were in the slums of Bwiza, a place full of poverty and every kind of reckless behavior imaginable. They were *in distress . . . in debt, and discontented.* After the onset of the war they grew into the same kind of people that David's mighty men in the Scriptures had become. Our people, just as these men did, became great warriors who stood their ground and never turned and ran when the enemy faced them.

One of David's mighty men listed in 1 Chronicles 11, Eleazar the son of Dodo, inspired me. His determination to fight for something that seemed to be worthless gave me a better understanding of why God had planted such a passion in our hearts for Bujumbura. In verses 12, 13, and 14 the Bible states:

> *After him was Eleazar the son of Dodo, the Ahohite, who was one of the three mighty men. He was with David at Pasdammim. Now there the Philistines were gathered for battle, and there was a piece of ground full of barley. So the people fled from the Philistines. But they stationed themselves in the middle of that field, defended it, and killed the Philistines. So the Lord brought about a great victory.*

I asked myself why this man would position himself in the middle of a barley field. In that time barley was of little value. It was reserved for the poor to eat or for the livestock; therefore, no one saw it as having enough value to defend, let alone cause the death of any man. But Eleazar knew better. He did not want to give one inch of ground to the enemy. He *stationed* himself and defended the land. Because he did, the *Lord brought about a great victory.*

Through these verses I believed the Lord was speaking to me. We were participating in the same kind of fight as all those years ago Eleazar was. Bujumbura was a small city. What was of value in that city that was worth us laying down our lives? No one seemed to care that we were in the throes of war; thousands were dying. Why should we care when the rest of the world turned a blind eye? We decided to station ourselves in the middle of our barley patch. For the sake of our people we had to stand up to the devil. If we were not going to fight in the spirit for our city, who else would? God had to bring about a great victory!

A bad-hair quarter

 In much of Africa power cuts or outages are a normal part of life. Sometimes the authorities are nice enough to give early notice that the power will be cut, but often that is not the case. Over the years we had grown accustomed to these power cuts. God even had blessed us with a generator to use when we had long periods—sometimes days—without power. At that time we thought we had learned to manage with or without electricity. When the war took an unexpected turn, we were about to learn how mistaken we were.

The struggle to take the city of Bujumbura seemed to have reached a stalemate between the fighting parties. Apparently neither side could overthrow the other outright, so they began to use other tactics to trouble each other. Since Burundians are known for raising cattle, in the violence frequently their cattle would be targeted. Wealth in that part of Africa often is measured in the number of cattle owned. The increased risk of losing wealth, the cattle, caused many to bring their herds into Bujumbura for safety. Not only were displaced people in the capital, we now had a daily encounter with displaced cattle. During midday traffic, cars would stop so the cows could cross. No one seemed to mind, as we all understood the importance these animals held to the people and their culture.

Despite the presence of cattle in the city, life seemed to be changing in Bujumbura. While the Burundi "symphony" still would play its music, the crescendo did not seem to happen as loudly or as often. So one day when the power was cut, none of us took much notice. Dealing with power cuts

215

was part of life, so we simply waited for the electricity to be turned back on. By the next morning, when the power still was off, we began to ask our friends in other areas of town whether they had power. The resounding response was that no one had power.

Some time passed before news trickled out to the community about what exactly had happened. Finally we learned that the opposition, in an apparent attempt to further cripple the capital, had attacked the main electrical poles leading to Bujumbura. Their attack was so effective and their subsequent hold on those electrical poles so powerful that for three months Bujumbura did not have power. We have heard women say that they are experiencing a "bad-hair day". I refer to this time of our lives in Burundi as a "bad-hair quarter" because without power, I had no blowdryer to manage my hair!

Life goes on, even without power

 I was so irritated by this new development. Even our early morning prayer sessions, which played a major role in the life of our church, were affected by the lack of power. For us to have up to 150 people meeting for prayer, which was more like a revival service than it was a prayer meeting, was not unusual. But because our facility was purposed to be a theater, we had no windows in the building. Without electricity to power the lights, the auditorium was pitch black. On top of that, our generator at the time was in a poor state of repair; we reserved its use for Sunday mornings only. We tried leaving the access doors open; this allowed for some light and ventilation, but the building still was hopelessly dark without the lights. Finally we set up candles and kerosene lanterns. Despite the fact that the light they gave out was minimal in the large auditorium, it was enough for us to keep praying every morning. So pray we did.

Jamie's determination during the most difficult days we faced in Burundi gave all of us courage to face every day head-on. The fact that I had no power for blow-drying my hair drove me to acts of desperation that only can be known to a woman who for any length of time has been deprived of a hair dryer. Until the power was cut, I had not learned how to start a generator, let alone learn how to fill the fuel tank. But when the desperate times, in which I had no blowdryer or husband nearby to start another generator we kept at our house, occurred, I learned how to fill the fuel tank and start the generator—because desperate times called for desperate measures. Our generator at home did not have an automatic starter; with all my strength I had to pull the cord—but I succeeded! When I had no other choice, I was able to start the generator and blow dry my hair!

Not only did I learn how to use the generator, the power outage forced me to learn how to cook many different meals on an African charcoal stove called a *jiko*. I was not very good at starting the coals; we did not have starter fluid for lighting barbecues. To get the fire going often took me an hour.

Tom, Mandy, and Steve took everything in great stride. They enjoyed our time together as we made dinner in the back yard. Watching them run around happily in the yard helped me forget, just for a moment, that we were in what, naturally speaking, was a hopeless situation. I did not have much time for reflection, because cooking dinner on the little charcoal stove was a process. Barbecued spaghetti bolognaise was my personal favorite when I made meals outdoors; this was followed closely by barbecued chicken and gravy. People may ask, *how do you barbecue spaghetti or chicken and gravy?* Live in Burundi; you will learn!

One day, several weeks after the power had been cut, I was driving downtown and saw a gas stove on display in a storefront. I raced home to tell Jamie about my incredible find. Imagine! A gas stove! No more sitting on the steps outside to cook dinner or having to wait for the rain to stop before I even could start dinner. The whole thing seemed too good to be true. Jamie was not home when I got there, but the moment he walked into the door, all he heard about was the gas stove and how if I had one, his life and culinary experience would be enhanced greatly! Not much time went by before one afternoon he returned home with a gas stove in the back of the vehicle. Life was good.

The power's on

 As the first few weeks without power turned into two and then three months, we grew accustomed to living without electricity. Once during those three months the power flickered on momentarily; this gave us the hope that the power would return full time. But that was short-lived as the power on that day only flickered and did not return for many more weeks.

Several months before the power cut Jamie's parents had scheduled a visit to see us in our new building. As the time for their visit drew near, they would make periodic phone calls to ask us whether the power had returned. Each time we would have to reply, "No, it has not."

The greatly anticipated day of their visit finally arrived. More than a year since we had seen them last had gone by; we all were thrilled by the prospect of having them with us—even if the power was turned off! Just as we were setting off to collect them from the airport, the power did more than flicker on as it had many weeks before; it returned and stayed on. On hearing the good news on the way home from the airport that the power had been turned on, Mom said, "It's because Jesus loves me." We did not laugh too robustly at that, for we knew that He did love her. Jesus probably did turn the power on that day just for Mom.

Church growth

We were blessed to spend time with my parents. During those difficult days in Burundi not many missionaries had the opportunity we had to have close relatives visit as often as my parents did. I believe God brought Dad and Mom as often as He did not only to encourage us but also to let them see firsthand the fruit of their labor. TCI in Lake Worth, FL, is a missions-minded church. The people give generously to works all over the world. At present, 28 percent of the church's income is given to missions. My father once believed he might be called to the mission field, but God instead directed him to raise up a missions-minded church. Whenever they came to visit us or any other missionaries that TCI supports around the world, my parents have been able to see the fulfillment of the call of God on their lives as well as see the scope of TCI's outreach worldwide.

During the time my parents were with us when we first were in the Odeon, we were beginning to enter a season of great change in our church. For the church to grow from 200 did not take long. By the time Mom and Dad visited, our attendance had increased to nearly 700 people. Often in our services we might see more than 20 people trust the Lord. One Sunday in particular we had more than 90 people answer the altar call. During that period of time a great grace that drew people to the Lord was present. In addition I am sure the war had something to do with the great hunger the people had for God. Times were so uncertain; people were driven to call on Him.

For the least of them

Our growing congregation fueled our feeding outreach with new volunteers; this enabled us to work more efficiently. I also was relieved to be able to finally hire a driver, Papa Marcel, which gave me much-needed assistance. As the church was growing, so was our ministry to the children. But as it grew, we had to find a way to work smarter, not more diligently. To streamline our feeding outreach we asked for and were given permission to build simple kitchen facilities with bamboo at the displaced camps at which we were feeding. Each day all we had to do was to transport the uncooked food and feeding teams to the site; we did this after early morning prayer. No activities were begun before we made sure we were spiritually ready to cope with anything that we encountered. Attending early morning prayer was a requirement for all those who worked with the outreach to the children in the displaced camps.

Our new setup for feeding was well received by the camps. Most of the time we had no trouble cooking and serving the meal of porridge to the children. On some occasions something would stir up the people in the camps. On those days the tension was almost palpable. No one ever explained to us what would happen to change the atmosphere, but most certainly it had something to do with security. Often rumors surfaced that opposition fighters had infiltrated the people in the displaced camps; this would bring great fear. If word ever got out that opposition forces were present among the people in the camps, the consequences would have been devastating.

Early one morning as we were cooking and teaching the children in one of the camps, fighting broke out in a nearby residential area; the people scattered amid the explosions and gunfire. A grenade was thrown into the camp and exploded; several people were wounded. The explosion was so close to our makeshift kitchen that the blood of the wounded splattered into and onto the pots. For many weeks afterward we were unable to continue cooking on site and had to return to the practice of transporting cooked meals to feed the children.

The setting in the camp in which the grenade exploded was extremely poor—probably the worst in the city. Many of the displaced in this particular camp had lost all of their family members. I paid special attention to the needs of the children in this camp. With the help of many national and international donations we were able to put up a simple schoolroom in which children could study and provide them with books. I never saw another church group or aid organization working at this site.

One little boy in particular, Daudi, pulled at my heartstrings. Daudi could not tell you how old he was. His mother, his only relative, said he was 7-years old. Daudi was blind and was unable to sit, stand, or walk. He suffered from a severe case of hydrocephalus (unusual swelling of the head because of insufficient drainage of fluid from the brain). At the onset of the violence in Burundi he and his mother had fled their village in the interior of the country and had ended up in this displaced camp. While I spent a great deal of time at this site, I had to divide my day among all the feeding sites as well as with our newest outreach to the street children. Mostly to check on him and his mother I did, however, manage to visit Daudi's camp two or three times per week. This little boy's mother, "Mama Daudi", as she was known, displayed a rare strength of character. When I saw scars from previous surgeries on his head, I asked her what had happened to her son. She said that, before the war arrived in their part of the country, Daudi received care at a Catholic mission. There they were able to perform the surgery necessary to address his condition. While at the mission he had improved because the doctor had placed a drain in his head. This enabled Daudi to gain strength. At one time, she said, Daudi moved around by himself and even managed to play with other children.

With the advent of the war she fled with her son for their lives. Mama Daudi did not know what happened to the rest of their family; she assumed they were killed in the fighting. Since the Catholic mission was abandoned, she had no choice but to make her way to Bujumbura to survive. By the day Daudi's condition grew worse; I attempted to find help for him in the local hospitals. Occasionally someone would show interest in his case, but no one was willing to take it on, as he was "not treatable". I took this to mean he was not of the right tribe.

Each time I visited, Daudi always was pleasant, never was angry, and talked about Jesus. His head, swollen with fluid, would move from side to side as he talked about how much he loved the Lord. He asked me once, "*Je, unamjua Yesu?*" ("Do you know Jesus?")

I said, "*Ndiyo, namjua, Daudi.*" ("Yes, I know Him, Daudi.") He said the fact that I knew Him was good, because that meant one day we would live forever in heaven together.

I did not know how soon Daudi would go to heaven, but I knew that without a miracle, he soon would be with his Savior. Not long after our little discussion, a surge in violence erupted; for more than a week I was unable to visit Daudi and his mother. When things finally were calm enough for me to go, I went to the spot in which I usually found Daudi and his mother. His little bed was gone, but his mother was there. She said her son died the week before when I was not able to visit. The truck arrived and carried his body away for burial together with the others that had died that week. Instead of me comforting her that day, I found she was comforting me. "God gave Daudi to me; but now, I am returning him to God."

Rest with your Savior, little one. One day we all will be together in a place in which the pain and tears of this life will be wiped away.

> *And God will wipe away every tear from their eyes; there shall be no more death, nor sorrow, nor crying. There shall be no more pain, for the former things have passed away* (Rev. 21:4).

Chapter 10

Friends of Our Lifetime

"A relationship that has not endured crisis is unproven and unreliable."[36]

The most important vehicle we, as church leaders, have in our hands is that of relationship. The relationships we strategically build with our co-workers represent what enable us to strengthen our base as well as to extend the scope of our outreaches. We believe that our job as soul-winners is the most important job on the planet—but we cannot win the world alone! We must multiply ourselves in others, so we can mobilize entire communities, cities, and nations. As important as our calling is to win the lost, we must not lose sight of another truth that plays a vital role in this calling of ours: the importance of relationship building in light of world evangelism.

> "Teacher, which is the great commandment in the law?" Jesus said to him, "You shall love the Lord your God with all your heart, with all your soul, and with all your mind. This is the first and great commandment. And the second is like it: You shall love your neighbor as yourself. On these two commandments hang all the Law and the Prophets" (Mt. 22:36-40).

According to Jesus the two greatest commandments in the Law have to do with relationship.[37] The first commandment deals with our relationship with God. The second commandment deals with our relationships together. When we get these two greatest commandments in order, we can work effectively to fulfill His last command:

"Go therefore and make disciples of all the nations, baptizing them in the name of the Father and of the Son and of the Holy Spirit" (Mt. 28:19).

Building relationships, especially cross-cultural relationships, is no easy task. They take time; time is what everyone seems to lack. However, no other way exists to fulfill effectively the Great Commission Jesus gave in Matthew 28:19. To reach the world we need each other.

A time of proving

An unexpected byproduct of the war was the strengthening of our relationships with our congregation. Going through the tough times with our people helped us to gain their trust. They believed us when we said we loved them and cared for the wellbeing of the nation. This newfound trust proved to be fertile soil for the establishment of real relationships that went far deeper than what we ever had experienced before war had arrived in Burundi. In the days ahead when the scope of our vision would reach beyond the borders of Burundi, we would draw from the reservoir of wartime relationships.

Embargo

In 1996, added to all the other trouble we had already faced, an economic embargo was leveled against Burundi by its neighboring countries in an effort to prevent the violence from escalating further. While the sentiment of these nations was a noble one, their method of enforcing their wishes did little to change the situation in the country. Under the economic embargo very little business took place. Fuel was rationed to 40 liters per month per vehicle, food prices soared, food often was scarce, and medical supplies (which were supposed to be off-limits concerning the embargo) often were unavailable in the clinics and hospitals. In reality it simply made things worse in the nation and served as a catalyst for the rapid expansion of illegal trade in goods. If you had the money, you could get just about anything. Fuel, which was rationed, could be procured for triple the normal price; food items normally difficult to find were available to those who were willing to pay for them. The rich simply got richer; the poor got poorer.

He makes a way through

 The U.S. Embassy was not too happy with our decision to re-main in the country. The embassy's "non-essential" personnel (spouses and children of embassy officials, etc.) already had been sent out of the country. When the embargo was leveled against the nation, the embassy did its best to scare us out of our commit-ment to stay. Flights in and out of Burundi were restricted to aid flights during the embargo; thus, all international commercial flights were can-celed. Word reached the ex-pat community that only a few more flights would be available for those exiting the country. Afterwards, Burundi would be cut off from the rest of the world. We were told, "Get your names on the list before it is too late to leave."

Just as we had gotten somewhat accustomed to the complicated way of living in Bujumbura, things grew increasingly difficult with the leveling of the embargo. The potential for violence to escalate into another round of full-blown war in the city bubbled constantly under the surface. Rumors abounded about the city being overrun by rebel forces. During this time a friend of ours from Scotland briefly visited us. He has a great heart for the world; one day after morning prayer we all went out for a cup of coffee, at which time we poured out our hearts to Hugh about the situation. He knew our family and had forged a special bond with our youngest son, Stephen, who loved sitting on his lap. That morning we wondered aloud to our friend about our future in the country. Tears welled up in his eyes as he answered us with a word from God that through many trials we have encountered since then has stuck with us: "I feel the Lord saying that He does not make a way out, but He will make a way through."

Not long after our visitor left, our lives went on, despite the undercurrents of fear and imminent danger being spread throughout the city. Our main concern at the time obviously was the welfare of our children. We recently had moved them from attending the French school (that had closed because of the situation in the country) to the Belgian school. On several occasions the consular officer at our embassy told us that the Belgian school's teachers would not return to Burundi, so we had no other option but to leave. In the event that the teachers actually did not get back into the country, we considered the option of homeschooling our children. Yet we realized that we had no way to get school supplies in and out of the country because of the embargo. This unforeseen complication brought us to our knees in prayer. At that time two international flights were going to be allowed into the country. If we were going to leave Burundi, this supposedly was going to be our last chance to leave.

The consular officer at the embassy continued to call us at our home and put pressure on us to leave. One Saturday morning as I was picking up things around the house and spending time with the children, I saw our front gate open. A large, white, Toyota Land Cruiser pulled in front of our house. Before I reached the door to welcome whoever it was, into our living room walked the consular officer from the embassy. I knew who he was; on many occasions he had helped us with renewing our passports, voting, and other such business that could be done only at our embassy. I did my best to give him a cordial greeting. It was obvious he was not at our house on a social call. His tone was somber; his expression almost was angry. Not a moment passed before this man began a verbal tirade that lasted several minutes. Watching him as he carried on, I thought he was very rude to enter our home in such a fashion and to speak to me in such a tone in front of our children. "How could you even think of staying in the country with young children in the middle of such a crisis? You need to put your names on the list for the air evacuation next week." He continued his assessment of our character by adding insult to injury and said, "You might be the worst parents I have ever encountered in my life!" On he went with his accusations and assumptions; I did my best to keep the hot tears that were forming at the back of my eyes from flowing down my cheeks and revealing the hurt at that moment I felt. When I was able to control my emotions, I cordially saw the man out the front door and told him that we would be in touch with him if we saw fit to do so.

Jamie was not at home that morning. Since the day was Saturday, he had gone to a small apartment we rented and used as a guesthouse for our many visitors. There in peace he prepared his Sunday-morning message. Since the apartment was not far from our home, I hopped into the car and drove straight over there to see my husband. I found him oblivious, of course, to the verbal assault I experienced moments earlier. I burst out in tears and did my best to explain what had just happened at the house. Once my anger and hurt subsided enough for him to get a word in edgewise, Jamie suggested we think about evacuating the children and me, so I could take them to safety and have them continue on with their schooling. He added that perhaps once the situation in Burundi calmed down, he would join us and we would pray about our next step.

Jamie had the children's and my names added to the evacuation list, but neither of us had any peace about doing so. For several nights sleep was difficult; as the day of our scheduled flight drew closer, we put a call in to Jamie's father to ask his advice. After he heard our explanation, Dad said, "Son, your mother would not be happy with what I am about to tell you, but I do not think you should go." That was all the confirmation we needed. We summarily called the embassy to remove our names from the list.

Before long our friend at the embassy was on the phone. He was hurling at us his now-familiar insults and insisting that the city was going to fall.

Jamie and I both tried speaking to this man, but we somehow could not get him to understand that our calling to Burundi was greater than that of a worldly job or profession. I finally told him, "If God wants us out of Burundi, it does not matter what the external circumstances are. He can make a way just like He did when He parted the waters for the children of Israel to pass through the Red Sea. The embassy did not call us here, so the embassy cannot take us out." The irony of the whole story is this: the Belgian schoolteachers arrived on the last flight into the country; our kids' education went on uninterrupted. Although the fighting did continue, the city did not fall. God had made a way through!

Pastors on staff

The church, despite all the trouble in the country, continued to grow. We desperately needed help in bearing the ever-increasing load as pastors of the church. Wilondja, who had been with us since the second Sunday in Bwiza, had grown into a powerful worship leader as well as a great youth leader. Both the choir and youth grew under his tutelage; naturally this young man was chosen to serve the church as youth pastor. Not long after joining the church staff as a full-time pastor, Pastor Wilondja met and married his wife, Christine. Under their leadership we saw the youth of the church grow both spiritually and numerically. On both their lives the hand of the Lord was great; we often found ourselves wondering what God had in store for their future.

Emmanuel and Jackie, who joined the church a year or so after Pastor Wilondja did, continued to serve the church as lay leaders. We were blessed by their commitment to TCI; at the right time they both joined the church staff. Emmanuel joined as a pastor and his wife as the church secretary. Later we learned that Pastor Emmanuel's brother-in-law, who lives in France, had offered to set him and Jackie up in business if they would join him in France. They turned down his offer; they said they knew God's will was for them to stay and serve in Bujumbura.

Others ministered at the church as well, but these two families were especially close to us. Both of them gave up a great deal to serve at TCI: Pastor Wilondja was a gifted musician and could have had a great musical career; Pastor Emmanuel gave up a future in Europe. We began to form lifelong ties with them as we lived through war together, raised our children together, and had the time of our lives growing the church together.

Cell groups

 We always believed in building relationships in the church and wanted to see this dynamic reproduced in the lives of our people. Dad encouraged me to initiate cell groups (small home groups). I had complied with his wishes—but the three cells we started did not do very much except exist. This gave me the chance to tell Dad we had cell groups. Not until we had a meeting in Nairobi, Kenya, with Pastor Don and Amy Matheny of Nairobi Lighthouse Church did our perspective on cells radically change.

While the embargo prevented us from using commercial airlines to travel by air out of the country, we learned that the U.N. allowed missionaries to travel on its plane, if it was not full with U.N. personnel. We traveled to Nairobi with the U.N. flight. As was our custom when we were in Nairobi, we went to worship at Nairobi Lighthouse Church. Once, during a previous trip to Nairobi, we happened onto this church and enjoyed the services so much that we decided, then and there, to worship with them whenever we were in town. That Sunday Pastor Don preached a great message; he made several references to cell groups; something "clicked" inside us. We knew we had to meet with them to learn more.

Pastor Don and Amy kindly agreed to meet with us over a cup of coffee; that meeting turned into a long one. They explained to us the basis for cell groups: to disciple believers and evangelize their surrounding neighborhoods. Our hearts beat wildly with excitement as this couple testified to us of the potential for building relationships within the cell groups and how new believers are cared for within the cell setting. The dynamic created within the cell-group setting sounded as though it was something we had yearned for our people to experience. The cell strategy helped us find a better way to get our members involved in evangelizing their own neighborhoods.

Our time with the Mathenys ended too quickly, and we found ourselves with more questions than we had answers—but we knew we had found a key that would unlock many doors.

From house to house

> *So continuing daily with one accord in the temple, and breaking bread from house to house, they ate their food with gladness and simplicity of heart* (Acts 2:46).

The Sunday after we returned, I stood in our pulpit and explained the change that our church was about to undergo. I said that, with the three cells we had going for a couple of years, we had been a church with cells. But from that day on we no longer were going to be a church with cells; rather, we were going to be a *cell church*. That meant we no longer were going to be program-based; we were going to be cell-based. Initially our people did not understand what being a cell church looked like. As with most parts of the world we had been a church with a multitude of programs: evangelistic programs, youth and children's programs, and the list went on and on. I had grown weary of organizing the same 10 volunteers to run the programs of the church. Many of those people grew weary and experienced burnout. With all the outreaches of the church becoming cell-based, we opened the door of ministry wide to everyone who wanted to test the waters.

Once the church understood how a cell-based church operates, delightedly the members embraced the vision! Of course this energized my determination to see the vision of cells saturate the church and in turn saturate our city for Jesus. Weekly we called in all our cell leaders for training. These times were more like during-the-week revival meetings than they were leaders meetings. The Holy Spirit often fell on us in a powerful way. We also found this same atmosphere of revival flowing in the cell meetings themselves. At some cell groups we attended, the presence of the Lord was so intense no one could do more than sit or lie down and soak in all His glory.

Leaders were being raised up more quickly than ever before. I realized the Lord was doing this to help safeguard the great harvest that was being added to our church. During Sunday services a noticeable difference also existed among the church members. Not only would people sit alongside their fellow cell members in church, they planned activities together with their cells and worked to see their cells grow and win the lost to Christ. To accommodate the ever-growing congregation I regularly was installing new cell leaders and releasing them into cell leadership. Before we knew what was happening, in less than three years our three cells had multiplied to more than 300 cells.

The street children

 The outreach to the children of Bujumbura grew at the same time and as exponentially as the church did. God placed strategic people in the ministry to help shoulder the ever-increasing number of children we were touching. The urgency to reach the children in the streets was overwhelming, so our outreach expanded to feeding the street children in Bujumbura. The culture of Burundi was such that, before the war, street children (compared to other major cities in Africa) rarely were seen. Their presence in the capital was an enigma. No one really knew how to address their problems, which were numerous and complicated.

With our landlord we had negotiated and received permission to rent out another part of the Odeon Palace that in times past had been a restaurant. There we built a large kitchen with very large sinks that could accommodate the huge cooking pots we had for the outreach. Early in the morning we started the fires; as soon as morning prayer was finished, we began cooking. The street children arrived in the morning as well; to try to reintegrate them into normal society we began holding classes for them. Slowly we saw them change; when they were ready, we enrolled them in local schools. At our center more than 100 street children received help.

As the weeks turned into months, we began to know the stories of these children. During the war most simply had been separated from their families. When the war hit their areas of the country, their families scattered. Some of their family members were killed, so the children were left to themselves. When they searched their villages but were unable to find their families, they assumed their loved ones were dead and then one way or the other found transport to the capital, in which they hoped to find some kind of help. Since by this time the violence had been taking place for several years, many of the children had grown and remembered little of what it was like to live with their families. Simple things, such as brushing their hair, bathing, changing their clothes, or sitting down for a meal, had been forgotten in their quest just to survive on the streets. Many rumors of sexual abuse were rampant. These included credible reports of foreigners prostituting these young street boys for profit. As a result many of these children were severely traumatized and seemed beyond hope.

One special young man who had been part of the church since the early days of meetings in Bwiza was Richard Tumbu. He joined the choir, served as a cell leader, and had a passion for helping the children. Richard himself had been reared without a father and had a personal understanding of the children's pain. He faithfully served on the feeding team at the church as well as initiated his own outreach to orphans who lived near his home in Bwiza. We had the blessing of supporting his outreach to about 10 orphan children and knew God had special plans in store for his future. Each afternoon Richard always was home on time to take care of the children, pray for them, spend time with them, and make sure they received a good meal. He was not (and is not) a man of many words, but his actions spoke louder than anything else he could have said.

Peace negotiations

 As happens in war, people grew weary of the fighting. Toward the end of the 1990s peace negotiations began to take place in Tanzania. Nelson Mandela, the former president of South Africa, spearheaded these negotiations. Because he was the leader, Burundi's peace became a prominent African issue. We began to see a decrease in violence, which dramatically reduced the stress levels all of us on a daily basis faced. While we still heard the occasional "music" and the embargo remained firmly in place, a definite change permeated the country's atmosphere.

Reunited

 Because of the increased security we all felt, we began to look beyond emergency relief for the children we were serving with our outreaches. I was invited to attend a weekly meeting of NGO workers that was chaired by UNICEF. While for the most part I found these meetings useless, I was able to garner some local support from UNICEF and other NGO's for our outreaches. One specific need I had been eager to address was the reunification of lost children with their families. Not many organizations were actively searching to reunite families. UNICEF, on hearing of my desire to attempt to address this need, offered to donate a small motorcycle for us to use if we began tracing family members.

Not long after that meeting we started our search throughout the country. Tracing lost families, while difficult, was not impossible. The tentative peace that was beginning to arrive in Burundi allowed us to travel more freely throughout the countryside in search of lost loved ones—but freedom of movement was only a small part of tracing families. We began our trek by talking to the children to learn as much as we could about their histories. This started with the obvious: learning where they had lived, dates of separation from family, how they arrived in Bujumbura, and everything and anything else we could gather from the children themselves that was critical for our success. Once we believed we had enough information from a child to travel to his or her village, one of our people would travel by motorcycle (thanks to UNICEF!) and begin the search. Often several trips would be required to several different areas before we had any information. Unfortunately many cases did not uncover family members; bringing this news back to the children was very difficult.

However, sometimes our news was not bad. On one such occasion we had been searching for a boy's family, which he assumed had died when the war reached his village. The child fled from school and figured his family was caught in the violence. After making his way down to Bujumbura and through a series of events, he became one of the children to whom we ministered on the streets. As days turned into weeks, we were able to gain his trust; in turn this led to our learning his tragic tale. This boy was not born on the streets. He was from a good home. His living on the streets simply was a byproduct of war.

Our outreach already had begun looking to reunite the street children with lost family members, and we were experiencing good results. Usually at the very least we were finding extended family members who were willing to provide foster care for their dead relatives' children. When this young boy heard of our reunification efforts, he was interested in trying to find any of his lost family. So we began the arduous task of searching for any remaining relatives. Initially we obtained what information we could from the child (who was nearly 14 at the time and for nearly four years had been separated from his family) and sent out one of our young men to investigate. His report on returning from the village was good; violence in the area had subsided. However, he told us that on a future visit he needed the boy to accompany him. Within the week we sent this boy along with our colleague to find what might remain of his family. Burundi is not a large country. Travel from one side to the other can be done in a day. Driving to the part of the country in which this young boy was from was only a two-hour drive. However, the bus did not take them to the village, which was in a remote setting about an hour from the bus stop. As they walked from the bus stop toward the village, people began to question them as to who they were and why they were there. Hearing that the boy was from the village but had fled years earlier during the violence elicited the villagers' cries. They recognized this boy; they knew his family. Amid the cheers that surrounded them, they drew near to the house that years earlier had been home to this boy. People ran ahead to alert the family members of the return of this long-lost son. All semblance of order was lost when Mom and Dad, both alive and well and assuming that years ago their son had died, received their child back to life.

The family refused to allow our church member to return home the same day; they said that at least for the evening they had to care for him. Accounts of the war that separated everyone were exchanged. We learned that, on the day war erupted in their village, the entire family fled in different directions. While some family members were killed, for a time the parents had sought refuge in the forest. They searched for their son to no avail and assumed he, along with so many others, had died in the violence. For a long time after the reunion this family sent gifts to us. Each time the mother and father sent word that they could not thank us enough for returning their son to them.

Hawkins home

 Unfortunately we were not always able to find families for the children. As a result we would try to put them in foster homes among our church members. This worked well for some children, but not every case was suited for placement in a foster family. Some of the children needing placement were of mixed heritage (their parents hailed from both tribes). This made placement difficult. Children from a mixed background could put the foster family at risk of violence. While peace slowly made its way in, it still was a work in progress. On occasion sporadic fighting could be heard; if radical elements were present near a family that was known to be fostering children of mixed descent, both the foster family as well as the children could be possible targets of violence. As illogical as this may sound, it was part of the reality of living in Burundi.

We had done well in placing many children, but a handful of unplaced children whose families could not be traced remained at our outreach for street children. At that time we opened a home for these unplaced children. Early on we decided the home would not be called an *orphanage* but rather a *children's home*, which was more in line with our vision of giving the children a place to call home. Some of the feeding-team members volunteered their time to serve at the home; slowly we began to see a long-term solution for them.

The children's home grew and developed and in time came to be known as "Hawkins Home" after a dear couple, Harold and Dolores Hawkins, from our home church in Lake Worth, FL. They donated a large sum of their retirement money to be used toward the purchase of a home for the children. Thank you, Harold (who passed away not long before this writing) and Dolores, for your love and care for the children; because of you their lives have been eternally changed!

Neema

 All of the children who lived at Hawkins Home have incredible stories, but one little girl's situation demanded our attention. One morning just as we were opening Hawkins Home to receive children, I became aware of her case. I received a phone call from some missionary friends who were staying in an area of Bujumbura called *Kamenge*. Kamenge often bore the brunt of violent outbursts; as a result, many civilians were caught in the crossfire and wounded or killed. Our friends asked us whether we could take in a 6-week-old baby girl whose mother was a casualty in some recent fighting. The child had been found tied in the customary African way to her dead mother's back; the fact that she had not perished along with her mother was a miracle. Under such incredible circumstances we believed taking the baby into the children's home was only right. Thankfully this little girl's health card (her medical record) was found with her mother and brought to us. While the girl's name was not indicated on the records, we were able to find out her age and area of origin.

When brought to us she was incredibly small—almost skeletal—but she had a strong cry. We called her *Neema*, which in Swahili means *Grace*. Under our care Neema slowly gained her strength. When we brought her to the clinic for the first time, we requested an HIV test (as we did for all our children who stayed at the children's home); the test was positive. This result devastated us, but we kept praying over our little girl. We knew that in small infants HIV tests could change from positive to negative. While this is not a common occurrence, neither is it uncommon. At that time in Burundi the only test available was a rapid test that had to be repeated every three months until the child was 18 months old. Until she was just 18-months old, Neema's tests for the virus continued to return positive; then they turned negative. For a child to be considered negative, three consecutive negative results were required. So we continued to send

Neema for periodic testing. When the final test returned negative for HIV, we knew we had named her in the will of God, for twice she had escaped certain death: the first time from a bullet when she was on the back of her mother, who was shot and killed, and second from HIV. Today Neema is 16-years old and is thriving.

Baby David

 HIV and AIDS seemingly overnight had become a global issue. Obviously for years before the time we were in Burundi, it plagued our continent, but in the mid to late 1990s, the world began to understand how widespread the disease had become. Obtaining the life-saving antiretroviral drugs in Burundi for those who were afflicted with the disease nearly was impossible. In the beginning days of the pandemic children bore the brunt of the neglect, because no one seemed to understand that, to save a continent, we had to save the continent's children.

In the middle of 1997 another child, a baby boy, was brought to the children's home. He had been left on a garbage heap that was hidden behind some bushes. By dumping him in the trash the parents of this child seemed to wish him away. The same day we received him, we brought the baby to the clinic. He had all the signs of what those at the clinic called a "sick" baby. When a child was said to be "sick" in this manner, everyone understood it to be HIV/AIDS. When such a diagnosis was made, we found the caregivers to be less than compassionate. This "give-up" attitude angered me to no end. I argued, "Isn't this child a life given to us to care for as long as he is to be with us, no matter what disease he may be fighting?" The day we brought our little baby, whom we named David, for his first checkup, the clinic gave us little hope. While they did tell us he was no more than a month old, they treated him as a hopeless case, despite the fact that they did not test him for the virus.

"He is so sick," the nurse said to us, "we do not even want to waste using one of our tests on him." We were given a bottle of antibiotics to treat a stomach infection they had found during the examination and then told to go home and not to bother treating him beyond the stomach infection. In effect they were saying just let him get sick and die naturally—nothing more can be done.

I have no way to describe the emotions that churned within us—we decided David was worth whatever we could do for him. He was a fighter and surprised all of us by gaining weight and strength. So great was his determination that even the greatest pessimist at the clinic began to show interest in his case. For the first few weeks he was with us, David was plagued with minor bouts of diarrhea, which we later learned was common in children infected with HIV/AIDS. Despite his poor condition we saw his first smile, heard him coo, and felt the joy of having a baby at the children's home. The other children knew David was special and were just as concerned about his condition as we were.

One Saturday morning the women at the home messaged me that David was very unwell. We brought the baby straightaway to the university hospital, at which the doctor diagnosed him with a kinked intestine. The pediatrician referred us to a pediatric surgeon who said he would see us later that same day. After we waited several hours, the baby was admitted, but we did not see the surgeon. I prowled the halls and tried to find anyone who could help us. Baby David was in agony and had no pain relief whatsoever. I also knew he was beginning to dehydrate and needed intravenous fluids—but no one would stop and listen to my pleas for help.

The next morning after David had lain in pain throughout the night, the pediatric surgeon decided to examine the child. I had great difficulty remaining calm as, without as much as a glimmer of compassion, the doctor poked and prodded David. "The child needs surgery," he said, bluntly.

Under my breath I growled, "Obviously." The surgeon was vague about the timing of the operation. At this point I lost my composure and nearly shouted at him, "Can't you see the child is suffering? Please help him! Please do the surgery today! We will pay whatever cost is related to the surgery and his care. We just cannot bear to see him in this pain any longer!" My vociferous pleas were heard down the hall; the normally quiet, Burundian atmosphere was charged and at attention.

David did have surgery and responded very well. In fact after only a few days he did so well that he was discharged; this once again brought us down the tenuous road to recovery. For a week afterwards David ate and drank normally. He bounced back; we all relished his turn for the better. Our joy was short-lived, however. As quickly as the baby seemed to be healing, he took a dramatic downturn and had to be hospitalized.

Simultaneously I contracted a severe case of malaria. While I was out of commission, Jamie did his best to keep me up to date with the baby's condition. But one morning, Jamie approached me quietly with the news that little David had died in the hospital. The site of the incision had weakened and opened; this allowed the infection to overtake him quickly and caused his death. I closed my eyes and cried for David and all the other babies who suffer. I imagined our little boy, free from pain, neglect, and sorrow, in the presence of our Lord.

The hospital would not release the baby's body from the morgue to anyone but me. We did not want to leave the body there for long, so that same morning, the women who helped care for him in the hospital and I went to retrieve David's body. I never had been in this particular hospital's morgue and was thankful to see working refrigeration units in place. One of the doors of the units was opened; I was unceremoniously handed the body. Tears flowed freely down all of our faces as we laid the body on a table in the morgue and washed him for burial. As they attended to him, some women sang quietly in the background. We were David's family. We were the ones responsible to take care of all these details. We had no funeral directors to take over for us—this last task had no frills attached to it.

On our way to the hospital Jamie had purchased a small casket. We laid the little body, together with his blanket, inside it. We had little to say. Here was a life that we had opportunity to touch; now he was gone. Jamie used the car's jack to hammer the coffin shut, since we had not thought of bringing a hammer along. At the gravesite, gravediggers already prepared a hole and were waiting as we took the small wooden coffin out of the back of the vehicle. No words were fitting for this occasion. We simply left David in the hands of the Lord.

As difficult as many of our experiences in Burundi were, what we gained was far more valuable to our futures and to us than we could imagine. War served to teach us patience and faith, which were the qualities we needed to foster for the future. Not only did we grow in our faith, far beyond our wildest dreams we also grew in relationships. Trial and blessing alike are temporary, but those with whom we have worked and served during those times have become friends for our lifetime. Together with them we have labored and will labor for this continent until Jesus returns.

> "... but truly, as I live, all the earth shall be filled with the glory of the Lord" (Num. 14:21).

(above) Moving from Kalemie, Zaire, to Bukavu, Zaire, 1989

(right) The bridges in Zaire, 1989

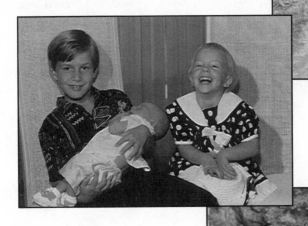

(above) Tom, Mandy, and Steve, 1993

(right) Jamie, Lea, Tom, Mandy, and Steve, 1995

(left) Sunday-morning
service, Odeon Palace,
Bujumbura 1997

(right) Hawkins Home, 1997

(above and right)
During the wars of the
1990s the telltale signs of
war were littered throughout the Great Lakes Region
(Burundi, Rwanda, and
Zaire)

(left) Pastor Emmanuel and
Jackie Nkunku, leading TCI in
Bujumbura, Burundi

(right) Ministering to
the street children, 1998

(left) Life in the
displaced camps was difficult
for the children.

(right) Feeding the
children in the
displaced camps, 1998

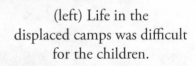

Part 3

Bigger, Better, More

"Enlarge the place of your tent, and let them stretch out
the curtains of your dwellings; do not spare; lengthen your cords,
and strengthen your stakes. For you shall expand
to the right and to the left . . ."
(Isa. 54:2-3a).

Chapter 11

The Way Forward

"For I am prepared to go anywhere, provided it be forward."
–David Livingstone

N ew vision is not always what we seek, especially when things are working. When all is going well, we prefer to sit back and enjoy the blessings of a restful season. Something we have learned about God is that He never sits back and does nothing. He always is on the "cutting edge" and doing something new. When the "newness" of what we are doing wears off, the time to dream again has arrived.

> For a dream comes with much business and painful effort . . .
> (Eccl. 5:3a AMP).

The church in Bujumbura had grown; with the advent of peace we enjoyed a season of great fruitfulness. Sunday sported multiple services; the congregation exploded from a few hundred to nearly 1,600 every week. Cell groups were flourishing; the children's outreaches touched more children than we could have hoped. For the first time in years we were able to relax. During this season of our lives we felt a familiar stirring for the lost in other nations throughout Africa. We knew this feeling far too well to shrug it off. Visible on the horizon was the next assignment; it brought us to the realization that the time to move on had arrived.

A bigger dream

 During our years in Burundi we visited neighboring Tanzania to start the process of registering the church in that nation. We reasoned, since the registration process took time to complete, we could get the paperwork going and then at the right time send someone from Bujumbura to plant the new church (time would not be a factor, since we would be out of the country and visit only occasionally to check on the status of the church file). Gradually Pastor Wilondja and his family became the obvious ones to spearhead the Tanzania plant. A fire of excitement was lit in us as we thought about new churches being planted in new nations!

As we sent Pastor Wilondja and his family to start the work in Dar es Salaam, Tanzania, we began to consider our family joining him and helping with the new church plant. Not only did we think we could help with the new church plant; we also thought that Dar es Salaam could be the perfect city to serve as a hub for TCI in Africa, from which we would oversee the work on the continent, because it is a larger city with greater access to international flights than Bujumbura.

The stirring we were feeling in our hearts neither was new nor was it going to subside. We could not shake it. On many occasions in the past God had moved us "suddenly"; we were ready for whatever the Lord was asking us to do. While our vision always has been to raise up national pastors to oversee the churches that we plant, the prospect of leaving our first church was very painful. Going through a time with our people as dramatic as our time was in Bujumbura had bonded us to them and them to us. Leaving Bujumbura was going to be even more difficult than leaving the U.S.

In late 1999 we broke the news to our leadership that we knew our time in Bujumbura was ending. Some months earlier Pastor Wilondja and his family had been sent to Tanzania to begin planting the church and to continue following the church's registration process. We learned that the process was nearly complete; we became increasingly eager to make the move.

The children

 The children took news of the move in stride. On one hand they were excited; on the other hand, they were deeply saddened by the prospect of leaving loved ones behind. Bujumbura had been the city in which they had grown up. For the greater part of their young lives it was our home.

All of Tom, Mandy, and Steve's schooling had been done in Burundi until 1997, when we began to homeschool them because Bujumbura's schools had begun to wane in quality because of the war and its accompanying hardships. Again God saw our need and provided a colleague and qualified teacher. In 1998 Cate Barker arrived to work with our children for a year. During our children's primary years God provided for their education. However, we were of the conviction that as they grew older and entered into high school, we had to find them the same quality education in Africa that they would have had in the U.S. While our lives were called to serve in Africa, God placed in us the conviction to make sure our children would be able to transition to the U.S. when the time arrived for them to pursue higher education. A quality school (Haven of Peace Academy) run by missionaries in Dar es Salaam was ready to accommodate our children. We felt confident that this school more than adequately would meet their educational needs. The atmosphere was warm; because the teachers were missionaries, they understood our children. The time was a critical one in their development; we realized that this move was as important for their needs as it was for the expansion of TCI in Africa. We did our best to prepare them—but the best thing we could do for them was to obey God.

The younger brother

Of the church leaders Pastor Emmanuel and his wife, Jackie, were the ones whom God raised up to become the senior pastors of the church in Bujumbura. This couple had the determination required to oversee the church in the often-stressful situations that presented themselves there. When he arrived at our church, Emmanuel had been a young Christian, but we watched him grow and mature. His wife provided the constant support a husband needs when he serves as pastor of a church. She not only was a wife to him, more importantly she was a colleague in the ministry.

One evening, as was our custom in those days, we had the pastoral team (more than 20 people) over to our house for a meal. Lea often prepared many dishes the team loved; that night, she prepared spaghetti (a favorite of several members of our team). After the meal we spent a long time fellowshiping and recounting stories. On such evenings in the past we often would laugh for hours as different ones would recount stories of their childhood or the goings-on in their neighborhoods.

This night was no different until the mood turned serious. One-by-one team members began to recount their memories of our years together. One brother said, "I never had a father; you have become my father."

Another said, "Everything I learned as a Christian has come from you." Tears were shed as each one shared what was in his or her heart.

One pastor's wife, who normally was very quiet, gestured that she had something to say. She was one who during the day of war fled across the border of Zaire to Uvira. "One day," she said, "after we had all escaped the violence in Bujumbura, we heard that a white pastor in a blue Pajero had come to the camp where we were and was looking for his 'lost sheep.'" With tears in her eyes she continued, "At that point we knew you loved us. No other pastor would take the time under those circumstances to look for those of his congregation in a refugee camp." While she was not there that day I went looking for members of our church, she said news filled the camp about the big *mzungu* pastor who cared enough to look for them.

At the end of that story all of us began to weep together and embrace one another. Frustrations and little irritations did not seem so important when we looked at these, our spiritual children, and realized they had grown up and were ready to take up the mantel that was about to fall on their shoulders.

I took my Bible and read from Acts 20:31-32, 35-37, . . . *I did not cease to warn everyone night and day with tears. So now, brethren, I commend you to God and to the word of His grace, which is able to build you up and give you an inheritance among all those who are sanctified . . . I have shown you in every way, by laboring like this, that you must support the weak. And remember the words of the Lord Jesus, that He said, "It is more blessed to give than to receive." And when he had said these things, he knelt down and prayed with them all. Then they all wept freely, and fell on Paul's neck and kissed him.*

I explained that the time had arrived for us to move to the next step God had for our lives. However, this did not mean that God had forgotten the church in Bujumbura. In fact this time was exciting for the church. The time had arrived for the church to reach the point we always had desired to see: the church was able to stand on its own and move forward with what God's plan was for that body of believers.

In African culture when the head of the family leaves, he will place the rest of the family under the care of the "younger brother". This younger brother, in effect, becomes head of the family; his word becomes the deciding factor for the family. That evening I explained to our team that Pastor Emmanuel and his wife, Jackie, were to stay in our stead and stand as the head of that church. His voice was the voice for the church; he was to become the leader among them. We were leaving him in charge as the "younger brother".

The tears running down our cheeks reflected the deep connection we all had forged through the years of war and hardship in the nation. How could any of us forget months without power, the sleepless nights filled with the sound of gunfire and mortars, the children we fed and had seen saved, the growth of the church, and the subsequent move of God in the church that sustained us? Yet that was, in effect, exactly what God was calling all of us to do—to look forward and not consider the past.

> *Brethren, I do not count myself to have apprehended; but one thing I do, forgetting those things which are behind and reaching forward to those things which are ahead. I press toward the goal for the prize of the upward call of God in Christ Jesus* (Phil. 3:13-14).

On a Sunday morning not long after our meeting at home we installed Pastor Emmanuel and Jackie as the senior pastors of TCI in Bujumbura. Present with us at that time were Pastor Paul and Perrianne Brownback and Pastor Duane and Kris White (who time and again in Bujumbura during the heat of the war had held revival meetings). Their presence in so many ways helped support us as we began to make the break from our beloved Burundi.

The feeding program and the oversight of the Hawkins Home, which was so close to Lea's heart, was shifted to Jackie, who was more than ready and capable for the task. We could not help but reflect on, time and again throughout the years we had served in the country, how good God was in providing for these outreaches. On one occasion when the food was nearly gone, we received a donation from Dr. Lester Sumrall's organization of 32 metric tons (or three planeloads) of relief. Dr. Sumrall himself visited to document some of the distribution and then ministered to our church. At times answers to prayers for the church and children literally fell from the sky. Yet at that time we had to grapple with the fact that obeying the call of God can bring more questions than answers!

Chapter 12

The Journey to 1,000 Begins

"A little one shall become a thousand, and a small one a strong nation. I, the Lord, will hasten it in its time" (Isa. 60:22).

When God gives vision, this does not mean the vision automatically will move to fruition. In fact, when God has given you a dream or vision, you can be sure the word God gave will be tested and fought. In our lives we have found that God often will give us vision in the driest of places—in a situation in which all seems to be lost with no future to what we are doing. We often felt as though we should give up when all seemed to be lost, but whenever we got close to that place, the question resounding in both of our sets of ears was the same one Peter in John 6:68 asked: *"Lord, to whom shall we go? You have the words of eternal life."* Retreating to a safe place never was and never will be an option for us, because we knew then as well as now that the only "safe place" to be was in the middle of the will of God.

Dar es Salaam, Tanzania

 After we closed our house and liquidated most of the possessions we accumulated while we lived in Zaire and Burundi, in early 2000 we arrived in Dar es Salaam with 13 pieces of luggage. We had few mementos left of the 13 years we had spent in Central Africa.

Moving in Africa is a very different experience to that of moving in the U.S. Besides the complexity of finding an adequate way to move household items, the roads are bad; the chance of losing everything to bandits or a car accident is high. Our only real option was to start over again from scratch; on several occasions we had done this and once again were ready to do it. Lea had insisted only that we save the rocking chair we had made in Zaire when Mandy was born, so it was stored in the church's container in Bujumbura. We wondered when we would see it again.

Our colleague, Cate Barker, who was teaching our children, joined us on the trip to Dar.[38] She had committed to teach our children throughout the move that took place in the middle of the school year; she held firm to her commitment. We were thankful that, even though the move was exhausting in every way, throughout it all the kids' education was covered.

In the hustle and bustle of the move we were able to arrange temporary accommodations at a house MAF had rented for its missionaries. It was empty for about a month; we were able to stay there while we looked for a more permanent solution to our family's housing. Lea did not complain, although I knew she wanted to do so; she put on a brave face even when the dirty, brown water entered the bathtub at a trickle and when the toilet occasionally overflowed into the hallway. She quickly found her way around the city and learned the locations of the market and where to purchase the best meat. Meanwhile, as Lea mustered herself up to adjust to her new surroundings and to run the household, I worked with Pastor Wilondja (who by this tiime had been in Dar about a year) in completing the registration of the church. This was going to be a great place for us to settle; we were ready to see another Bujumbura church born.

Starting again

Before we arrived, Pastor Wilondja and his wife, Christine, had started a cell group in their home. The group had grown to nearly 20 people. With that, we all decided the time had arrived to start Sunday-morning church services. The small house was filled to capacity; we all were bursting with excitement about our young congregation. Soon, the Sunday service moved to our new house, which had a room large enough to accommodate our growing congregation. One cell grew to two cells; so began the church in Dar es Salaam. Eventually we moved the church to a rented warehouse downtown. Even though the government did not officially recognize us, it granted us verbal permission to rent a place for our church to meet.

After Cate's commitment for the school year was done, she returned to her home in the U.K. Later that year the children started their new school year. Tom soon found his niche with his fellow classmates and often played goalie when he and his classmates played soccer after school. Mandy always has been our gregarious child; she has found friends everywhere she went—Dar was no exception. While she struggled to get schoolwork done, she made many friends and loved spending as much time with them as possible. Stephen was only in second grade and made friends quickly. Many children of similar ages as our children were there; while we worked to plant the church, the Lord made sure our children's needs were met.

Not so fast

Soon we learned that our church's registration in Tanzania was going to be a more complicated process than we thought. While we had done everything the government requested and had paid the $500 registration fee (we had the receipt to prove it), no one in the official Tanzanian offices really knew what to do with us. Together with Pastor Wilondja, I went to the offices—sometimes more than once a day—to check on the progress of our file. What was bizarre about our situation was the fact that we had this official receipt issued to us; it indicated our request had been accepted. Everyone with whom we had a conversation said that such a receipt was issued only when the government had approved the registration. However, day after day, we went back and were told, "Tomorrow; come back tomorrow." We did not realize how many tomorrows we were going to have to face.

Because the church was not yet registered in Tanzania, for us to get resident visas with our organization was impossible. Initially we stayed in the country on three-month tourist visas. This worked for a while, but we were unprepared for what would be required of us to stay in the country.

As the months went by, all of us (our family and Pastor Wilondja's as well) had to get special visas that allowed us to stay in the country. These special visas cost $400 per month per passport; in just a few months' time those visas added up to several thousand dollars. Our confidence slowly eroded away as these months passed; keeping ourselves positive about the whole situation was difficult.

Humble pie

 While we were in Tanzania, we had several groups of visitors. Most of them wanted to visit Bujumbura as well; this worked well for us because Jamie would go periodically to see how the church was transitioning to the new leadership of Pastor Emmanuel. I did not want to return to Bujumbura; I was glad I needed to stay behind with the children. Returning to see our beloved church, which we had left behind for this difficult place in which we found ourselves, simply was too painful. At times the water was brown, the power was off more than it was on, the weather was hot, without power we had no fans, and the government was not making things easy for us. *Was the government not happy we wanted to be there to help the nation? When was the church registration going to finally be approved?*

The U.S. embassy in Dar and the embassy in Nairobi both were bombed the same day in 1999. While the death and destruction in Nairobi was extensive, the bomb in Dar had not caused as much devastation as in Nairobi. Nevertheless, the anti-Western flavor in the air was undeniable. This atmosphere did little to help my nearly depressed self. I had not been prepared for the loss I felt after having left Burundi; everything paled in comparison. I tried to rejoice in the little victories we experienced, but nothing seemed to give me any real relief.

In those days we had many talks on the subject. We had many tears, many questions, and little news to report to our supporters in our newsletters. Gone were the days of dramatic news—of the sound of gunfire, mortars, embargoes, feeding hundreds of children, and multiple Sunday morning services. Every month, when time arrived to write our news, we drew a blank and struggled to manage a victorious report. For many, many months in a row we did not feel victorious.

The Journey to 1,000 Begins

 In early 2001 our home church was hosting a world-missions conference. I hoped Lea could join me, but at the time—with the situation of the church file and the children being in school—we decided our best plan was for her to stay behind and support Pastor Wilondja and Christine. Pastor Emmanuel and Jackie were supposed to join me on the journey and arrived a few days before our scheduled flight. We had an unexpected hiccup in plans, as we found out just before the trip that a visa would be reqired to transit through Europe. This was our first attempt to bring any of our national colleagues to the U.S.; we were uninformed of this little, yet important, detail. As an American I was not required to have a visa to transit through most countries in Europe, but this was not the case for our co-workers. Normally, the type of visa they needed took a number of days to process; we had only a day or two before our flight was scheduled to take off. Despite heroic attempts we were unsuccessful in obtaining the required visas. Pastor Emmanuel and Jackie were unable to join me. Instead they stayed behind with Lea and the children in Dar.

As things turned out, having Pastor Emmanuel and Jackie with me while Jamie traveled was a great blessing. I had done my best to put on a brave face but several times had dissolved into tears as he was preparing for the journey. Under most circumstances crying was an abnormal thing for me to do—Jamie must have been at a loss with what to do with me.

Just about everything that could go wrong while Jamie was away did go wrong. Our little laptop burned out, the spare water tank that was stored on the upper level of the house overflowed and leaked all the way into the living room, the power was off more than it was on, and because of an unusually heavy rain our driveway caved in! I vividly remember the rain that morning. Together with Emmanuel and Jackie I watched in amazement as water began to flow over the perimeter wall fence of our property. After some minutes we collectively gasped as the driveway gave way to a kind of sinkhole that had formed underneath.

Despite rain, sinkholes, and burned-out laptops, we did manage to survive the daily curves that life in Dar threw at us during Jamie's absence. I anxiously counted the days to his return and the day he arrived prepared his favorite meal. All I expected to hear was an "I missed you." I had not entertained the thought that at the conference perhaps God had spoken a word to him. In my selfish, self-pity mode I had no time to think of what God might say. I simply wanted my husband to be home and the nightmare of visa renewals, constant checking on the church file, and caved-in driveways to end!

After I picked up Jamie from the airport, we found that something deep had happened to him at the conference. Shaken from my self-pity I silently listened to him as he tearfully began to describe the vision for TCI Africa that God had given him. He read from Isaiah 60:22:

> "A little one shall become a thousand, and a small one a strong nation. I, the Lord, will hasten it in its time."

TCI Africa, he said, was going to expand far beyond any of our dreams. We had thought that a handful of churches might be our destiny to fulfill, but this was not the case. While today things might seem that we are a "*small one*", the day would arrive in which we would plant 1,000 churches on the continent. Therefore, now was not the time to turn our backs, even though things looked bleak in Tanzania. Time to move forward had arrived; retreat was not an option. We still had people to be won, churches to be planted, and a continent to change for Jesus.

Chapter 13

Scattered

Therefore those who were scattered went everywhere preaching the word . . . and there was great joy . . . (Acts 8:4, 8).

When we hear the words *abundance* or *prosperity*, we usually equate them with money. While money certainly is an important part of God's provision or prosperity, it is not the all-in-all of these words. In fact we are convinced that when we finally can get our eyes off of money and on to what real abundance and prosperity are, God freely can bless us with everything that is necessary for us to accomplish our purpose here on earth.

Real abundance and real prosperity are not bound up in what we have here on earth. They are measured in what is known as the true riches of heaven—that is, souls. We cannot take our possessions to heaven; our bank accounts do us no good in the grave. But the souls we affect for the Kingdom of God are the non-perishable "goods" that accompany us on that final journey into the presence of God.

An unexpected change of plans

 Our time in Tanzania nearly had brought us to bankruptcy in every sense of the word. While we had seen a good core of believers established in the Lord, we basically were at a standstill; if we were to continue in the nation, the registration of the church was paramount. Renting the facility for the church, added to the thousands of dollars we were paying out for visas for both our family and Pastor Wilondja's family, severely depleted our budget. For us to move forward, something had to change.

In the weeks that followed my return from our home church's missions conference in the U.S., we continued in prayer and in brainstorming sessions. The nations were in our hearts; we could not continue doing "nothing" while the world was waiting for the gospel! Lea and I discussed the possibility of moving to another nearby country to register the church. Such a move potentially could ease the extreme financial situation in which we found ourselves as well as could expand the church into another nation. When we approached them with this idea, Pastor Wilondja and Christine arrived at the same conclusion as we did. Our conclusion was to venture out on a "spying-out-the-land" trip into the neighboring nation of Zambia. That being decided, in April 2001 we made plans to fly to Lusaka, Zambia.

A God-thing

 At the time of our trip Audrey Partlow, a friend of ours who for some years had served the Hagemeiers faithfully, was working with us for a short season. She graciously accepted our request that she stay with our children for the week while we were away visiting Zambia. My utmost concern was for the children and their education. Stephen already was in ninth grade and needed to be well-grounded; soon the time would arrive for him to move to the U.S. for his college education. For days I had scoured the Internet and looked for schools available in Lusaka; I found that four schools offered internationally certified curriculums. One school in particular, Lusaka International Community School, caught my attention more than the others did. I contacted the head teacher (principal) and explained our desire to visit the school. He was kind enough to reply and even to arrange guesthouse accommodations for us. This was an answer to prayer, as we had no contact in the city. Not only did the school offer to help us find the guesthouse, but it also arranged for the guesthouse driver to collect us from the airport when we arrived.

When we landed in Lusaka, Jamie turned to me and said, "I just feel in my heart that this thing is of God."

With that encouragement I smiled, tried to pull myself up from the seeming defeat we had just experienced in Tanzania, and said, "I agree with you then."

In comparison to Dar es Salaam, Lusaka was a very modern and clean metropolis. We found a supermarket—in fact, several supermarkets—in the city. We found a shopping center called "Manda Hill", in which one could shop for everything from clothes to groceries—all in one spot! Lusaka was not as big as Dar es Salaam was, but it was growing. We hardly could contain our excitement over the possibility of seeing a church planted in this new place.

The day we arrived, we found we had enough time left that very day to start inquiring about the place in which the government offices were situated. We have found that each country's process for registering a church is different. Some countries require church registrations to be processed at the Office of Home Affairs and others at the Registrar's Office. We guessed that either office in Lusaka at least could direct us. After we drove around and asked several individuals, we located the offices, but the hour had grown late; everything was closing for the day. Questions would have to wait until the following morning.

Early the next day we began our research again. After we entered several offices and made inquiries at each, we were given the exact procedure to follow once we decided to start the process. Making note of all the necessary required documents, we thanked those giving us the information and began to make plans for our move and application for registration of the church in the country. At the time no one had told us that registrations were known, even in Zambia, to be precarious dealings that not always were successful. We simply believed, according to the word Jamie had received at the airport, that God was in this move.

The schools in Lusaka all were great options for our children. However, the best option we found for us was Lusaka International Community School. It was not a Christian school, but the warm reception we received from the head teacher and staff who spoke with us on the day we took our tour of the school won us over. We enrolled all three children—Tom, Mandy, and Steve—for the following year.

What was that all about?

The decision had been made. All that remained was facing what we had not expected: another international move. Feelings of failure washed over our hearts as we closed our house, gave Pastor Wilondja and Christine most of our household possessions, zipped our suitcases shut, and in June 2001 stepped onto the airplane destined for Lusaka, Zambia. Puzzled, as the plane took off we looked at each other and silently wondered, *What was that all about?*

Throughout the years one of the most valuable lessons that we have learned is that for the believer, no ultimate defeat exists. Each and every experience, good and bad, can be an opportunity for learning and growth. While many of life's experiences are painful, something always can be gained and learned from them. Even those experiences that seem to have been sent from hell itself for the express purpose of destroying us actually can serve as stepping stones to bigger, better, and more in the Lord. By saying this we do not mean that God is the Author of all bad experiences in our lives; that is not the case at all. What we are saying is that what the enemy means for our destruction, God can turn it around and use it for our good. The believer never experiences true defeat; ultimately, we win.

Lusaka, Zambia

As suddenly as our time in Tanzania ended, our time in Zambia began. Cate (who had returned to work with us once she heard about Zambia) and Audrey met us at the airport. Before our family arrived, Cate and Audrey had gone to Lusaka to begin the process of house-hunting. Our family, together with Selenie, our co-worker from Burundi, without incident passed through customs with our 13 pieces of luggage. In Burundi Selenie had trusted Christ and subsequently for several years had served our family and church. Her familiar presence somehow eased the emotional process of this unplanned move. All of us made our way to the guesthouse, at which the now-familiar process of starting over was to begin.

While I received a word from the Lord that this move to Zambia was a move orchestrated from heaven, we had a tough time staying strong in our faith while we walked through another church-registration process. From our Tanzania experience we learned that being in the country for as much of the registration process as possible was necessary. Our passports had three-month tourist visas stamped in them. We were not sure what would happen if the registration took longer than three months.

On a deeper level Lea felt this. She did her best not to agonize over our situation in front of anyone, but many times I knew she yearned for things to break through to bring stability to our situation. None of us possibly could be settled until the registration of the church was complete and our work permits were secured for us to work legally in the country.

Since we made this move with no furniture, we had to find some "interim" furnishings for the house. Before we moved to Tanzania, we packed a 20-foot container full of ministry and household supplies, but this container still was sitting on our home church's property in the U.S. and waiting to be shipped. While we were in Tanzania, we had not been able to send for the container and had to wait to have it sent to Zambia until this process was complete. Basically all of us had lived in limbo since we departed from Burundi.

To have something on which to sit, locally we purchased some used chairs and household items. This opportunity occurred rather quickly after we moved into the house that Cate and Audrey so graciously worked to find for us before we arrived. A guesthouse was closing down and at reasonable prices was selling its beds, chairs, tables, and other basic items. Jamie was thrilled when we walked into the guesthouse and for $300 purchased a set of living-room furniture, a water filter, and a few other small items! While the items were far from new, they were usable and would help us until our shipment arrived.

Jamie's excitement over the price of our "new" furniture was obvious; I did my best to be excited with him.

Zambia was a beautiful country with beautiful people. It had grocery stores, fresh fruit, and a great school for our children. Zambia even had a cooler time of the year. We never enjoyed cool weather in any other part of Africa in which previously we served. This was a wonderful, new place. Despite the great surroundings I felt tired and useless. Tanzania had left me wondering whether we ever again would be effective on the continent. I was fearful that our registration would fail and that we would end up leaving Africa under the worst of circumstances. I did not voice these fears to anyone, but they bubbled constantly underneath the brave face I tried to put forward for everyone else.

We all looked forward to our "new" furniture arriving. The guesthouse needed it for another week or two after we purchased it; because it was such a good price, we said we gladly would wait for the week or so until the guesthouse no longer needed it. For another week we could use for tables the cardboard boxes we brought over from Tanzania and use other bits and pieces of luggage as makeshift furniture.

The big day when our furniture was to be delivered did finally arrive, but in my eyes it was a disappointment! As Jamie and Tom carried the simple couch into the living room, I saw that not only did the cushion covers need replacing, the couch itself was broken and unusable without being repaired. I unexpectedly burst into a flood of tears and wondered aloud what in the world was I going to do with a broken couch. Jamie consoled me and said we could recover the cushions. He then brought to my attention the fact that we had someone at the house right then who also was a carpenter and could fix the couch; it was the person who was helping us move the couch "Really?" I sniffed miserably and trembled under the effect of the ugly, broken couch.

Jamie held me close and said, "Yes, we will cover the cushions and fix the couch. It will be all right."

With that I reclaimed my composure and somehow got through the rest of the day.[39]

The green light

 American citizens were allowed to stay in Zambia for up to three months on a regular tourist visa. During this three-month window of time we began the process of registering the church. Applications were filled out, a board was formed, documents were submitted, the fees were paid, and we waited and prayed.

While the government was determining the status of our application, we decided to start meeting as a cell group with our family, Selenie, Cate, Audrey, and whoever else might want to join us. Our first Sunday we had eight people meeting under a small hut in our front yard. Before long we moved our little group indoors, in which we grew to 30+ people.

The swift growth of our unofficial congregation gave us cause for joy as well as apprehension. We had people but no official church. Our apprehension soon was assuaged when, three weeks after filing our documents, we received news that the church had been approved to operate in the country. Within hours of receiving the news of our approval we gathered all the necessary documents to apply for our work permits, which were approved within two weeks of our applying. The light finally had turned green!

The new academic year had begun; Tom, Mandy, and Stephen all started at their new school. The curriculum proved to be a challenge for the kids, but they rose to the occasion. This school used a different curriculum than the kind that was familiar to them. But God gave them grace; as time went by, they adjusted very well.

Huts, houses, garages, and tents

The apparent standstill had ended; we worked "full-steam ahead". During our first months in the country another couple, Danny and Amy Wells, along with their baby daughter, Carly, joined us. They had a burden for Africa and had arrived to work with us for a time in Zambia.[40] Together, with their help as well as with help from Cate and Audrey, we saw the church move from the hut into the house; when the house grew too small to accommodate the crowd, we took our congregation out to meet in our garage, in which I preached as if I were in a stadium seating thousands. We called these church meetings (in Burundi our Sunday-morning services had been called *celebration services*) our *garage-a-brations*.

Cate took on the children's ministry. Audrey, who had experience working with bookkeeping, helped in the initial setup of our church's books.[41] Danny organized setting up a large piece of tarpaulin to extend the garage to better house our ever-increasing crowd. Amy volunteered to oversee the music. The church was growing and vibrant!

Before long we were looking for an alternate place to meet. On Sunday morning the church had grown to 100; the garage simply could not hold any more people. Our container had arrived; contained therein were a used tent and some metallic folding chairs that a church had donated to us. A local school agreed to rent us a piece of its property next to its football pitch (soccer field), on which we could set up the tent. Not only did the church agree to rent us property for the tent, it also allowed us to use one of its classrooms for our children's church, which under Cate's direction had flourished. Danny organized a crew of church members to assist him in getting the tent set up. Our hearts were full of gratitude to the Lord for His obvious leading in bringing us to Zambia. However, our hearts never were far from Pastor Wilondja and Christine, who were left working in Dar.

Lubumbashi, Congo

 A few months after our move we invited Pastor Wilondja and his family to visit us in Lusaka. He arrived with news that he had received a letter from the government in Tanzania, which stated that our church was "not wanted" in the country. This letter was devastating to all of us. With this news we all arrived at the conclusion that we needed to "wipe the dust" from our feet and set our eyes on a different horizon.[42]

After prayer our unanimous conclusion was that TCI's next church plant would be in Lubumbashi, Congo. Pastor Wilondja and his family are Congolese citizens who very easily made their move to the country. To live there they would not have to apply for visas. While they visited with us, a scouting trip was set to take place. As they got on the bus for the day-long trip, our hearts began to pound with excitement; we knew another church was about to be born!

Before our departure from Burundi nearly two years earlier, we had purchased a small piece of land in an area called *Gatumba*; we had done this for the purpose of planting a church in the timing of the Lord. We had many church members from this small town that was near to the Congolese border. During the war Gatumba had been the site of many skirmishes; we had waited to plant the church until things settled down. After the peace negotiations began, the small town grew relatively peaceful. Together with Pastor Emmanuel and Jackie we believed the time was right to plant TCI in Gatumba. Years earlier in a container we sent a tent to Bujumbura; for many years it had gone unused—but the time to break out the tent had arrived.

I made a trip to Burundi with Danny (who by then was well-versed in setting up tents) to kick off the new church plant in Gatumba. We had a wonderful time in the Lord as we rejoiced over the new church that was number three of 1,000.

Pastor Wilondja and his family members set their eyes on moving to Lubumbashi and on planting another TCI church around the same time that the church in Gatumba was planted. This would be our fourth church in Africa and our first in the Congo.

We know a great church in Dar—Shining Light Church—whose pastors, Dan and Melinda Koehler, are former colleagues of ours from the time we had served under the Hagemeiers. While we were sorrowful to leave the country under such circumstances, we knew that the best place to steer our people was to Shining Light Church. They quickly settled under the leadership of Pastors Dan and Melinda; to our delight many of them are, to this day, thriving members and leaders in the church.

In about one year's time we had moved from a place of nearly giving up to witnessing the establishment of three new TCI churches. While we were "scattered" from Tanzania, we used that dispersion to our advantage and planted churches everywhere we had a mind to do so, or so things seemed.

> *Therefore those who were scattered went everywhere preaching the word . . . and there was great joy . . .* (Acts 8:4, 8).

Growing pains

The church in Lusaka had grown faster than we had expected. We simply thanked God for the growing pains of needing more chairs and space. In 2003 God blessed us with our own land; we moved our operations to our own property. Apart from the land we purchased in Gatumba in Burundi before we left, this was our first time to experience the blessing of having our own land, We scarcely were able to contain ourselves over the joy of it all! Together with this property we also acquired land for the TCI Bujumbura church and a house for the children's home (we previously had been renting a house). This all happened within the period of one year.

Not only were our churches growing, our own family also was experiencing its own growing pains. In 2003 Tom graduated from high school (secondary school); the whole church celebrated with us as our firstborn son transitioned from child to young man. Jamie's parents traveled out for a short visit to celebrate with us—only yesterday when Tom was a toddler they seemingly had accompanied us on our first journey to Zaire. Now our little boy had turned into a man, was packing his room, and was saying his goodbyes. Soon the time would arrive for us as a family to take our last plane ride from Africa; that was a trip I was not ready to face. One evening a few days before our departure I stood by the doorway to his bedroom and took in the sight of him and his father playing video games together. I scarcely could breathe as I realized that room was soon going to be empty and that my boy would be far away. I asked God for help to face the greatest challenge of my life: leaving a child on another continent to go and do the will of God.

All of us flew to Florida to spend Christmas 2003 with our extended families and to help Tom get started as a college student. I remember sitting on the plane next to Jamie. Tom, Mandy, and Steve were seated in the row opposite ours. As the plane took off, I watched the Lusaka airport grow dim in the distance. Tears ran unchecked down my cheeks as I closed my eyes and remembered my son when we first arrived in Africa. He was 18-months old and in my arms as we disembarked from our chartered MAF plane in Kalemie. As he took in the strange sights and sounds, he then clung to me; he was totally dependent on his father and me. *Now, I thought, he is 18-years old. How did I miss his growing up?* A tangible, deep pain occurred in my chest as I glanced across the aisle and caught his eye. Somehow I managed a smile; he smiled in return. Quickly, I leaned back. I did not want him to see the tears I could not hold back. Looking out the window I held Jamie's hand tightly as we both wept tears of gratefulness for the wonderful son we had but also over the great separation that we were about to face.

During those few weeks in Lake Worth much work was to be completed before we had to return to work in Lusaka. Tom had lots of things that needed to be done: enroll for the winter semester at the community college, get a bank account, and purchase a car. Each step he took cut the proverbial umbilical cord a little bit more. The busy-ness of the time helped us get through the deep emotion of it all. In those days we experienced many heartfelt, impromptu hugs.

 Christmas Day 2003 our family was together, with each one in turn giving thanks to God for the past year. Tom's turn was first; what he had to say brought everyone to tears. "When I was growing up in Africa, all I thought about was moving here. Now that I'm here, all I can think of is moving back there." When we have children, every step we take is to help them grow into healthy adults who love God. That day I realized my little boy had grown up. While still young and inexperienced he now was a man. But most important of all he was a man who loved God.

On the day the rest of our family was to return to Africa, at the church offices we met with Tom and other family members to say our goodbyes.

Long ago we decided that family cannot accompany us to the airport. (A great couple in our church, Keith and Lynn Loving, were kind enough to drive us to the airport in Miami and waited for us at the office as we tried quickly to part from Tom and the rest of the family.) My father led us in prayer; we all took turns embracing those we were leaving behind. Hugging both of us and in turn his brother and sister, Tom, contrary to his nature, cried openly. He held us and said, "I'm sorry for all the times I disobeyed you. I'm sorry, I'm sorry . . .. " Holding on, we told him that he is not to worry about what he did as a child; children act as children. We were proud—so proud of him—of who he was . . . our son.

For nearly the entire hour that we spent getting to the Miami airport, the Lovings endured our family's weeping. Mandy and Steve took the separation with as much difficulty as we did. Tom, while he could be their nemesis at home, at the same time was their hero. Crying, they clung to us; we could not hush them or comfort them, because we, too, were crying. While we somehow mustered the courage to leave our son in Florida, in spirit we never were far from him. Never have we prayed for Tom as we did after we left him. We had to leave him entirely in God's hands; that took more faith than anything else we had experienced up to that point.

(left) Ministering with my
father in Dar es Salaam,
Tanzania

(right) Our first cell meeting
in Lusaka, Zambia, June 2001

(left) Meeting in our house
in Lusaka, September, 2001

(left) Trinity Church International, Gatumba, Burundi

(above) Our garage at home worked very well as a meeting place in Lusaka.

(right) Pastor Wilondja
and Christine
Kingombe leading TCI
in Lubumbashi,
Congo

(left) TCI's land in
Lusaka, Zambia

(right) TCI's tent in
Lusaka, Zambia

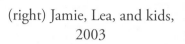 

(right) Jamie, Lea, and kids, 2003

(left) Sunday-morning service in Lusaka, Zambia, 2003

Part 4

Perfect Timing

"*Therefore the Lord will wait, that He may be gracious to you; and
therefore He will be exalted, that He may have mercy on you.
For the Lord is a God of justice;
blessed are all those who wait for Him*"
(Isa. 30:18).

Chapter 14

Moriah

" . . . Take now your son . . . whom you love, and go to the land of Moriah, and offer him there . . . " (Gen. 22:2).

Offering and Worship

Then He said, "Take now your son, your only son Isaac, whom you love, and go to the land of Moriah, and offer him there as a burnt offering on one of the mountains of which I shall tell you." So Abraham rose early in the morning and saddled his donkey, and took two of his young men with him, and Isaac his son; and he split the wood for the burnt offering, and arose and went to the place of which God had told him. (Gen. 22:2-3 NKJV)

The process of offering, while painful, requires obedience. God does have compassion for us (Ps. 86:15), He remembers our tears (Ps. 56:8), yet He requires us to obey His commands. When God asked for Isaac, the Bible does not record Abraham arguing with God. It simply states that the very next morning after God spoke with Abraham, Abraham went to obey the command of the Lord. During his journey to Moriah, Abraham surely had questions. He must have thought about God's promise that his descendants would be as numerous as *the sand on the seashore* and *the stars in the sky* (Gen. 22:17). Yet Abraham knew that God does not renege on His promises. He knew that somehow through Isaac, the promise would be fulfilled.

Then on the third day Abraham lifted his eyes and saw the place afar off. And Abraham said to his young men, "Stay here with the donkey, the lad and I will go yonder and worship, and we will come back to you." So Abraham took the wood of the burnt offering and laid it on Isaac his son; and he took the fire in his hand, and a knife, and the two of them went together. (Gen. 22:4-6 NKJV)

At this juncture every promise God gave to Abraham apparently was being fulfilled, yet Abraham said that he and his son were going to "*worship*". While he was facing what the rest of us reading the story would see as the loss of his promise, Abraham went to worship. Worshiping God is more than singing songs; worshiping God is a lifestyle. If Abraham's love for God was measured by his obedience, that love had to be proved in obedient worship—true worship that did not hold back because he could not understand how God would fulfill His promise.

Back to Zambia

 Leaving Tom in the U.S. undoubtedly was the most difficult personal event we had experienced up to that point in our lives. For months after we left him, Lea would not walk by his old bedroom. Before his departure, for his graduation we had set up a volleyball net at our house. At the party people used that net and played for hours. Once we returned from leaving him, for months Lea refused to let me take it down. I never had seen my wife grieve this way before and was at a loss for how to comfort her, especially because I also was struggling with the fact that our firstborn son had grown up and left the nest.

Change

The year 2004 was one of great change for us as well as for the work in Africa. The church in Zambia was growing, people were trusting the Lord, and the congregation was maturing. The worship leader and his wife from our Bujumbura church (Richard and Nadine Tumbu) had arrived to serve in Lusaka to help establish a praise-and-worship team. Their initial commitment was a temporary one. But *temporary* quickly changed to *permanent* as the congregation connected with them on a deep level. We recognized what was taking place—God had singled out His choice for senior pastor; that unsettled feeling we recognized all too well had returned. We understood that God was about to change our assignment.

Lake Worth, FL

The possibility of returning to the U.S. and working with my father in Lake Worth, FL, for some years had been an ingredient of the discussion with our leadership in Florida. While Dad was far from retirement, we acknowledged that a part of us always had yearned to serve under him and Mom. They are steadfast and consistent in their service to the Lord; once again we yearned to be a part of their ministry in Lake Worth. After prayer and much counsel with the leadership we all concurred that the next year, 2005, would be the year for us to transition from working in Africa to serving once again in Lake Worth, FL.

The reality of it all . . .

We began working with Richard, who in the interim had become Pastor Richard, to help him step into the senior-pastor role. Our experience of handing the church in Bujumbura over to Pastor Emmanuel and Jackie taught us many valuable lessons. Since we had nearly a year to prepare the church for this transition, the first thing we did was to have Pastor Richard preach on a regular basis. He also was given an increasing load of responsibility in front of the church. While we did not want to announce our move a year before we left, we wanted to make who the senior pastor was going to be increasingly obvious to the church. We desired to make the transition as natural a process as possible.

Cate, who since our time in Bujumbura had been a dear friend and colleague, also sensed a change arriving in her ministry and well before our departure transitioned out of Zambia. God had begun to lay a new burden on her heart for another region of the world; with great sorrow we let her go to do the will of God. She is a dear friend whose help, especially during the days of war in Burundi, enabled us to keep working the vision God had given to us. We knew whatever God planned for her life was great—but she was, and is, sorely missed! Thank you, Cate!

In the interim as we were transitioning out of Zambia, Cathy Exley from TCI in Lake Worth, FL, for a season arrived to work with the children's ministry. Working diligently she partnered with Cate's team, which had grown tremendously under Cate's tutelage, in preparation for the upcoming transition of leadership. Thank you, Cathy, for your service! What a time it was!

Goodbye . . .

 Breaking the news of this change began with our leadership in Zambia as well as in Burundi and Congo. No one was surprised, but no one (ourselves included) took it lightly. Because we all craved for the will of God to be done, among any of our leadership we had no dissension—just simple surrender accompanied by many tears. The church in Zambia showered us with gifts and prayers; we looked to our Lord in heaven for the grace to make this shift.

Mandy and Steve both were excited about moving to the U.S. and once again living as a family under one roof with Tom, who had gone nearly 18 months earlier. The kids were growing older; their needs were paramount. We reasoned that this move would enable us to minister to their needs as well as to oversee our African outreaches from Florida. We believed that, in some ways, our outreach even could be enhanced with this move. While this thinking may not have been flawed, the feasibility of doing so remained within the realm of the unknown. Although we had a certainty in our hearts that we had followed the leading of the Holy Spirit, we sometimes wondered—even out loud to each other—what God really was up to with this change of venue.

What about the kids?

 Throughout this process first and foremost in our hearts and minds were our children. At times people on the outside may have thought that we, as missionaries, had not taken our children into consideration and that somehow our eyesight focused only on the missionary task set before us—a task which blinded us to their needs. God calls families (Josh. 24:15). When the call arrives, God enables His people to fulfill the call. He gives grace—even to the children—to withstand any and all enemy attacks that surely will happen. Through all the years on the field we labored to include our children in the ministry and to impart to them the love we had for the people. Our first mission field was our family; if we lost our family members in pursuit of a continent, we would not have gained anything at all.

As Tom, Mandy, and Steve grew and matured, they developed friendships and ministry and cultural skills that not only helped them fit into the societies in which they lived but also to develop a love for the field in which we all served. This does not mean that they did not struggle or desire to see family and friends in the U.S. This simply means that they

285

learned to love, live, and function in Africa. Besides being obedient to the will of God, learning how to love the place in which you are is the richest inheritance parents can leave their children.

I learned this lesson from my parents, Pastor Tom and Mary Ann Peters. When I was a young child in elementary school, our family left a comfortable life and a strong, local church in Orange Park, FL, and relocated to Lake Worth, FL, in which my parents took the pastorate of a small church (Trinity Church International) of eight people: four women and four children.[43] I do not bear any resentment toward my parents for making this decision; in fact I cannot imagine how I would have turned out if my parents had not answered the call. I appreciate their teaching me this principle and leaving me a rich inheritance of faith. Forever I am grateful to them for rearing me in the will of God; this is one of the things that inspired me to dare to obey God when He called.

So many families today are in pursuit of a lifestyle that is supposed to bring satisfaction. In reality contentment can be found only in Christ Himself (Phil. 4:11-13) and in following His will. This is true whether a person is single, married, divorced, widowed, and with or without children. God is very well attuned to the places in which He sends people and of the risks, trials, and hardships they will face. We doubt that, during the times we have struggled living overseas, God was caught unaware of our situation. He did not suddenly turn around, snap His fingers in heaven, and say, "Oh, the Peters family is there with so much trouble around them. I totally forgot where I put them! How could I have sent them there with such small children?" People—well-meaning people—sometimes made comments to the effect that by living in Africa our children were missing out on life. Such comments, as painful as they were at times, tested our call and determination to do the will of God. In fact they actually helped us to grow stronger in our conviction. The comments worked for the "furtherance of the gospel"[44], because the pressure those comments put on us just increased our determination to fulfill the call. While the kids may have not had as many things or distractions available to them as did their peers in the States, what they gained by growing up in Africa far outweighs any inconveniences they may have endured.

Through the years filled with the dangers of civil war, economic embargoes, and separation from loved ones, we learned that the most satisfying and secure place in the world is in the middle of the will of God. During some of our most difficult times, when the situations around us were potentially dangerous and frightening, God's grace enabled us to stay. At times—sometimes several times daily—we had to make sure we still were on track because of the circumstances around us. When you have children on the mission field, all the choices you make affect your children. A day will arrive in which you will be required to give God an account for your lives. We were profoundly aware of this fact as well as aware of the importance of staying on course with God's will—not only for our own well-being but more so for the well-being of the kids. Yet, as God assured us that we were on course, He gave us the strength to go on with the work. God promises His blessing to rest on us when we obey Him, but those promises hinge on our obedience to His will.

> *"If you are willing and obedient, you shall eat the good of the land; but if you refuse and rebel, you shall be devoured by the sword; for the mouth of the Lord has spoken"* (Isa. 1:19-20).

This understanding of the great importance of following the will of God caused us to pull up our stakes from African soil and move our children to the U.S. after having spent most of their childhoods on the continent. So once again we closed up house and went to another field in which another assignment awaited us.

Reunion 2005

 By the time our family was reunited in Florida, Tom was well into what we now know is the experience of "re-entry." Re-entry is a phenomenon that no returning missionary can escape. It is difficult to articulate, impossible for others to understand, and an experience that especially is marked with emotional shock and pain. When in 2003 we left Tom, if we had known about the pain of re-entry, we would have taken more care in helping him to adjust. During those weeks we were together before we returned to Lusaka, I noticed he was anxious and that emotions were running high. I did not suspect that re-entry was playing any role at this point. We can only thank the Lord that Tom did, by the grace of God, navigate through that experience. While he was well ahead of us in the re-entry process, we were just beginning ours.

As we landed on the airport runway in Florida on that hot summer day in June 2005, a great expectancy and trepidation filled our hearts as the magnitude of our decision washed over us. *This was it! We were to have no turning back to Africa–the house had been closed up, our household items either were given away or sold; everything down to the bathroom scale had been liquidated!* Silent prayers were offered as we exited the plane—prayers for strength and grace to deal with what lay before us individually and as a family. That day we met the future not knowing at the time what stage God already was setting in motion.

With hearts and arms open wide our families and Tom were waiting for us at the airport. To hold them and be welcomed back was so good—18 years living on separate continents from our families had made us appreciate them so very much. Hugging Tom once again especially was gratifying. We all marveled at how he had changed—how he had matured. During our time apart he lived with Jamie's parents, who opened their door to him. The sting we felt at the time he returned to the States to continue his education had been overwhelming. Now the happiness we felt in seeing him overshadowed any residual pain. Some rightly have said that being a parent is the only profession where your heart can walk outside of your body. In our case this has proven to be true.

As we drove from Miami toward Lake Worth, I reveled in the fact that the interstate in Florida was paved smoothly; compared to where we had been, cars drove in a definite order. The traffic lights worked, grocery stores stood on every corner, a gallon of milk could be purchased at any time of the day or night all year long, and while the water in Africa that emerges from the faucet often is full of dangerous bacteria, Florida water even can be used to brush your teeth. I arched my neck and hoped to find a Starbucks coffee shop. On occasion in the past whenever we visited the States, I had the opportunity to indulge in the odd Starbucks coffee. Now, I lived in the land of Starbucks! While my hope of sipping that unmatched blend was not realized on our way to Lake Worth that day, I made a mental note and assured myself that I would find a way to indulge myself in a cup of specialty coffee before my first week in the States was over.

As we studied the landscape along the highway, the children chatted nonstop with their family members. Florida, with its palm trees and sand, is very similar to many areas in which we had lived on the continent of Africa. Even then we grew nostalgic for what, naturally speaking, was now home—Africa. Even with the similarities we somehow felt ill at ease and began to ask ourselves questions: *Were we going to be all right? Would we learn the ropes of serving in a great, established church? Would we meet their expectations? Were we needed?* Then, looking at the children and remembering our reasons for moving included their needs, we sat back to take in all the emotions that were assaulting us.

A *houseful of what?*

In the months before our move God made a way for us to purchase a house. On several occasions we actually had the opportunity to stay in this particular house; the church used it as a guesthouse for missionaries and ministers. The owner of the home lived out-of-state and decided to sell, so God stepped in and enabled us to make it our own. The timing was perfect. On our return we were going to need a place to live; the house precisely was what we needed at the time. One of the most amazing aspects of the transaction was that before our return the sale was accomplished via Fedex between Lake Worth and Lusaka. Because of the fact that we had not been physically present during the transaction, understanding that we owned a home was surreal to us. Driving into our own driveway brought tears to our eyes. Nearly 18 years had gone by since we last had owned a home. Before this provision we had no natural hope of ever having the ability to purchase a home; yet, here we stood at the threshold of the front door. A few days before we arrived, Tom had moved in; this made us feel really welcome to the new surroundings. Internally I smiled at the fact that he apparently was happy about our being together again. This was a moment for us to remember and enjoy, which we did.

Because of jet lag the first days we were home, I would wake up at strange hours—between 2 and 2:30 a.m. I seem to have tried every remedy for jet lag that is out there and regretfully never have found a cure for the condition. It does not leave in a jolly mood those suffering from it. I was annoyed that I was the only one in the entire family who was not sleeping soundly. Four of us had taken the same trip; I was struggling not to be jealous when I heard their contented snores drifting from the bedrooms. The second night we were home, I was awake watching a wildlife documentary on TV in the living room, which was adjacent to the kitchen. I suddenly heard a grinding sound emerging from the ceiling over the refrigerator. It was not a normal sound at all, yet, I recognized it; I had heard similar sounds in Africa, in which many creatures can infest your house. One of the most common and most difficult to remedy is rats; this sounded as though it was rats. Inwardly I groaned, walked into the kitchen, and listened intently. Suddenly, the grinding stopped; the squeaking began. My heart beat hard and fast as images of rats crawling out of the kitchen cabinets and running all over my feet filled my mind! As I turned on the lights, I hesitantly surveyed as much kitchen area as I dared and then entered the garage from where I heard more sounds emanating. In the garage I found rat droppings. All over the world rat droppings are the same; rats leave these "calling cards" of theirs everywhere. They also like to squeak, grind, scurry, and chew holes in walls, wires, and wood. I had seen the "calling cards", heard the sounds, found the chewed hole in the wall next to the clothes dryer, and was certain we were infested. I shook my husband out of his sleep and loudly whispered, "We have rats!"

Jamie, a sound sleeper, growled, "Well, what can I do about that NOW?" He then turned over and continued enjoying a good sleep. I do not know whether I was angrier at him for sleeping well while I suffered sleepless nights watching shows on Animal Planet or because of his apparent irritation at my rat-based fear. When my suspicion later was confirmed, I felt a sense of triumph. The next night the rats could be heard squeaking in the wall that separated the master bedroom from the garage. By this time the re-entry process was starting to take hold in me. With everything I could muster within myself, I said to Jamie, "I left rats in Africa! If I wanted rats, I would have stayed there!" *This is America,* I thought. *We are not supposed to have rats in the house.* I astonished myself with the magnitude of my reaction to this familiar scourge. Apparently re-entry was having a greater effect on me than I thought.

As we reflected on our departure, we understood God had asked us to lay down our promise and trust Him to fulfill it in His way, in His time. However, the dream of 1,000 churches on the continent faded as a dream fades when you wake up from sleep. We had offered our Isaac, but we had yet to learn how to worship God in the offering.

Chapter 15

Surrender

"Faith is the bird that sings while it is yet dark."
–Max Lucado

O ne exeriences power in surrendering to the will of God, especially when we do not understand His will. Truly surrendering to God—as if to raise our hands and shout, "We give up!"—is what empowers our relationship with Him. He sees the end from the very beginning, but He also sees everything that lies in between. When we surrender, He is free to lead us forward because no longer are we resisting.

Mixed feelings

Turn and answer me, O Lord my God! Restore the sparkle to my eyes or I will die (Ps. 13:3 NLT).

After only a few days in the U.S. we already had been experiencing mixed feelings. To comfort ourselves we held that these feelings were natural and to be expected. After a history such as ours how could we immediately fit in and flow with life in the States? In 1987 when we made our initial move to Africa, to Kalemie, Zaire, I immediately found my place. Although I was very young (24) when we moved to Africa, at the time I felt as though I had waited all my life to be a missionary. When the door opened to me, I finally was at the place in which I was destined to be. Sometimes to the disappointment of my family, with a vengeance I dove into Swahili studies. One situation in particular sticks out in my mind when Tom was not even 2-years old. At that time I easily could spend eight hours daily studying and memorizing vocabulary lists and passages from the Bible in Swahili. Tom, barely being able to speak himself, said to me, "No more 'wahili, Daddy!" His plea that day, if only for a moment, did cause me to pull away from the books.

Moving to Africa had not been difficult for me. From the very first day after we landed, I felt as though I had always been there; I knew where I was and what to expect. The day we arrived in Lake Worth, however, brought a different experience than that of moving to Africa.

As the days passed and our jet lag began to subside, we found ourselves slowly beginning to flounder, as if our focus, which for years had been crystal clear, had been lost. We felt confused, as if our life's mission and purpose were missing. While we endeavored to fit into society and work in our wonderful church, something was chipping away at our souls. I would tell Lea that I felt as though I was "drying up inside". She was sympathetic but at times grew impatient with me as she struggled with her own questions. At this stage we continued to believe that these feelings must be part of re-entering American culture and that we needed to give ourselves time to allow the experience to run its course. Everything that had a beginning surely must end. Our prayer was that the end of these disoriented feelings would occur sooner rather than later.

Dishwashers

 The responsibility of making our house a home distracted us enough from the re-entry process to enjoy some of the amenities of Stateside living. The first weeks were spent cleaning house, exterminating rats, purchasing furniture and cars, and re-learning the ropes of being U.S. citizens. For many years we lived as foreigners; living as citizens almost was a new experience. We also had at our disposal many shops from which to choose as we searched for various items needed to set up our home. Not only did we have a choice of stores, we also had a great variety of each product readily available; often within 24 hours they could be bought and delivered. For instance the main shop in the center of town didn't have just one couch we could buy, it had hundreds of couches readily available in a variety of styles and colors. Imagine first our shock, then delight, but ultimately our confusion at having to decide which couch to purchase for our living room. We more easily could have selected 20 couches we liked than to have to narrow our choice down to one. *Who can decide which couch he or she wants with so many from which to choose?* Our selection finally occurred one rainy afternoon, possibly more out of fatigue than anything else, because we were so weary of looking. Everything available was beautiful; how could we possibly go wrong when everything (even the most unappealing choice) was beautiful? Perhaps the greatest acquisition of those early days in Florida was our purchase of a dishwasher. To have the chance of owning and using a dishwasher (after years of washing dishes by hand) nearly sent me over the edge. Washing up after meals may not sound as though it is a big deal; it isn't, but in Africa, washing up is another story. Picture this: cleaning everything had to be done with precision. By precision I mean that every food type had its own process. Vegetables eaten raw first must be rinsed of visible dirt, then cleaned with filtered water and a bleach solution, and then rinsed again in filtered water. Meat must be thoroughly cooked; even eggs needed to be washed. Definitely more to washing up exists than just washing plates and a few pots—in Africa this is an all-day event. Now, a dishwasher sat installed in my kitchen in Florida. It was a very light beige color; best of all, *it made noise!* The salesperson tried to sell us a model that was "silent" and that wouldn't bother us. Imagine his reaction when I said I wanted to hear the noise! I wanted to hear that a machine was washing my dishes and that they would emerge clean. Obviously the "silent" dishwashers are more expensive; Jamie met with approval my choice of a less-expensive dishwasher, but the price was not what moved me. I simply wanted to hear the hum of the machine emerge from the kitchen. After we loaded the machine, the kids and I often "high-fived" each other; we would push each other out of the way to press the "start program" button. Having a dishwasher was not a difficult part of re-entry; it was a little bit of heaven.

A normal life?

 The time arrived for us to assimilate totally into a normal life—to work and live as Americans. At the church Jamie had an office ready, but his first days there he was not really sure what to expect. His absence from my side brought great anxiety to both of us. For a long time we had served side-by-side. We learned what made the other "tick" and learned to function comfortably as a team. Many married couples often do not enjoy working together as closely as we had; at first, in Africa, we were forced into it. But over time we grew very comfortable working as colleagues. It ultimately became our preferred choice. Neither of us knew of anyone with whom we'd rather have worked than the other. In one day we not only were in a different nation, our working environments changed drastically.

In America on that first day of Jamie's going to work, I no longer shouldered, as I had done for many years, with my husband the same ministry burden. To say that this upset me is an understatement. The first day Jamie was to leave for work, I stood and asked him and myself, *"Who am I, and what do I do?* I always had been the one who answered the phone, written reports and newsletters, and ran the offices. One afternoon I cried openly when Jamie said that any secretarial duties he needed to have done had been assigned to someone. I was not upset at the person who had taken the duties; I was mourning for my lost identity and the loss of teaming up in ministry with my husband. Financially our family needed me to find work of some sort, so I was blessed to work at our church's academy, which our children attended, as a substitute teacher as well as working as a translator. I also found refuge in teaching once a week at our church's Bible school. Teaching is a joy; if only for one night a week, teaching at the Bible school helped me avoid feeling useless. Substituting at the academy allowed me glimpses into the daily lives of our kids; translation offered me the opportunity to sharpen my language skills while I was away from Africa. These activities were a welcome distraction and helped me cope with my new state of things.

 I grew up at Trinity and had been a staff pastor from 1984-1987. As a young man I almost fought against going into full-time ministry. I wanted to be sure that, if I was going to be in ministry, God had called me and that I was not simply doing what I thought people might have expected from me because my father was in the ministry. However, the pull eventually became too strong for even me to resist; I eventually jumped wholeheartedly into full-time service. Once I made that decision, I could not get enough of church and everything that had to do with church. I was involved in every ministry that was available: nursing-home outreaches, youth ministry, ushering, choir—I did it all; my thirst for God could not be quenched. My first position on staff was to serve our youth pastor, Mel Rolls, who not only was a good friend but also was an invaluable mentor in the faith. The youth organized a mission trip to Haiti; I eagerly waited for the day of our departure. After one night in the capital, Port-au-Prince, our group traveled to the interior of Haiti with a national pastor, Pastor Preval, who I believe is an apostle to that nation. This first trip forever changed the course of my life; from then on I was incurably infected with the missions bug. I knew that, in some way during my lifetime, I would serve in missions. While I still was on staff for three-and-a-half years before I became a missionary, all the while my heart was expanding beyond the realms of Lake Worth.

The move to the States, after we had served nearly half of our lifetime of focusing our attention on Africa, challenged us to change on many levels. Perhaps my experience best can be described as an identity crisis. Everything I had grown to become changed the day I stepped back onto American soil. My first day to work at the church office after our return sent me reeling; I no longer knew who I was. Because of the fact that I had been gone from the church office for so long, I knew I had to take time to re-learn the ropes. During my first time to enter the office designated for me, I stared with awe at the desk, the empty shelves, and telephone (and its many extensions). Apologies were made for the fact that my office was not yet decorated, but I was more than happy with it! My offices in Africa mostly had been, at best, "fixer-uppers" compared to the room I had just entered. I had secretaries to write letters, make photocopies, take care of plane tickets, make hotel reservations, and even order my lunch for me. These were conveniences that on the other side of the pond I never had the opportunity to enjoy. In Africa we had to do most things by ourselves; Lea took care of most of the office work (and lunches, of course); I dealt with airline reservations, preaching, and official business. Work held its challenges, but we learned how to navigate through them. The challenge that lay before us now was to learn how to steer through a very different way not only of living but also working.

One of my major responsibilities remained the oversight of our African churches. This required me to be in close email contact with the church leaders. When I saw their emails in the inbox, I often wished reading them had not been necessary. Somehow even reading emails hurt. How I longed once again to be "on the front lines" with them. Nevertheless, I had to remain in close contact with the African churches; I, who for years had been computer illiterate, began to learn how to navigate the computer. This was new territory for me; throughout the years Lea had done most of the correspondence. I embraced the challenge since I knew I had, at some point, to enter the world of cyberspace. The first time I did an Internet search, I was amazed! All of this information at my fingertips was exciting! I also was introduced to the idea of online banking. At first I was wary of the idea of going online with my banking because of the horror stories I had heard of identity theft. But I not only mastered the banking part but also became good at surfing the whole Internet.

Working with our African churches no longer was the only activity assigned to me. I had to expand my thinking beyond Africa. I also began to attend pastors' meetings and to participate in the church's other ministries. This gave me more exposure to the heart of the church as well as to the people we were serving. Neither Lea nor I ever felt ill at ease with the people of Trinity in Lake Worth. From the moment we arrived, the outpouring of love from the congregation was amazing. We were honored and still are honored to spend time with the people and to get to know them anew. So much time had passed since we had spent any lengthy period of time with the people of our home church; getting to know them again was like being introduced for the first time. My heart, while missing Africa, was to serve this great house that over all our years on and off the field had been a source of spiritual energy and support for us. I know of no other church than Trinity in which I would rather serve. My parents, by the grace of God, have seen the church grow and mature into a body of believers that has influence all over the world. They honored me by making room for me to serve with them and someday to serve as co-pastor with my father. Dad recognized the pain I was in and wisely counseled me to refrain from traveling back to Africa until the initial stages of the re-entry process had passed. Recognizing the wisdom of his words I determined to work through the process and make my first visit back in the early part of 2006. The routine I established—attending early morning prayer, office work, etc.—was helpful as I worked through re-entry. The busier I was, the better I found myself coping with the ache I felt.

I began to work with our church's cell ministry, which for some years was moderately successful but needed a fresh touch. We had much experience working with cell groups, as all of our African churches are cell churches. Most recently we had implemented in our churches the Principle of 12 strategy[45] and greatly appreciated the effect it had on the health of individual believers as well as on the church as a whole. My father long had planned to transition the church's cell strategy to the Principle of 12 and assigned me to oversee the transition. I am thoroughly convinced of the scriptural integrity of the Principle of 12 and was eager to work with the cells. Slowly I began to enter the process of finding my way in a place outside my comfort zone. My first step was to open a men's cell group. In the Principle of 12, cells generally meet by gender. I excitedly looked for members to start the first group. Lea, as eager to work with cells as I, was slower in the process of starting a cell group, because she was involved with working and teaching and for some months until her responsibilities ended could not start a ladies' cell. When I did open my cell and established relationships with some men in the church, I found a place in which I fit; I found my place to serve.

"This is temporary . . .. "

In September 2005, after we had been in the U.S. for nearly four months, the women's ministry of our church invited Kathy Lechner to be a guest speaker. On the weekend of September 9 she spoke in several meetings; this weekend took us by surprise. By this time we were in the thick of our "process", which in some ways seemed only to grow more painful as time passed. Jamie and I had spent many hours in tearful conversations with each other and in counsel with others in an attempt to find our way through the fog that had settled over us. However, no amount of conversation or counsel seemed to be able to alleviate, even for a moment, the constant ache we felt for Africa. For people who have not gone through re-entry, understanding its implications on the returning missionary is impossible. For anyone (other than another missionary who has gone through the experience) to give help in navigating its course cannot happen. Well-enough we understood the dilemma in which we found ourselves, but for others to identify with our situation was difficult. For us to experience what had (and still has) no words that fit its description was tougher.

The weekend of Kathy Lechner's meetings had arrived. The first Friday evening she was to speak, I found myself especially tired even though I loved church and ministry, I believe the weariness was more a part of my "processing" than it was true fatigue; at the time I was fighting depression, which was extremely unusual for me. In my youth I struggled with feelings of depression, but when God got hold of me, I found the joy that had evaded me! Therefore I was surprised when these feelings re-occurred; I no longer was accustomed to feeling down and was distressed at once again having to fight depression. Often in the afternoons and evenings I would retreat to my bedroom and did not want to emerge unless necessary. While I did not lock myself in my room, I sorely was tempted to do so. At the time of these meeting this was my state, yet somehow that evening I found my way to the church.

On my arrival I went to the pastor's study, in which I found several of the women leaders and my mother-in-law speaking with Kathy. I never had met Kathy before that evening but found her to be genuine. She had brought some of her children with her; we enjoyed a few minutes of conversation. Before that evening I never had heard Kathy speak but had heard how powerfully the Lord moved in her ministry through her teaching and prophecy.

Kathy gave a wonderful message on having passion and fire as we press ahead in the grace of God. She encouraged us that God's people can go through anything as long as they drink from God's wells of living water. I hung onto every word. God seemed to have written the message for me. Certainly others were blessed, but I was sure God had thought about me that night when He sent Kathy. After the move the fire I had in Africa had seemed to disappear; I once again began to yearn to feel the fire inside my heart. I felt refreshed as the presence of God hovered over not only me but the whole gathering of women. As the teaching ended, Kathy began to pray for a woman and prophesied over her. The woman obviously was touched deeply. As Kathy ministered, all of us in the audience prayed together with her.

With my eyes closed and praying alongside everyone else I heard Kathy's voice calling, "It is Lea, right?" I rarely had received a prophetic message from anyone. At times in the past, as a couple Jamie and I were called out from a crowd and prayed for; in this type of setting, together with my husband, I would receive a prophetic word. Yet for me to be called by name for prayer was highly unusual. At the sound of Kathy's calling my name I was startled into consciousness. Shaken, I stood and walked to the front to hear what the Lord had to say. She said, "Lea, I don't know how this fits . . . " and for about 15 minutes continued to prophesy over me. God certainly wasted no time in getting my attention. I almost immediately heard her say the words, "This is temporary . . .. " I wanted to stop everything and ask the question, "What did that mean?" She went on to "read my mail", so to speak, and said, "You have not been put on a shelf", which is exactly how I felt at the time. But I continued to think about the "temporary" word—my mind was reeling! In her next breath she said, "I've pulled you out to re-fit you, to take the dents out of your armor . . . so when you go out next time, next year, when you are standing in a land you never had thought of going to before . . .. " Finally I just stopped thinking and listened to the rest of her prophecy. I had to restrain myelf to keep from crying out loud.

That evening I was not the last person for whom Kathy prayed, but as far as I was concerned, no one else after me was left in the building. Others' reactions to the word I received ranged from "Yes, that's right" to "No way!" I felt surprised, curious, and eager to share with Jamie the word I had received. That evening the people in the media department were kind enough to give me a CD of the entire service. I rushed home to share it with my husband.

 I listened to the CD of Kathy's prophecy; initially I felt confused and attempted to interpret what was said in light of our move to Florida. So much prayer had gone into this relocation; I was confused to think that God would bring us back to the States only to send us out again. *What did all that mean in light of the plans we had made to oversee our African outreaches from the States and eventually co-pastor with my father?* Together we talked about the word Lea received and even had different leaders and friends listen to it. We hoped someone had something to add that would help us make sense of it all. Finally the CD was put away in a case somewhere as time made the words (which seemed to intrude on our world like a loud explosion might) fade into the background of daily living.

Holidays

 The children were in school and learning how to adjust to American living. As time passed, they began to fit in and make friends. Mandy joined the church dance team and then the choir. At first she had shed many tears; she missed her friends (especially those she had led to the Lord), school, and the work in Africa. In Lusaka she had been a youth cell leader and was one of the church's key youth leaders. Born in Nairobi, Kenya, Mandy is as African as anyone could be. Yet with her outgoing, friendly personality, she found places to serve and quickly made good friends. Steve also had grown up in Africa and had spent all, besides a few weeks, of his 12 years on the continent. He had good friends in church and school in Lusaka and had appointed himself as head children's usher, which he took seriously. When we moved back to the States, Steve found the move tougher than Mandy did. Some time was necessary for him to adjust and make friends at school. He often lamented that he missed Africa because that is where he "fit". We understood how he felt and sometimes ached when we had to send him to school, because we saw the sadness in his face. However, in time, Steve was befriended by a trio of boys in his class and began to do very well. We rejoiced to see both children happy and settled in, but from time to time they would say to us, "Remember in Lusaka when . . .. " At times we saw the distant look in their eyes and knew they felt the same pull we did.

Just as we were becoming accustomed to life, Thanksgiving was on us. Being home together for the holidays was wonderful; many years had passed since our last Thanksgiving with family. We spent the holiday weekend in Georgia at Frank and Tina's cabin (Jamie's sister and brother-in-law) with our family; the food was as wonderful as the company. Being together with Tom was a special treat; the year before, we had been in Lusaka and away from him; we nearly missed celebrating. Observing Thanksgiving in Africa was a bit different than what we had experienced in the U.S. growing up. Most of the time we took the kids out of school (because Thanksgiving is not observed in countries besides the U.S.), invited friends over, cooked whatever we could find, and had a great time. The year before,when we were in Lusaka and separated from Tom, I did not have any heart to cook for anyone. As "Turkey Day" drew near, Jamie asked on several occasions, "What are we doing for Thanksgiving this year?"

I lamely answered, "I don't know."

The day before, Jamie, intent on celebrating, said, "You know, other people are here, too!" Grudgingly, I went to town and found a turkey (a real treat in Africa) and other necessary supplies. I really had no heart for it, though. On Thanksgiving morning, the kids went out to the local shop to purchase some cookies. While they were away, I was attempting to clean up and stuff the turkey.

While I wrestled with the slippery bird, Jamie walked in. When I saw him, I took the raw turkey in my hands, slammed it into the sink, and cried, "I miss Tom! The time we had with him was too short!" I was not taking this separation as gracefully as I had hoped; that, in itself, was an embarrassment. I always have thought that I could put on a brave face and get through the tough times—but being apart for the first time on Thanksgiving was as close to unbearable as anything I ever experienced. God has a strange way of breaking down the walls we build to secure ourselves! That year He proved I was not really as tough as I wanted people (myself included) to think.

Then, in Georgia and enjoying Tom's company and playing games with family, we were unable to shake the emptiness. We were so happy to be with our family, yet we felt a sense of emptiness that always was lurking close to the surface of our hearts. This was puzzling not only to us but to those around us. *Why did we not love life in the States? We should be happy, right?* Here we were, enjoying the conveniences that were not available in Africa (dishwashers) and living together in the same city as our extended family, yet we were not rejoicing every day! We felt guilty in our quandary; we had no excusable reason for not loving our lives! Keeping our emotions in check was a daily struggle.

Christmas and New Year's Day arrived and went; though we loved our special times together with family, to find some kind of security we had to put ourselves on "autopilot". To this point we had not found any solution and found ourselves laying Africa down and closing the door to that part of our lives, so we could look for something else. Weariness had set in as we searched for answers and saw the bewildered look on people's faces when we tried to explain the events of our lifetime on the other side of the world. The once-vivid conversations we shared together became frustrating; neither one of us wanted to hear how the other was feeling, because no resolution was in sight. Eventually we even stopped talking about "how it used to be" and tried to find "how it could be" instead.

Vision

> *Where there is no vision [no redemptive revelation of God], the people perish; but he who keeps the law [of God which includes that of man]–blessed (happy, fortunate, and envied) is he* (Prov. 29:18 AMP).

 Somehow we could not stir ourselves to be excited about the New Year 2006. Our normal anticipation was replaced with weariness. Exciting things were happening: the men's cell was doing great, the women's cell had opened, we were in a great church with a world vision, and we were honored to be even a small part of that vision. Yet, our own ministry vision, which always had been lively and full of anticipation, was gone. In years past we wrote our own personal vision as well as a vision for the work; each year would have a "theme". This year was different. We had no title for the year—nothing for us to reach. In times past, we knew God was moving; that brought joy to us. But even as January went by and we saw our cells grow and the lives of our members change, joy was not there. When anyone would ask us about Africa, that is when the lights really would turn on. One of our cell members mentioned how we would change when the topic of conversation turned to missions, as if something that was "locked" inside was let out! Truly we drew much energy from our cells and the life that was taking place in our meetings. Without those meetings and the relationships we forged in our groups, we most certainly would have been lost!

Moving forward

> *I press on toward the goal to win the [supreme and heavenly] prize*
> *to which God in Christ Jesus is calling us upward* (Phil. 3:14
> AMP).

Our first scheduled trip to Africa was February 2006; we took inventory of how we were feeling and prepared ourselves to be met with upheaval. We knew this first trip would stir up things we had been able to compartmentalize. We might have been better off emotionally not to go at that time, but necessary business on the other side of the world awaited us. Every year we are required by the governments (where our churches are present) to hold board meetings and to report the churches' activities for the year. Since we are on our churches' boards, we needed to travel to take care of these reports.

We landed first in Bujumbura and took time to minister in our church and spend time with our leaders. As we walked the streets of the city in which we had spent nearly 10 of our years on the field, memories flooded our minds. This was the city in which we had lived during the days of civil war and great unrest. In this city we saw mighty movements of the Holy Spirit; during the most difficult times of war many people had been saved. We left when peace had returned but had never seen the city so vibrant—so full of life and potential. We were tempted to think what "could have been" in Bujumbura if we had not gone! But we had gone in 2000. The church, under the capable leadership of Pastor Emmanuel and Jackie, moved on; so had we—to plant other churches.

After our work in Bujumbura was finished, the next part of our trip was to Lusaka. As we landed, memories of our first flight there in 2001 and the feeling of excitement we had at that time for our new church plant rushed over us. We found ourselves in 2006, nearly five years later, visiting the church that had been born and that we had seen grow from a small meeting of eight people in our front yard to a full-fledged church. Members of the church met us with singing and dancing at the guesthouse (owned and run by one of our church members in Lusaka) in which we went to stay. Intent on enjoying the moment we joined in and for the first time in many months felt very much at home.

In Lusaka we had scheduled five days, which were full of activity. Besides board meetings we held leaders' meetings, preached on Sunday morning, and met with old friends; all too soon we needed to return home. As we took our seats on the plane, the all-too-familiar feelings of "Who are we?" returned to us. During the past two weeks in Africa we felt at home; we believed that we knew who we were and what our purpose was in life.

 At that point we began to consider that the time was right to return to Africa. During this trip I had sprung alive and believed that perhaps God had yet more for me to do on the continent. We spent time in prayer and discussion with my father as well as with our kids and began to make tentative plans to return. When we approached them with the possibility of returning to Africa, they were uncertain; they did not know how they felt about going back. While not adamantly opposed to heading back to Africa, they did have reservations. This was coupled with our own inner reservations (we believed perhaps we were being influenced by the emotion of the trip), so we decided that as good as we felt being on the continent, we could not get a clear word from the Lord that returning was His plan. At some level we held out hope for returning to Africa, especially as we remembered the prophecy given over Lea. Yet because we had no strong indication from God to return at that time, we sorrowfully concluded that this may very well have been the end of the African chapter of our lives.

On our return from the trip in February we gave ourselves totally to the work in Florida. A kind of peace settled over us as we offered our Isaac to God—the vision and all of what had been done in Africa. Our children continued to do well in school; we were comforted in being obedient to the will of God. To most people we may have seemed that we had begun to acclimate to life in the States—that the reverse culture shock and re-entry experience was beginning to ease. While to some extent this may have been true, more than recovering from re-entry, we had given up fighting for Isaac and decided the time had arrived to lay him on the altar and worship God—after all, the vision was His.

Worship

> *Then on the third day Abraham lifted his eyes and saw the place afar off. And Abraham said to his young men, "Stay here with the donkey; the lad and I will go yonder and worship, and we will come back to you." So Abraham took the wood of the burnt offering and laid it on Isaac his son; and he took the fire in his hand, and a knife, and the two of them went together* (Gen. 22:4-6).

 The cry of our hearts remained strong for the continent—perhaps stronger than ever before, but we began truly to worship as we offered our hearts to God by laying our "Isaac" down as an offering before Him. Everything that had been done in Africa in the past was past; we had to lay it down to receive vision so we could move forward. We desired to follow Him wholeheartedly without reservation. Before we truly could worship, we had to realize that we had to give up everything for Him. This process took months to accomplish; once it was done, we ceased struggling and simply enjoyed loving God and each other.

A desire accomplished

In May 2005 we had another short trip to Africa. On the way we passed through England, where we attended the wedding of our dear friends,

Cate (previously Barker) and Will Scarlett. Cate trusted the Lord to bring her across the path of someone who loved missions as fervently as she did; true to form, God did just that. Witnessing their marriage was a joy to us; we gladly took a few days in England on our way to Africa to take part in the festivities. Along the way we met with several friends and acquaintances—many voiced their amazement with our relocation. We were as amazed as they were with this relocation but assured everyone that we had left Africa on God's altar; He knew what He was up to; we trusted His judgment more than we did our own! The wedding was a great occasion; many tears were shed as we were witnesses to the hand of God at work in the lives of our dear friends. Almost as soon as we arrived, the festivities were over and we went on with our journey.

Two years before this visit the Bujumbura church had acquired land and was in the middle of an ambitious building project in which we were heavily involved. This was to be among the first permanent church buildings in Africa; we believed that visiting the project as it was under way was important. Strangely enough while we dealt with the various details of building, we felt more at ease during this trip than we had on our trip in February. On several occasions we commented on how we felt the grace of God all over us as we took care of all the business that required our attention. The deep sadness we felt on our earlier trip gave way to peace; maybe we were going to make it after all! While we felt peaceful, tears were not far from us as we said our goodbyes at the airport. These tears were not tears of sadness; rather, they were tears of joy. The church was moving forward; life was going on. That is, in effect, what we always had wanted to see from the churches we planted after we left. Had we left and the work folded—that would have been a failure! Instead of failure we were witnessing fulfillment of our life's work and our dream: the establishment of an indigenous, autonomous, local church.

A desire accomplished is sweet to the soul . . . (Prov. 13:19a).

Chapter 16

Isaac

"God, send me anywhere, only go with me. Lay any burden on me, only sustain me. And sever any tie in my heart except the tie that binds my heart to Yours."

–David Livingstone[46]

What???

 hat a relief to return from Bujumbura with peace in our hearts! We went, expecting to meet with another emotional challenge, much like the one we encountered in February. The change was so remarkable that we nearly were surprised! We actually were able to go for several days at a time without feeling the familiar pain of leaving the work in Africa. Our attention increasingly was drawn to the cells we were overseeing, which had multiplied from two cells to nine. We were ever more taken with establishing the Principle of 12 within the church in Florida. And with our renewed energy we were able truly to give ourselves to the fulfillment of that goal. The next two months were full of activity as we settled in permanently (or so we thought) to work at the church.

Together with the rest of the leadership at TCI we were eager to learn from other churches in the U.S. that successfully had made the transition to the Principle of 12. While we made several trips to visit other churches that already had navigated these waters, one of the connections was with Alex Clattenburg, pastor of Church in the Son in Orlando, FL. A few years before Church in the Son successfully had transitioned into the Principle of 12. The counsel of the people there was an invaluable resource to us as we maneuvered through the waters of transition at TCI in Lake Worth. Not only had their counsel helped us in Florida, it proved to be of vital assistance to our churches in Africa, in which the Principle of 12 already was in use. Pastor Clattenburg and his wife, Judith, planned to hold a luncheon for churches that had embraced the same vision. We felt honored to be invited and looked forward to attending.

Two weeks before we were to attend the luncheon at Church in the Son, I began to feel unsettled. The impression I had was unlike feelings of re-entry but still was familiar and very puzzling. However, so much time had passed since I last experienced this unsettled feeling that I was unsure of its meaning. I remembered the last time I felt this way: it was December 1986, when God first dealt with me about moving to Africa. As a couple we had taken a mission trip to an island off the mainland coast of Haiti, in which TCI assisted in building a church facility. The trip was very difficult, yet during that time was when God dealt with me about moving to Zaire. On a sandy beach, together with the pigs and chickens that roamed freely and under the moonlight, I told my husband I believed we should pray about moving to Africa. I remembered the look he gave me. We both had visited Kenya in 1985 and then he had gone alone for two months to Zaire in 1986, but neither time had God given us the "green light" to become missionaries. Yet, there I was, telling him we should pray about going! Before long Jamie began to feel the same as I; perhaps God had to deal more with me about moving to Africa with a baby than He did with Jamie (at the time Tom was only a year). So there I was, again having the same unsettled feelings as I did in 1986; I remembered that some months later (June 1987) we landed in Kalemie, Zaire, to serve as missionaries. To say that I panicked is an understatement. *How could this be happening?* I did not want to face the inevitable repercussions that would result in moving back to Africa! Questions filled my mind: *What would people say? What would they think? Would people think we were "flaky"? How could we raise enough support to start all over again? What about the kids?* For two weeks in silence

I wrestled with these feelings before we were scheduled to drive to the luncheon in Orlando.

Setting off early the day of the luncheon, we stopped at a Starbucks coffee shop. As we sipped coffee we indulged in a few moments in silence as we stared at the road ahead of us. Slowly we began to talk; our conversation took a more serious turn as I carefully began to open my heart. Struggling with unsettled feelings alone had exhausted me. In the days before our trip my mood had grown increasingly gloomy; I believed I could not continue feeling this way alone. Normally such a trip would have ample time of silence for sleeping, but this was far from silent. After some minutes of dancing around the subject, I blurted out (in my classic demure fashion), "OK, I'll say it; it's time to go home. Take me home; take me to Africa!" Jamie's expression was a picture—he had the same look as he did years ago in Haiti when I said we needed to pray about our first move.

 When I heard Lea say the time had arrived to take her home, I was shaken. She explained how she had been feeling; at first all I could say was, "I thought we had dealt with this already!"

I remembered her approaching me on our trip to Haiti about our first move to Zaire and thought this might be a similar situation. I had always believed that God initially had to deal with Lea about moving to Africa more than He did with me because of her concern for Tom, who at the time was so young. She insisted she believed the time had arrived to return; I did not have difficulty agreeing with her. As the discussion progressed, I remembered the prophecy Kathy Lechner had given her so many months ago and reminded her of what had been said: that we would go out again.

My heart began to pound with anticipation—returning to Africa! *Where would we go? For what country was God preparing us?* While the prospect of returning to Africa was nearly uncontainable, I resisted being too hasty. My practical side began to kick in; I knew I had to consider church responsibilities in Florida, support, the children, the house, and so many other things. This was a big decision to make; I had to be sure it was the right one.

As we drove into Church in the Son's parking lot, our conversation was still in high-gear. We somehow had to return to earth and bring our minds back to what was at hand: the luncheon. Some of the church's staff was at the front door as greeters, but we found entering into normal conversation with others difficult and stood distracted from the activity that surrounded us. Just after our arrival Pastor Clattenburg greeted us and asked how we were doing (he had known of our re-entry experience). Our reply was, "We've just spent three hours talking about that!" No sooner than we spoke those words, the time arrived for us to go in to the meeting. After a light lunch and an encouraging word, we had a time of prayer. Different ones were prayed over as we all agreed together. We had a tough time, however, taking our minds off what God was doing in our lives. Toward the end of our time together, we were called forward for prayer and quietly, Pastor Clattenburg said to us, "You know what you need to do." This was a confirmation of what God that day had stirred in us along the Florida Turnpike. A light had been switched on; we knew exactly what was about to happen: God was going to open a door that no one could shut.

Isaac

Then they came to the place of which God had told him. And Abraham built an altar there and placed the wood in order; and he bound Isaac his son and laid him on the altar on the wood. And Abraham stretched out his hand and took the knife to slay his son. But the Angel of the Lord called to him from heaven and said, "Abraham, Abraham!" So he said, "Here I am." And He said, "Do not lay your hand on the lad, or do anything to him; for now I know that you fear God, since you have not withheld

your son, your only son, from Me." Then Abraham lifted his eyes
and looked, and there behind him was a ram caught in a thicket
by its horns. So Abraham went and took the ram, and offered it
up for a burnt offering instead of his son (Gen. 22:9-13).

 After our time in Orlando a momentum began to build. Before we approached my father, we spent a few more days in prayer. With understanding he heard our news; he almost knew beforehand that this day would arrive. We asked him not to discuss the issue with anyone, since we still were in the praying stages. The month was July; as a family we were preparing for a month-long trip to Africa. We would be going with our missions director, elder, and dear friend David Briggs, and were to depart in less than a week. After our trip we hoped to discuss the matter further with all the elders to hear what they felt about our possible return to missionary service. At that moment our main concern was our children. We decided to let God Himself speak to the two younger kids about returning; we trusted Him with their hearts. Tom was not surprised when we approached him with this news. He laughingly told us, "Make up your minds!" This move, if it were to happen, would affect him as well as us. He needed not only to be informed but also in prayer about making this decision.

A man fighting bees

 The first leg of our travels took us to Nairobi, Kenya, at which I was set to preach at a conference held by our good friends, Pastor Don and Amy Matheny of Nairobi Lighthouse Church. My first step on African soil this time barely touched the ground—I was home! As wonderful as I felt about our being back, I resisted the urge to tell everyone about the possibility of our returning; we still were waiting for the Lord to deal with Mandy and Steve. We also needed to hear from our elders in Florida. The atmosphere of those meet-ings was electric. I was slotted to preach three messages; Pastor Don said that I preached "like a man fighting bees"—as if I had not preached in years.

As we pondered our possible return, Malawi quickly moved to the fore-front of our discussions. Another nation we considered was Mozambique. During the course of this journey we planned to visit both countries. When we lived in Lusaka, we often had passed the Malawi embassy and said that, someday, TCI would plant a church in Malawi. At that time we thought we would send someone else to plant there—assuming that Lusaka was the last church plant we personally would do and that others from that time forward would do the planting. During the conference the Malawi flag, along with flags of other nations, was on display; our eyes often were caught gazing at it and dreaming of the possibility of TCI in Malawi.

 Throughout the first meeting of the conference I could do little more than cry. I had the impression that my spirit re-turned to me after it had been gone for a very long time. The joy and anticipation I felt at the thought of returning to Africa sustained me through the throes of jet lag; for once I was glad not to be bothered with sleepless nights! I anticipated every meeting and prayed fer-vently for the kids, who seemed to be enjoying themselves as much as we were. Nothing is so precious to parents as is witnessing God deal with their children. Jamie and I watched as during nearly every service Mandy wept and as Stephen danced and lifted his hands as he joined into the African worship. God is faithful. He did not need our help in dealing with them—He knew how to get their attention.

Toward the end of our time in Kenya the kids began questioning us about the possibility of ever returning to work as missionaries. At that time we explained to them we already had been praying and had asked the Lord to speak with them Himself. They were elated with the possibility of returning; we, however, waited to see how they felt at the end of the trip. We also cautioned them to be in prayer. The ultimate decision would be made according to the counsel we would receive from our elders at TCI. If the elders had serious reservations about our returning, then we would submit ourselves to them and not return. Also, we knew this was just the first stop of several; we were aware that the days ahead could bring frustrations and setbacks that are common occurrences in day-to-day life in Africa. We knew this also could affect them.

Building in Burundi

 On the final Saturday morning of the conference, we boarded our flight and headed for Bujumbura, where we were going to check on the progress of the building project that was well under way. David Briggs, TCI's senior pastor in Bujumbura, Emmanuel Nkunku, and I together poured over the plans for the building. The dream that the first church we planted would have its own building soon was to be a reality! A contractor with his own company in Bujumbura was hired, but we wanted to look over the plans before the major portions of the structure went up. The building was drawn to seat 1,000 and to have ample office space and classrooms for educational outreaches to the community. The day we took part in the actual groundbreaking, the dream moved closer to reality. While people outside our circle may have thought that it was a small and meaningless ceremony done with little planning, it could not have held more meaning had it been held with pomp and circumstance and all with the bells and whistles one could imagine. God allowed us to see and take part in it; we were so thankful!

Crossing the border

As we landed in Lusaka, our excitement was increasing. A day might be about to arrive in which we would be returning to join the front-line battle for souls in Africa. We were only in Lusaka for a couple of days as we prepared to drive from Lusaka to Lubumbashi, in which another TCI church was planted in 2003. Our plan was to visit the Lusaka church after the Lubumbashi portion of our trip. Since we had visited only the Lubumbashi church once before, we felt an urgent need to go and encourage the senior pastor, Pastor Wilondja, and his congregation. The drive to Lubumbashi, Congo, from Lusaka, Zambia, is 11 hours. While the roads in Zambia are quite good, traveling at night is unsafe. We felt pressed to leave early in the morning; we not only wanted to avoid driving after sunset but also to arrive at the border before it closed at 6 p.m. The car was full of luggage and passengers, but we laughed almost all the way to Congo.

On our arrival at the border we were met with vendors of every type: one young man offered to give us a haircut, another was selling kitchen knives, and yet another offered to wash the windscreen for a price. Everything in Congo has its price; distinguishing between what is extortion, bribery, and actual legal fees is difficult. Jamie bravely circulated from office to office to obtain one stamp and the other; because of our obvious "foreigner-ness" he got the unavoidable run-around. One hour of waiting turned into two. Three hours later we were allowed to pass through but not before the officials at the border took our car papers. This was curious, but later we learned common practice in Congo is for visiting vehicles to have their papers confiscated at the border and then returned to them as the visitors leave the country. The entire process, between one fee and another, cost us around $300—each one, of course, had its own receipt and was difficult to argue. Just as we pulled out, relieved because we believed all the chaos was behind us, we drove up to a little building, at which we were told to stop and pay a $50 road tax. That $50 is more than most Congolese see in a month. How could the people there possibly expect every car passing through to pay $50? The answer to that question never was answered; the tax was coughed up; an official receipt was issued. Being officially "had" did not feel good, but we could do little more but pay! David Briggs later remarked that an invading army could not attack Congo because it could not afford the border crossing!

The next morning when Pastor Wilondja arrived at the hotel, we followed him to the place in which the church was meeting: a tent shipped from Bujumbura to Lubumbashi. This was the same tent that the Gatumba church had used when it first was planted. The team then met together with the congregation, which was alive with Congolese enthusiasm. We do not believe any other group of people can sing and dance as the Congolese do. The church choir had prepared special songs and dances for us; we were thrilled to meet in the tent—this made the border crossing worthwhile and only a memory that paled in the face of seeing our people. Over the course of several days we held meetings in the morning and evening; the kids never complained! Mandy sang a special song in Bemba (one of the languages used in Zambia); this caused the crowd to roar with applause. She was precious to watch. But while she loved her time in Congo, she was ready to return to Lusaka. As we were driving, we told the kids that only real missionaries go to Congo. Mandy, quick to reply, said, "Smart missionaries go to Zambia!"

Worth the effort

 The 11-hour journey back to Lusaka from Lubumbashi was uneventful; we enjoyed settling into the same guesthouse that during our last trip in February had received us. During those days in Lusaka many church members visited us; among them was Joyce. In 2001 I had led Joyce to the Lord. Each day in our neighborhood she set up a little shop, in which she sold eggs, bread, sugar, and other basic groceries. I would jog around the neighborhood (a spectacle in and of itself) and attempt to communicate with Joyce as I rounded the corner by her shop. After some time we learned the local language (Nyanja). Then I was able to present the gospel to Joyce, who eventually gave her life to the Lord. Joyce now sat before me; she was a cell leader in the church and helped many new believers grow in the Lord. I thought of how all the years of work had been worth the effort for this precious soul.

Mandy and Steve quickly reconnected with their friends; for both of them the fit was easy. One evening after a long day of meetings I passed by Mandy's room, in which I found her and Steve in tears. Concerned, I asked them what was wrong. Steadying herself Mandy asked me, "What if we do not get to come back?" Sitting down with both of them I explained that we trust our leaders; they never have led us down a wrong path. If, on our return to the U.S., they said that in their spirits they did not feel good about us returning, then we would follow their wishes. I further explained to her that God had placed these advisers in our lives for our safety and not to hinder us! We have to trust that they will hear from God, just as they always have before. If this feeling of returning to Africa is right, they will release us to the will of God because they are people of prayer. So all we could do was trust God. Inwardly I rejoiced because the call was hitting both of them hard. I knew God was working; we all were in unity about this. Even further this assured me that this move really was a work of the Holy Spirit.

We're not just praying about this anymore, are we?

 Our plans had us driving to Lilongwe, Malawi, after our time in Lusaka had closed. Lilongwe is a full-day's drive from Lusaka; the border closes sometime around 6 p.m., so we got off to an early start. As they had to Lubumbashi Pastor

Richard and Nadine accompanied us on our trip. Together with our family and David we made our way to Malawi. Even during the dry season the landscape between Lusaka and Lilongwe is particularly beautiful. We enjoyed the view of mountains, traditional villages, and miles of uninterrupted African scenery. By this time we should have been travel-weary, but we had boundless energy. This was Africa!

Tucked into one of our bags was a copy of our constitution we used when we registered our churches. We had not necessarily planned to enter a formal request for registration, but we had the constitution just in case. The next morning, leaving everyone else behind at the hotel, we went to find out information about registering the church. Every country in Africa is unique; what works for registration in one country will not necessarily apply in other countries. Therefore we began our quest by asking the hotel receptionist where the government offices were situated. After we heard some explaining, we learned that the government offices in Lilongwe were in an area known as "Capital Hill." Taking our time to negotiate the unfamiliar city we eventually found Capital Hill and entered a building we hoped housed an office that could give us some information. The first one we entered actually was the Office of Immigration; however, the people there were able to direct us to the proper place. Some minutes later we found ourselves at the Ministry of Home Affairs, in which all registrations of churches took place. There we were directed to go to Blantyre (four hours by car), the point at which all files first are received. Once files are received in Blantyre by what is known as the Registrar General, they then are sent back up to the Ministry of Home Affairs in Lilongwe. Initially we viewed the news with disappointment. But we did not take long (perhaps five minutes at most) to conclude that that very afternoon we would drive to Blantyre. We rushed back to the hotel to eat lunch and pay the hotel bill so we could get on the road before the hour was too late.

Not long after hearing that we were going to drive to Blantyre, David said, jokingly, "We're not praying about this anymore, are we?" Laughing, we agreed we had no reservations about returning. Even if we did not return for whatever reason, registering the church in a new country would not be a wasted effort. We have a vision to see 1,000 churches planted; the church eventually has to be registered in many countries on the continent! Eventually someone who would start the work if we were not going to be the ones to establish TCI in Malawi would be found.

Plans to fly to Mozambique after our trip to Malawi were made before this side trip. However, with our path being led to Blantyre, we knew the trip to Mozambique was going to be taken at another time. As we canceled the flights to Mozambique, with every passing hour the burden we felt for the nation of Malawi grew stronger.

One evening, as I was talking with David, he began to cry as he said, "Jamie, I've seen dead bones come to life here!" He went on to say how sometimes God asks us for our "Isaac". When we have given Him what He has asked, He returns it to us. His perception of what God was doing in me was uncanny; I had sprung back to life again. God had returned to me; He had provided the sacrifice for Himself.

We soon found the Registrar General's office and, with the help and counsel of a local lawyer, filled out all the paperwork and made the necessary adjustments to our constitution to make it legal according to Malawian law. On our second day in Blantyre we finished the application and submitted it. We had such favor with those at the Registrar General's office that they allowed us to courier the file, after it officially had been received at their office, to the Ministry of Home Affairs in Lilongwe. Normally the process of getting the file to Lilongwe could, in itself, take weeks. This way we cut off a potential weeks-long delay. We left those offices amazed at the favor God had given us before all those officials. The next morning we drove to Lilongwe and deposited the file at the Ministry of Home Affairs. What remained for us was to wait for its response, which we hoped would occur sooner rather than later. We arranged for our lawyer to communicate with us via email about any news he would receive about the file.

The end of our month-long journey swiftly approached. Driving back to Lusaka from Lilongwe we left in the hands of God the entire dream of returning. The possibility of everything we were planning was very real; we could only trust God with the outcome. Also our elders at home had yet to give us their point of view in the matter. A burden for Malawi had been set into our hearts and spirits; it was like a fire that could not be put out. We were as sure about Malawi as we had been about Zaire in 1987. Likewise the kids were as sure in their conviction; this only fueled the fire! If God truly was returning our Isaac to us, we still were in the "faith stages" of the process, because we had yet to face everyone else in the U.S. with the news. We prayed for strength and grace to meet the task, which we knew would be massive.

On Thursday, August 10, our plane arrived in South Florida. Almost immediately after our return I spoke with my father. I wanted to talk with him about what I strongly believed to be the leading of God—returning to Africa. As I sat before him, before I said anything he knew that this was what I was going to say. Dad, in his wisdom, already had talked with the other elders. They unanimously released us to do the will of God.

The nuts and bolts of moving

Those who never have experienced it often take for granted the nuts and bolts of arranging such a move. While we waited for the lawyer in Malawi to give us news about our file, we focused on making arrangements for the house and cars, closed out Internet accounts, and set out tying up all the other loose ends. The kids had been set to start school, but with the move we decided they would do better to pursue their education via a DVD curriculum by the accredited A Beka Academy in Pensacola. While the switch to DVD school was an adjustment for them, Mandy and Steve did not waver once in their commitment to return to Africa. This amazed both of us, because most teen-agers immediately would balk at the thought of leaving the U.S. for missionary life in Africa. What a supernatural time in the life of our family! All of us were totally committed to the fulfillment of the vision God had resurrected in our hearts for 1,000 churches on the continent.

Tough choices

 As we prepared for our move, we eagerly waited to hear from the lawyer in Malawi. Our tickets were purchased; our departure date was set for November 4, the day before Tom's 21st birthday. We purchased our tickets by using the travel points we had accumulated throughout many years of traveling. The only date available for us to use our points was on November 4 or later in December, which really was not an option in light of where the church's file stood in Malawi.

When we left, Tom, still in school, would move back in with his grandparents; the sting of being apart once again began to rise up. From the outside looking in this decision to move could have been translated into neglect of our older son with no thought given about him and his future. On the contrary we were painfully aware of its repercussions on not only ourselves but also Tom and the other children. Moving again meant we would be separated from Tom. It also meant that two to two-and-a-half years down the road Mandy would finish high school and be leaving us, too. We were determined to use the experience of leaving again as a means of teaching our children a very valuable lesson. Over dinner one evening we explained that the most important thing to do in life is follow the will of God. We believe that God was using this experience to teach them to follow His will, no matter what they will face in the future. This was, perhaps, the most important lesson we ever had taught them.

The complications brought on by moving were far greater than any comfort we may have felt in returning to the continent because we were accustomed to African life. We simply had the assurance that the choice we made was the right one, even though it was more painful for our family. Additionally that choice brought with it much pain at the thought of separation, not only from our own parents, but even more so from our own children. Growing together on the mission field brings a kind of uncommon intimacy and camaraderie within the family. When the time arrives for a child to move on and further his/her education, it is extremely painful. A missionary child who moves away is not moving to another city or state; he/she is moving to another continent and away from parents who had to work extra diligently to raise that young person in foreign surroundings. This was definitely not the easier path to take.

Hiccups

Time quickly was passing; we wondered what was happening with our file in Malawi. To try to get some information we made several phone calls to our lawyer, who, after some days, was able to give us some news. Sadly, it was not the news for which hoped, which would have been the approval to start the church. He explained that the file had been sent back to Blantyre for "corrections". Some issues had cropped up with the constitution and other things that were difficult to understand over the telephone or email. This news put increasing pressure on us to get to Malawi quickly. Our experience taught us that registrations must be followed through with persistence. Following through from the other side of the world was difficult. We did not share this news with anyone except my father and David Briggs. We knew these were normal "hiccups" that were to be expected in the registration process. But those who did not know the routine could have misinterpreted the "hiccup" as a "sign" that we possibly were out of the will of God.

Not only were we pressed to get on our way, we also found ourselves in a hurry to sell our house as well as to liquidate what was in the house. Some furniture was left, other pieces were given away, some were sold, and finally, a buyer for the house was found. The sale was not yet settled, because the buyers were waiting to qualify for their loan, which was not going to happen before our departure date. We agreed for the buyers to pay us rent in the amount of our mortgage payment until the loan was approved. While we were not happy about leaving while the sale of the house was still "up in the air", our tickets already were bought and nonrefundable. Most important of all, we had a peace in our hearts that all was well.

Our cells held going-away parties for us; we felt closer to those we were leaving behind than we had the first time we left in 1987. These people were the ones who had comforted us when we cried for Africa, were patient with us when we were adjusting to living in the U.S., and now were the ones who with tears were sending us off. We were humbled to be loved by these wonderful people; we forever are grateful to them for their support and encouragement throughout this process through which God had brought us in the States.

Saying goodbye never gets any easier

As we watched Tom move his things, I felt the familiar lump begin to rise in my throat. In classic Tom fashion he waited until the day before we left to begin moving his things from his room. Actually for him to do things that way probably was better; I don't think either of us could have dealt with seeing him leave before the actual day of our departure. We all decided that our goodbyes the day we left would be quick. Tom had work; we had to finish tying up the loose ends that inevitably occur during such a move. For his birthday we ordered him a gift, which, for some reason, had yet to arrive. Disappointed with the delay, that morning I checked on the status of our online order and found out that, because of our address change, the order had been canceled. Tears stung my eyes as I explained the order had been canceled but that we would give him money instead. When I ordered his gift, I ordered a happy birthday message to be put into the box. Now here we sat with no gift, no card, and a miserable me, who berated myself for being a poor parent. Tom is a forgiving soul and said it was not a big deal; but it was a big deal. Internally I scolded myself for not having checked on the order sooner. Had I done so, perhaps I could have avoided this scenario. Instead, the day before our son's birthday—his 21st birthday—we were handing him money with no card instead of a gift we carefully had planned and one we knew he would have liked. At that moment I was inconsolable.

As a family we prayed together; we understood that this most likely was the last time we would live together. This made us pray all the more fervently for our son who was staying behind. He would have adjustments to make as well as we would. We were conscious of that fact and hoped somehow he understood that we understood! After prayer we all attempted, through tears, to make light of the separation. We would be returning in just a short while to attend Trinity's World Missions Conference (we had long planned to attend together with our African pastors and their wives) and would see each other then. Internally this fact did not help us very much at all. As they said goodbye, Mandy and Steve, who loved and respected their older brother, shed many tears. We both steeled ourselves, but that did not help. We cried as we hugged him goodbye and watched him drive away. Somehow we had learned to let him go, but that did not make seeing him leave any easier.

Finally we said our goodbyes to family and friends. And as suddenly as we drove into our driveway just over a year earlier, for the last time we drove away from our house. The new owners (whose loan ultimately was approved) had the keys; our 14 bags and carry-ons were packed into the trailer being towed by the van transporting us to the airport. For us to be setting off again was surreal, because we felt as though our year and four months in the U.S. had been a dream and that we were being stirred to wake up.

Not knowing the things that will happen there . . .

> And see, now I go bound in the spirit to Jerusalem, not knowing the things that will happen to me there, except that the Holy Spirit testifies in every city, saying that chains and tribulations await me. But none of these things move me; nor do I count my life dear to myself, so that I may finish my race with joy, and the ministry which I received from the Lord Jesus, to testify to the gospel of the grace of God (Acts 20:22-24).

 When he went *bound in the spirit* to Jerusalem, Paul was in the will of God. He seems only to have known that he had to go to Jerusalem and preach the gospel. He was not sure about anything else that was waiting for him there on the other side of his obedience to the heavenly vision. He just knew he had to go. Later Acts records some of the difficulties Paul encountered not only along the way to Jerusalem but also when he arrived. He was arrested and jailed as he faced multitudes of angry people who were accusing him of blasphemy. Paul, knowing beforehand that complications most likely would arise, said, *None of these things move me.* He apparently believed that problems were not an indication of being out of the will of God. Problems were Satan's way of trying to dissuade him from finishing his course, but none of those things moved him. We knew that along the way, we would most likely face complications, troubles, and tests—but nothing persuaded us from going *bound in the Spirit* to the place to which we knew God had called us: Malawi.

Here was the Peters family

 Our trip brought us through Europe on our way to Africa. In Europe everything is small and quiet compared to things in the U.S. We were a great spectacle for everyone as we maneuvered around and transported all those bags. Most people in the airport were carrying one and perhaps two bags at the most. But here was the Peters family with 14 bags plus carry-ons in tow! We developed a system of having two of us wait with one pile of bags while two others undertook the process of moving the mound from one place to the next. Passersby would stare; others would lose their footing as they gazed at four people moving through the airport with our whole household in tow. Not only did we have to get our bags around in one airport, we had to move them by bus from one airport to another! Because of security reasons the airline no longer was handling bags between airport transfers; we were left to our own devices to find a way to get everything but the kitchen sink from one place to the next. Nothing is cheap in Europe; we did our best to move everything with as little paid assistance as possible. We found that even the women of our family, when inspired, could lift heavy bags!

All of the bags did arrive safely at our first destination—Lusaka, Zambia. Because of the fact that no direct flights existed from Europe to Malawi, we decided to fly into Lusaka, in which once again we could arrange to rent a vehicle to drive to Malawi.

It shall not come near you

> *A thousand may fall at your side, and ten thousand at your right hand; but it shall not come near you. Only with your eyes shall you look, and see the reward of the wicked (Ps. 91:7-8).*

After we spent the weekend with our church in Lusaka, we set out early on Monday morning, November 13, for Lilongwe, Malawi. Pastor Richard and his wife, Nadine, were accompanying us (we had planned to see to the church file together with them once we arrived in the country). Our good friend, Selenie, who had arrived from Burundi to work with us in Malawi, also traveled with us. Selenie had been with us when we planted the Lusaka church in 2001 and was a vital member of our church-planting team. The vehicle was a large, 15-seat van which held everyone's bags (now 19 in number with our additional passengers) and in relative comfort seated all seven passengers.

For the first leg of the journey I took the wheel. Since the vehicle was from Lusaka, Pastor Richard would have to drive it back. After driving it for several hours, I believed he should drive for a while to become accustomed to handling the vehicle when he returned. So he took over; I, sitting in the front passenger seat, rested while he drove. The road to the border is quite smooth except for one stretch that was riddled with potholes and was under repair. These areas require careful navigation, especially when a vehicle carries a load such as ours. As Richard, unaccustomed to driving under these conditions, worked his way around the potholes, he swerved in an attempt to miss a deep hole. In so doing he inadvertently hit a pothole, which caused the van to begin to roll off the side of the road. I cried out, "Oh, no!"

In the back the women screamed, "Jesus!"

This could not be happening! The only seats that were equipped with seatbelts were the ones in front in which Richard and I were seated (and we had them buckled). Everyone else in the back rolled unprotected with all the luggage as the vehicle turned over twice, slid on its right side, and finally rested on its roof.

Steve was the first to emerge out of one of the side windows. He was clutching his Game Boy™ in his hands and had the presence of mind to save his game before he put it away! I found myself upside-down and still buckled into my seatbelt. At first I tried to break open the window beside me to get out, but when I realized Steve had made his way through a side window, I unbuckled my seatbelt and followed his way out; Richard followed suit. Devastated by the accident and not knowing whether anyone was hurt or dead, Richard screamed, "No! No! No!"

Once I was out, I began calling out, "Is everyone alright?"

 Mandy, not realizing he already had climbed out, called for Steve. When he did not answer, she began to panic and cried out for him all the more. She thought something bad might have happened to him but calmed down after a moment when she realized Steve was fine. I was still in the van. Seeing her upside-down I asked her whether she was OK. She replied, "I think so." Seeing her panic I told her to begin climbing out of the side window. She again said, "OK." Everyone exited from the same window Steve found. I was the last one in the vehicle; I took a moment to gather my senses. I knew thieves often profit from these kinds of situations, so I had the mind to get Jamie's briefcase (which held all our passports and money) and everyone else's important bags. Jamie began to get impatient with me as I seemed to be slow in getting out. He thought the vehicle possibly might catch fire as oil and other engine fluids were leaking out of the car. I handed the bags out to him and Richard. They finally pulled me from the van; I stared in disbelief at the scene before me.

The van was upside-down, oil and other fluids were leaking from the engine, the front windshield was shattered, and the wheels still were spinning. I walked over to see how everyone was; I was blessed to find everyone OK. We had some bumps and bruises, which would heal, but generally speaking, no injuries needed urgent medical attention. Perhaps 100 times I hugged and kissed Mandy and Steve as the relief of their being alright rushed over me. Looking at the vehicle I understood we miraculously had been saved from serious injury or death. Had the front windshield not been shatterproof, the glass might seriously have injured us as it flew into the van. As things were, a scratch hardly could be found on anyone. Not only had we been saved from harm, no pedestrians were touched in the accident. In addition we saw neither trees nor deep embankments that could have made things much worse. This was God's protection; we saw with our eyes the reward of the wicked—but it did not touch us!

 At the same time we were emerging from the van, cars stopped and people offered to help us. An entire busload of people stopped to help us; their kindness was amazing. When something such as an accident occurs in Africa, people understand that emergency services are unavailable to bring help (especially in rural areas such as we were driving through). A woman who was a nurse in the next town called *Chipata* (about 30 miles away) examined us for injuries and volunteered to bring Nadine and Selenie to the hospital at which she worked. She wanted to make sure they were OK. We took her phone number and arranged that later on in the day we would collect the women.

Another vehicle stopped to help us and took Lea and Mandy to find a guesthouse in town as well as to bring the police back to begin writing up the accident report. Since the vehicle the people were driving was a pickup truck, we quickly were able to get most of our luggage transported away from the scene of the accident. That was very helpful because, by this time, a great crowd of people was standing by and watching everything that was taking place. I stayed at the scene with Steve and Pastor Richard and waited for Lea to return with the police.

I settled Mandy into the car and did my best to comfort my daughter who, without the intervention of God, just moments before could have been taken from me. Finding that my cell phone was not damaged, I sent a text message to Tom to have Jamie's father call me because we had an emergency. Dad called and I explained what happened. Together we had a quick word of prayer. He encouraged me to let everyone know that the church back home was praying. Those prayers certainly had their effect as we worked through that time.

Once we got to town, I left Mandy with the luggage at the guesthouse and then with the police made my way back to the scene of the accident. Meanwhile Jamie, waiting for me to return, worked with Richard and those who had stopped to help us to right the vehicle. Clearly the van could not be turned over without the help of another vehicle. A lorry passing by had a cable that the people in it hitched to the van. With the help of the lorry the vehicle was turned upright and set onto the road. Jamie met another man (who owned a farm nearby) who offered to use his truck to help tow our vehicle to town. As I was being escorted by the police to the scene of the accident, I met Jamie on the road with the van in tow. The van was taken to the police station; we finished filing the report. Thankfully, because no one else was involved in the accident, filing the report was less complicated than it otherwise would have been.

In the evening after we filed the police report and collected the women from the hospital, we gathered for dinner. The relief we all felt was tangible; we held hands around the table and gave thanks not only for our safety but also for how God in the hours after the accident had helped us. While several of the bags were destroyed and had to be replaced, nothing that was in the bags had been broken. The only thing that had been stolen was Steve's DVD player that Tom had given him for his birthday. In every way the outcome could have been much worse.

The hospital the women visited was little more than a small clinic; had someone been seriously injured, the hospital really could have done little. Additionally, without the help that local people gave to us, finding a safe place to stay, towing the van back to town, and filing the police report would have been very difficult.

The entire experience, while designed to slow us down or perhaps stop our progress, actually served to kindle the flame further as we saw God's hand guiding us the whole way. Satan obviously was mustering his forces, because he had reason to fear the work that was about to be born. We had to get to Malawi and plant the church.

The next morning, after we called Lusaka and notified the vehicle owner of the accident, we arranged to get on our way. The man who helped us tow the van to town had another vehicle, a Landcruiser. For a price he would drive us to Malawi. We agreed to pay him $250. At the time we were only 20 minutes from the border; the drive to Lilongwe from the border was only one-and-a-half hours. Since we had so many pieces of luggage, we did not have many other options in the matter. Pastor Richard and Nadine purchased bus tickets and planned to return to Lusaka. They did not have much heart to continue on the journey! The Landcruiser was loaded with all the bags—with about 10 suitcases tied to the luggage rack on top. The rest somehow fit inside. We insisted on the driver being very careful. With all the bags on top this easily could have caused that vehicle to roll out of control.

 We easily reached the border, at which I began the process of crossing into Malawi. For up to 90 days Americans visiting Malawi can stay in the country without special visas; before we left, in Zambia we had acquired a visa for Selenie. With the luggage we were carrying, I knew we were conspicuous. One cannot easily explain to border officials that (1) our registration was pending, (2) we were entering the country to see the registration procedure through, and (3) we were going to apply for work permits, which would allow us to live and work long-term in the country. Saying a prayer under my breath, I left everyone in the vehicle and entered the building. We followed the process of entering the country. Not one question was asked; not one bag was opened. We simply passed through quickly and were on our way to take back our Isaac.

Chapter 17

Someone Was Waiting

"There's someone waiting for you on the other side of your obedience."

–Unknown

Starting over again

We are hard-pressed on every side, yet not crushed; we are perplexed, but not in despair; persecuted, but not forsaken, struck down, but not destroyed (2 Cor. 4:8-9).

Planting a church in a foreign country is much more complicated than is simply renting a building somewhere, opening the doors, and having a service on Sunday morning. Not every country in the world allows churches to operate as freely as churches do in the U.S. In Africa churches first must be registered for them to operate legally. Not following correct protocol for opening a church could, in the long run, actually hinder its work. Much more was to be considered in moving than just having a church service; God had to keep parting the seas before us. I think He prefers to do things this way for our benefit, so we will not ever be tempted to think that to bring the victory we did something besides obey Him!

Travel-weary we drove into Lilongwe on Tuesday night, November 14, and spent the night at a guesthouse that we found during our last visit. The rooms were ready for us. As we once again worked to move the luggage from one place to another, we marveled at God's goodness—we had arrived! Despite all of the expenses we incurred with hotels, excess baggage, duty, the original rental car from Lusaka and its insurance deductible, the replacement vehicle that drove us into Lilongwe, and now all the expenses that awaited us as we worked to settle into life in Malawi, we were up to face the challenge. Each time God had supplied for each need. He paid for this journey so far; we were sure He would take care of the rest that was ahead of us.

Our first morning in Lilongwe in the guesthouse, we all sat together and had devotions over the breakfast table. With prayer for safety and wisdom we bathed the day, because we knew we had much work to do before we even could see to the church's file waiting for us in Blantyre. That morning the kids and Selenie stayed behind as we set out on foot to find a place in which we could rent a car. Everything hinged on our being mobile. Without a car we could not possibly find a house, furniture, kitchen utensils, bedding, or anything else. Thankfully the guesthouse was situated near a hotel in which we were able to get information on car rentals. By the end of the morning we were in a vehicle (with battery issues) and began working toward settling in.

By Saturday a house was found; a car was purchased; mattresses, bedding, cookware, and plates were moved in; and we began setting up our new home. Not until later did we understand that for us to get into a house so soon was a miracle. One of our neighbors told us their family members stayed in a guesthouse for two months while they searched for a place in which to live. In less than a week God had answered our prayer. Not only did we find a house, we also had so much favor with the landlord that for the first two weeks she allowed us to live rent-free. Much longer was necessary, however, to sort out the practicalities of life, but at least we were in a place we could call our own!

Once the family was somewhat settled and the kids were back to the grind of DVD school, we had to get busy and see to the church file. Early on a Wednesday morning we left for Blantyre and arrived there around noon. The lawyer was expecting us and explained all of the "corrections" that we needed to do. In fact getting them done was far less complicated than we originally had thought. All that needed our attention were two minor details that did not change any of the substance of our constitution. Once that was complete, we got back into the car and the same day drove home to Lilongwe. The waiting game began again; we fervently prayed for favor that before Christmas the church registration issue would be resolved successfully.

Meanwhile, we had met some people and led them to the Lord. Because of the stage in which we found ourselves with the church file, we could not have large-scale meetings. However, we legally could have small gatherings at home; on Sunday mornings we began to hold these as a cell group.

Swiftly we realized that for us to work effectively in the nation, we had to learn the local language known as *Chichewa*. Malawi was colonized by England, but only a small percentage of the population communicates effectively in English. While learning another language was daunting, we were comforted by the fact that Chichewa is closely related to Nyanja—the language we learned while we were in Zambia. Armed with the ability to speak Nyanja we tackled studying Chichewa and slowly grew in our fluency of the language.

Christmas was drawing near; we decided to have a small Christmas party for the members. We did this on Sunday morning. Forty-nine people showed up, so it became a very large "small" party! During this time we continued to be strong in our stance for the registration to be released, so we officially could open the church, rent a facility, and get things going.

During my years of missionary service I have learned to be very persistent when seeing to official church business such as registration. Files easily can be left to the side and forgotten, but in our case I was not about to allow that to happen. My persistence gave me entrance to the officials at the Ministry of Home Affairs in Lilongwe. I obtained phone numbers and began making telephone calls. Many times I was told to "call back in the afternoon" or "sometime next week". Obviously people did not realize that, when I was told to call back, I indeed would call back. At the office one person in particular began to lose patience with me and referred me to another individual with whom she would rather have me speak about the file. I thanked her for her help and called this man, who appeared to be sympathetic to our situation. I explained that we were missionaries and were waiting for the registration of our church to be released. I told him that without the registration, we could not apply for work permits, rent a facility, or do anything for the benefit of the people. Because the year was ending, he said, we would have to wait until the holidays were over before the minister (who ultimately approves and signs church registrations) was back in the office to see to business. Thanking him, I hung up and kept believing for favor!

"Because of his persistence he will rise and give him . . .. "

> *"I say to you, though he will not rise and give to him because he is his friend, yet because of his persistence he will rise and give him as many as he needs. So I say to you, ask, and it will be given to you; seek, and you will find; knock, and it will be opened to you. For everyone who asks receives, and he who seeks finds, and to him who knocks it will be opened"* (Luke 11:8-10).

 The will of God is not something that simply is handed to us on a silver platter. Rather it is something for which we have to fight. In Matthew 11:12 Jesus said that the kingdom of God has to be taken with force, which includes the will of God. We cannot take a kingdom simply by standing by and hoping it merely will fall into our laps. We must be forceful in the spirit; that force calls us to be persistent never to give up in the face of apparent hindrances or defeats. In this endeavor Satan was not about to make things easy for us. We had to fight back in the spirit and take by force the will of God for our lives. When our church's file was concerned, we kept on asking, seeking, and knocking on every door we could find. Somehow God was going to open a door of favor! We also proclaimed the favor of God over our file; we understood His Divine favor is what would protect us.

For You, O Lord, will bless the righteous; with favor You will surround him as with a shield (Ps. 5:12).

 We knew God had called us to Malawi. We knew our mandate had brought us this far. God brought us to this point by providing for us financially, protecting us in the accident, getting us through the border, and helping us find a house. At this point He certainly was not going to allow us to be defeated.

The New Year arrived on a Monday; we purposed to call our contact on Thursday that week. I realized that, after a long holiday, work would be piled up; a few days to sort things out might be necessary. Each day we prayed and rejoiced in faith that the approval was imminent. When Thursday finally arrived, I called the office. Once again I was told to call back tomorrow because the people in the office could not clearly see whether our file had yet been approved. Resisting the urge to be impatient I did my best to be gracious and hung up the phone, only to call back the next day (Friday). In the morning I held myself back from calling early. I wanted to give the people ample time to see to everything at the office. When I finally did call, I was given the news that the file indeed had been approved but would not be released until Monday. Keeping this good news quiet was difficult; but, we were wise to wait until the registration certificate was in hand before we announced anything. On Monday afternoon, we were told to visit the office, where our certificate of registration was handed to us with the minister's signature. We were approved! The best part of all was the date the certificate had been signed: December 22, 2006, three days before Christmas! We truly had our answer before we even saw it.

Not losing heart

> *Therefore we do not lose heart. Even though our outward man is perishing, yet the inward man is being renewed day by day. For our light affliction, which is but for a moment, is working for us a far more exceeding and eternal weight of glory, while we do not look at the things which are seen but at the things which are not seen. For the things which are seen are temporary, but the things which are not seen are eternal* (2 Cor. 4:16-18).

Not many people can say they have lived their life's dream, yet, here we were living the dream God gave us. We have lived through painful choices, good and not-so-good experiences, separations, wars, and times in which we had to live day-to-day—times in which we did not know how God was going to provide (which He always has and always will). In all that time we never have regretted a moment of the life God has given us. As agonizing as the experience of leaving Africa in 2005 was and then the subsequent experience of having to go through all the difficulty and pain that was involved in leaving the States in 2006, we do not regret the path we have taken. Everything through which we lived and for which we worked had brought us to this moment in which we stood ready to see another church born.

What could possibly be worth this path? What is . . . worth the price of leaving family behind—especially our own child—not only in another country but on another continent? What is . . . worth being misinterpreted and misunderstood? These things are, so aptly referred to by Paul, as *our light affliction*. They all are temporary and actually are working for, not against, us. These bumps and curves along the road are counted as that heavenly *weight of glory* we all are working toward and one day hope to carry. Even more so, what makes this life worth it are the souls affected for the kingdom of God. Everything else fades into insignificance in the face of the reason we are on this earth: for the saving of the souls of men and women.

> *Yes, and if I am being poured out as a drink offering on the sacrifice and service of your faith, I am glad and rejoice with you all* (Phil. 2:17).

Feeding the children

 As with all our churches, during the week after we initiated our Sunday-morning celebration service, we began meeting in cell groups. The celebration service was held at a local warehouse. I started a ladies' cell in a village on the outskirts of town in which we had won some people to the Lord. The first thing I noticed was the deplorable conditions in which the people lived; these were, in some ways, worse than what we saw during the war in Burundi. Many children had the telltale signs of malnutrition: discolored hair, distended stomachs, and general malaise. Until that time I did not realize the desperate condition of the people.

Malawi is one of the poorest nations of the world. Most of her citizens live below the poverty line and earn less than $1 per day.[47] Many households are led by children under the age of 16, HIV/AIDS has hit the nation especially hard, and reports put the total number of orphans at 850,000 to 1.2 million.[48] Of the children who are orphaned, hundreds of thousands live from day to day without proper shelter. The scale of the problem we faced was staggering and only could be addressed by a supernatural movement of God.

I knew that for me to sit by, lead my ladies' cell group, and not be part of God's solution for these people . . . for the children . . . would be impossible. On hearing of the children's plight Joyce Meyer Ministries quickly partnered with us. On Thanksgiving Day 2007 before we had our own Thanksgiving meal, we   and fed 200 little ones. The day was unique because we knew this was just the very beginning of a very special outpouring of God's love into the communities. The outreach swiftly took on a life of its own; within a matter of weeks daily we were feeding upward of 800 children. The chief of the village allowed us to build in a central area of the village a temporary, grass-roofed structure in which we concentrated our activities. While this was a blessing, it was not suitable as a permanent way to house the outreach. Young men who were drunk often troubled us; youth would show up and start problems. I wondered how God kept things in check. As we cooked and taught the children, we had no security whatsoever; only by the grace of God did nothing happen while we were feeding under those circumstances.

In April 2008 God once again blessed us when Joyce Meyer Ministries stepped in and purchased a piece of property in the village (called *Mtsiliza*) for the feeding outreach and had a wire fence put up for security. At our new site we swiftly settled into a rhythm. There we registered 800 children and continued feeding and teaching them the Word of God. An existing house on the property was the place in which we kept our cooking utensils, firewood, and a small stock of food. Daily God seemed to be working to ensure that the children were cared for and fed.

He lifts the needy

> *He raises the poor out of the dust; and lifts the needy out of the ash heap, that He may seat him with princes—with the princes of His people* (Ps. 113:7-8).

As we worked to feed and help the children of the community in whatever way we could and whenever we could, I knew I had to find people to coordinate our efforts within the city. Our experience of dealing with intense poverty during the war in Burundi helped us understand the value of working with others in the same field. We knew the possibility of having babies and children abandoned at the feeding site was high, so we sought out an organization that dealt with abandoned and orphaned children in crisis.

With the help of a neighbor I was introduced to a Christian outreach called the Crisis Nursery; this group reached out to babies and young children in crisis. This ministry seemed to be exactly the connection we needed in the event of an abandonment taking place at our site. I met with the director, who was happy to collaborate with us in any such case that might present itself at the outreach. I appreciated the dedicated staff who day and night at its facility took care of up to 20+ infants. Before I left after my meeting and visited the babies myself, I took time to read the notice board in the group's reception area. Posted there was a small sign saying that the babies needed volunteers to cuddle them. For some moments my eyes remained fixed to that sign as I pondered bringing Mandy and Steve to see the children. Both of them were older and soon would leave Africa; we wanted them to experience as much of Africa as possible. They served at the feeding site, they worked with kids in children's church, and both of them even had led cell groups. But they never visited anything such as the Crisis Nursery. I made a mental note to talk with Jamie about all of us going on the next Monday (the day after Easter 2008).

Church on Easter Sunday morning was great. We rejoiced and celebrated the resurrection of Christ. Yet my mind was not far from the Crisis Nursery. We often had talked about our family adopting a baby. The only difficulty I had in the process was how to choose a child. Africa has millions of orphans; how could just one be chosen? We knew that if He ever wanted us to adopt, the Lord simply would pick a child for us. That was our only request.

This one is yours

That Monday afternoon when we walked into the Crisis Nursery, the Holy Spirit had His hand on our visit. Mandy and Steve quickly found babies to cuddle, but Jamie simply watched, as if mesmerized by the beautiful children. (He mentioned that, if the Lord were to give us a child, he wanted a little girl.) Each child had a heartbreaking story: one was placed in a plastic bag and thrown into a pit latrine; others willingly had been surrendered by family members who were unable to care for them. Jamie sat in the middle of the sitting room, in which all the babies were lying together on the floor. Several very small ones, not more than six or seven pounds each, had desperate conditions that pulled at our hearts. Just as we were settling in and choking back rivers of tears that formed behind our eyes, one of the nurses picked up one of these painfully small babies. With a great laugh she placed the little girl on my husband's chest and announced, "This one is yours!"

Our eyes locked on this baby, whose name was Andreya. In all four of us something just "clicked". She was no more than six pounds or so, but her little spirit captivated our hearts. We learned that she ultimately was abandoned by her family. Her mother died shortly after childbirth; Andreya was placed under the care of an older family member, who tried to feed her raw goat's milk. Very quickly after her mother died, little Andreya developed pneumonia; the family caretaker brought her to a hospital, left her there, and never returned. At that point the Crisis Nursery was contacted; the child was rescued. When we visited her, she was 3-months old but weighed only six-and-a-half pounds. Besides having fought pneumonia, she also was born prematurely, we learned. While the odds had been stacked against her survival, she seemed to have hung on long enough for us to find her. We asked whether we would qualify to adopt her; the answer we received was a resounding *yes*. That evening, after we held the baby for as long as we could, we went home with forms to fill out officially to start the process of adoption.[49]

Immediately we contacted Tom and asked him what his thoughts were on our adopting a child. All Tom said was, "What has taken you so long?" Several days later we had gathered all the required documents. Before we took our little addition home, a mandatory test for HIV was performed. Imagine our heartbreak when we learned the initial test was positive. I knew this was a strong possibility, yet I had not been willing to entertain that thought. I had seen too many HIV/AIDS babies die in Burundi; I knew that should she remain positive, it was a terrible path to take.

Andreya's prognosis was tentative. The nurse at the clinic at which she was tested explained to us that, with her premature birth and the death of her mother (who obviously was positive), the chances of her remaining positive were high. Infants who are born HIV positive can, occasionally, turn negative. However, the process of their turning negative is not sure. No rhyme or reason seemed to be known why some babies stay positive and others do not. While we lived there, Chrissie, our friend in Bujumbura had adopted twins. Initially both twins tested positive for the disease. One child died shortly after Chrissie took her in, while the child's sister thrived and has grown up normally.

Several days passed as we adjusted to this possibly deadly news. *How could we cope with caring for a sick child? What about our other children?* As these and other questions whirled around and around in our minds, Mandy and Steve questioned why we simply could not take her home, pray for her, and believe God for her. Every day I found myself at the Crisis Nursery; I was unable and unwilling to remove this child from my heart and thoughts. There I surrendered to the will of God.

Homecoming

On Monday, April 15, 2008, just days after the positive test, we visited Andreya. As I held her in my arms, I was unable to bear the thought of our lives without her. Lea stood next to me; her eyes betrayed her inner thoughts that mirrored mine.

In turn each of us agreed that, even if the worst happened, what was wrong with taking this child home? We knew she was the will of God for us and for our family. Had any of our other children been born sick, we would have fought the fight of faith for them. How was this different? Our baby had been handed some very bad news and needed her mother and father to fight for her. *Let's go home,* we said, *and believe God for a miracle.* With that, joy filled our home and hearts. At full-throttle Mandy and Steve followed our enthusiasm; Tom told us, "Just believe God!" We went and purchased a crib, diapers, formula, and bottles. On April 16, 2008, Andreya went home with us.

I shall not die, but live

> *The voice of rejoicing and salvation is in the tents of the righteous; the right hand of the Lord does valiantly. The right hand of the Lord is exalted; the right hand of the Lord does valiantly. I shall not die, but live, and declare the works of the Lord* (Ps. 118:15-17).

Little D, as we began to call her, was painfully small, but she quickly began to thrive. After going home with us, she did not develop any of the characteristic infections that HIV babies acquire. Commonly infected infants (even when given therapeutic doses of antibiotics to prevent infection[50]) suffer with chronic ear infections, upper-respiratory infections, and chronic diarrhea, just to name a few maladies. We knew the only way to overcome was through the fight of faith. During a short trip Stateside for Mandy's high-school graduation[51], the elders of TCI anointed Andreya with oil and prayed the prayer of faith[52].

Our great friends and long-time supporters, Pastor Dale and Jean Gentry, also were visiting TCI at the same time we were. Pastor Dale moves strongly in the prophetic and on many occasions has prophesied over us and the work in Africa. His words always have proved to be right on the mark, so when he laid hands on Little D, we made sure carefully to listen to each word. He prophesied that, when she grew up, she one day would work with children in her home country—and we all said *yes* and *amen!* She would live and not die! All we had to trust in was God and His faithfulness. We drew great comfort in knowing that God fulfills His Word.

For some reason God gave this unexpected assignment to us. On many days we questioned whether we had what was required to face up to the challenge of believing God for Andreya's healing. Yet in our hearts we felt an almost tangible peace—even in the face of such a challenge as a potential HIV infection.

Three months passed; the time arrived to take Andreya for another HIV test. Despite local physicians' attempts to keep our hopes at bay, perhaps out of a need to help us brace for the worst, D's second test came back to us negative. The nurse simply said, "Your baby's status has changed to negative." While this type of test[53] (the same type of test as the first) was not conclusive, it was a turn in the right direction.

Armed with this good news I bolted straight to the doctor's office and almost dared him to quench our joy. "Mrs. Peters," he said, "I know of a test called a PCR test that would be conclusive, but I do not think such a test is available here in Malawi. Perhaps you could inquire at the U.N. medical headquarters near the hospital in town." Twenty-four hours did not pass before I found myself walking into the building. The people there confirmed that yes, they do PCR tests for HIV, but one must follow a certain procedure; I had not followed it. A familiar-looking woman walked by; she began to talk with me. Her children attended the same school as Steve did; she was one of the higher-ranking officials over the lab. She agreed to test Andreya's blood; in five days the results would return to us.

If we have ever prayed, those five days were filled with prayer. While emotionally at times we had trouble remaining focused, we continued to experience an indescribable peace. We knew God had everything under control.

One morning five days later, while we were out running errands, my cell phone rang. "Hello?" I said in as normal a voice as possible.

"Lea? I just wanted to give you the good news that Andreya's test is negative. No virus has been detected in her system. Congratulations!" I do not recall exactly what we all said that day in the car. We laughed and cried and wanted to shout, "LOOK what the Lord has done!"

That afternoon as we gazed at our little girl in the car seat, we all knew we had not moved to Malawi just to plant a church. Someone had been waiting for us to arrive . . . someone had been waiting for us to be obedient . . . for us to be there at the time in which she would need us. Her life showed us how much God cares for the needs of a single soul.

Chapter 18

Unfinished Altars

"Before we can pray, 'Thy Kingdom come', we must be willing to pray, 'My kingdom go.'"

–Alan Redpath

Building altars

" . . . build my altar wherever I cause my name to be remembered, and I will come to you and bless you" (Ex. 20:24b NLT).

When the will of God is concerned, we find no room for negotiation; we either will obey Him or not. We also have no luxury of choosing whether we agree with the way He leads us. The altars (places we serve as living sacrifices to God[54]) are the places in which we give our service and ourselves to Him. At certain altars we have served longer than at others. Some have called for greater sacrifices. Wherever we have been—whatever the altar or sacrifice—we have experienced the blessing of God. We know we can follow no other road except the one that leads us to the next altar.

Life and death

 In the latter part of 2007 and into 2008 the church in Lilongwe grew as we once again worked the ground to see a great spiritual harvest in the lives of our church members. Cell groups were growing; the feeding site (Hope Center) had become a well-established outreach in the area.

Our other churches in Africa were expanding as well. The Bujumbura church began making plans to start another church in Burundi's second largest city, Gitega. This new church plant was particularly exciting for us. Pastor Dale Gentry, praying for us at a missions conference in 2007, challenged us with a prophetic word that 1,000 churches were "not enough", the vision was not "big enough", and we needed to believe God for more. So we looked at each other and said, "Amen, so be it." One thousand churches plus, we're ready!

However, life changed dramatically for us when, in the middle of the busy-ness of life, Lea's mother (Kaisa) passed away in September 2008. For some months Kaisa's health had been tenuous, but she felt well enough to take a trip in August 2008 to Finland to see family and to attend a school reunion. On her return her health declined to the point of hospitalization. While we had been calling Lea's mother regularly, we relied on Tom to give us updates on her health as she, even to the end, did not want to worry anyone. Initially she seemed to be rallying, but as things turned out, she went on to the Lord's presence. This was our children's first experience with the death of a close loved one; it made our separation from Tom especially emotional.

We had witnessed the people of our churches deal with grief. While Africans do not grieve in the same way as Americans do, in some ways they have a better understanding of death than those of us from the West. From childhood they know a spiritual realm exists. When a loved one passes on to the presence of the Lord, they know that their parting is only a temporary one. Not only do Africans have a grasp on life after death, they also have a deep respect for those who are mourning and will spend hours and sometimes days just sitting with loved ones who are grieving.

Lea began preparations to fly to Florida for the memorial service. She planned to take Mandy and little Andreya with her. The morning they were set to leave, more than 20 church members visited our house and spent time singing and encouraging our family. No sound is as beautiful as that of African voices lifting praise to God. That morning without much fanfare the church members expressed how much they loved us, accepted us as they mourned with us as one of their own, and felt for us in the time of our sorrow. This gesture moved us deeply; we understood that this tragedy demonstrated our success at breaking down the cultural barrier and becoming one with our congregation. Lea's mother loved Africa; I could picture her singing as she had on this earth when she was young and now dancing, healthy and strong, in heaven to the beat of an African drum.

Co-workers!

In 2009 a new missionary couple, Scott and Jeannine Serra, and their children joined us in Lilongwe and began the process of entering into African culture. Their enthusiasm for the field was contagious; we breathed a sigh of relief as their presence greatly refreshed us. Slowly, a momentum was building, members were added to the team, and the congregation in Malawi was growing. We knew that, from the little church that began on our back porch, a great work was in the process of being established.

Mandy

 After she graduated from high school, Mandy remained in Lilongwe for another year. She worked as a cell leader, helped in the church office, and served at the feeding center. While her cell group continued to grow, she knew the time was arriving in which she would prepare her cell members for her imminent departure to the U.S. to further her education.

On the home front Mandy was a great office worker and an even greater babysitter. Naturally, she and little Andreya grew very close. When Andreya began to talk, she called Mandy her "sissy" and followed her around as though she was her shadow. We were blessed to have enjoyed the extra year we had with her before she was to set off for the "foreign soil" of the U.S. and begin the process of furthering her education and becoming an adult. In those days I often looked at Mandy and realized she was beginning to be drawn Stateside. This was inevitable—our baby girl had grown up; the day of separation from us was swiftly approaching. From time to time Lea and I would glance at one another and understand that our days with her were short. I had no answer for my wife's tears or my own—only the grace of God could sustain us.

All too quickly the day of departure arrived for us to make our way back to the U.S. to face the inevitable task of leaving our daughter there to begin her college higher education. The Lilongwe church, especially the girls of her cell group, had grown to love our exuberant daughter. For many years Mandy's reputation for enjoying life had been a well-established fact. When she was just in kindergarten, one day Lea asked her teacher how Mandy was doing in school. The teacher laughed and said, "On three separate occasions, I found Mandy today with her feet in the air and her head on the floor—it is the joy of living!"

Once Mandy said her tearful goodbyes to the church in Lilongwe, in May 2009 our family boarded a plane bound for the States. This trip was going to be full of activity. Stephen, who was attending a Christian school we had found in Lilongwe, had his bags full of work to keep him busy throughout our stay Stateside. He lamented that while others would be enjoying the journey, he would be "stuck in school!" I told him that soon enough his time would arrive; he was not to grow up quite yet.

The first order of business after we arrived was to attend Tom's graduation from Trinity International University on May 9, 2009. We doubt that the decidedly American crowd was prepared for the African shout when Tom's name was called to receive his diploma. This was one of the crowning moments of not only his but our lives as well—our son graduated with a bachelor's degree!

After the graduation we spent time helping Mandy buy a car, find a job, enroll at the local community college, and learn how to manage her bank account. In June and July we spent time visiting churches as well as taking a week to vacation with our children on the West Coast as we drove from San Diego, CA, all the way to Lynden, WA, to visit with my sister, Maria, and her family. The week we had together was the first vacation our family had taken in years and was the first time all of us, together with Andreya, had time off in each other's company.

In the airplane on our way back to Florida from Washington, I watched the "kids" interact and joke with one another. Tom, his whole life ahead of him, turned into a great preacher in his own right. Mandy, our little miracle baby whose life, halfway through my pregnancy with her, was in question, was beginning her life as an adult. Steve, though still with us for another couple of years, found his almost-adult rhythm and was not far behind the first two in reaching adulthood. As I held Andreya, I understood God's love for me all the more. As the older ones were leaving the nest, He had given Jamie and me someone to love and bring us comfort.

Living in Africa never has seemed difficult to us. We have loved living the overseas life God has given to us. But the prospect of our children living continents away from us has been a daunting one. Leaving kids behind while we returned to Africa is our first taste of ultimate sacrifice. The pain of war, difficulties of embargos, and the learning of new languages pale in comparison to the ache we felt when we left our children in the U.S.

Mandy found her first job and was becoming increasingly confident in driving on her own and relating to her friends at church. After we were scheduled to head back home, school was to start shortly. Things were falling into place for her; we began making preparations to return. Somehow filling suitcases and buying supplies for our return trip did not seem as exciting as usual. At this time Tom had been living in the U.S. for a little more than five years; we still were learning to live without him in the house. *How were we to adjust to both of them being away?*

As usual we did not have family take us to the airport; before our actual departure we said our goodbyes. Our flight was set to leave from Miami on a Tuesday afternoon, so we decided to say our goodbyes on Monday evening at Jamie's parents' home. I had avoided this moment and hoped it never would arrive, but it did and was right there staring us in the face.

All of us, having learned from the painful experience of leaving Tom behind, did our best to hold ourselves together for as long as we could. But after the prayers were voiced and we began to say our goodbyes, no longer could we hold the emotions back. I watched my husband dissolve into tears. His broad shoulders shook as he hugged Mandy in an embrace that I knew he wished would never end. Then Stephen took his turn with his sister. They were very close; he was going to miss all the things she did to annoy him. I mused, momentarily, that for a couple of more years at least I had Steve. Sometimes we joked with him and told him he was not allowed to grow up, but we knew that even Steve someday (soon) would take the same steps as his two older siblings had. I watched him hugging Mandy and marveled that he had grown as tall as his father. Before our eyes the little boy was turning into a man! Tears were running down his 16-year-old face as he told Mandy he would miss her. In that moment I decided to take in each day we had together as a family and enjoy it to its fullest before he left! Little Andreya was not really sure of what was going on, so she simply held on to her big sister as she said goodbye. How I wished this was not happening!

I purposely waited to be the last one to say goodbye, as if hoping that delaying the moment would make it go away. Finally facing my oldest daughter I marveled at how she was so grown and so beautiful. Her whole life was before her; we would miss so much of it! My words were inadequate: *I love you, I will miss you, I am proud of you.* Then I just held on tight and prayed that God would watch over my baby.

The rest of the family had gone on to hug Tom. Saying goodbye to him never has gotten easier, but at this moment, I drew comfort from the fact that he was there for Mandy to help her adjust to her new life. Looking into my firstborn's eyes I said, "Watch your sister."

"I will, Mom," he assured. He and I held each other close. We understood that the will of God was calling and that we could do nothing but obey.

We drove away from the house that evening and prayed, "Your Kingdom come, Your will be done." Once again we found that somehow, His grace was sufficient as we left the United States to return to Malawi, at which we left an unfinished altar.

(left) Pastor Richard,
Nadine Tumbu and
Baby Miracle, leading
TCI in Zambia

(right) The van after
the accident
on our way to
Lilongwe, Malawi,
November 2006

TCI church meeting first
on our back porch
2006/07 (above) and
later meeting in a rented
warehouse 2010 (right)

(left) Andreya comes home, April 2008.

(right) Andreya's adoption day, December 2009

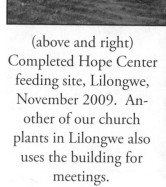

(above and right) Completed Hope Center feeding site, Lilongwe, November 2009. Another of our church plants in Lilongwe also uses the building for meetings.

(above and right)
Feeding 800 children Monday through Friday. The youngest ones often are brought to the feeding site by their older siblings.

TCI, Gatumba, Burundi (above) and TCI, Bujumbura Burundi (right) completed and dedicated 2008!

Our family, 2009

Epilogue

You crown the year with Your goodness, and Your paths drip with abundance. They drop on the pastures of the wilderness, and the little hills rejoice on every side. The pastures are clothed with flocks; the valleys also are covered with grain; they shout for joy, they also sing (Ps. 65:11).

S o many things hinge on our obedience to God. The paths down which He leads us are not always straightforward or well-lit, but He always is there to hold us and, step by step, to guide us. When we live this way, we can be sure of His provision in the *pastures* (our place of rest), on the *hills* (our times of victory), and in the *valleys* (where we meet with trial). Such faith is contrary to human nature and reason, but we no longer are meant to live by our own reasoning. We are strangers only passing through on our way to a city whose Builder and Maker[55] is God. Those who live this way and walk down the unchartered territory of God's will understand that their life is not the sum of eternity. We are on a journey; as we go, we are looking for what really is valuable—the souls of men and women.

Since Tom left in 2003 and Mandy left in 2009 to begin their lives in the U.S., our family has begun to adjust to their absences. Andreya's Malawian adoption was finalized in December 2009 (we presently are working on her U.S. citizenship); Steve suddenly has become the oldest kid in the house and enjoys his status as Andreya's big brother. On the horizon we see the inevitable empty nest, so we are enjoying each day we have with Steve and Andreya at home. Truly children are a blessing and heritage from the Lord.

In the middle of our learning to live without our kids at home God has been faithful; the work has gone on at an almost remarkable pace. Our first Hope Center (feeding-site facility) was completed in the latter part of 2009. We were honored to receive Dave and Joyce Meyer in Lilongwe, Malawi, for the dedication of the building that Joyce Meyer Ministries built. We also are working on developing another piece of land in Lilongwe to house a community center, feeding center, school, orphanage, and church. Besides these projects we also believe God will fund the construction of similar community centers in other nations of Africa. TCI Africa churches also are expanding and growing. This year (2010) we have planted another church in Lilongwe; our other main churches will plant at least one more church in their nation. This will give us 10 churches on the continent. For the first time we will have broken into the double digits —1,000+ churches, we're on our way.

How can we possibly fund such projects? We do not know. But one thing we do know is this: when in 1992 we planted the first one, we did not know how to plant even one church; now we have seven. How did we get here? We really are not sure except by the grace of God. Our missions director and dear friend, Pastor David Briggs, often has asked us this question: "How do you eat an elephant? . . . One bite at a time." We will plant more churches, build more centers, feed more children, and bring the gospel to the lost, because that is what this life is all about. It is not all about us—but it is all about Him.

> . . . *for in Him we live and move and have our being* . . .
> (Acts 17:28a).

Notes

[1] Some estimates have the death toll as high as 400,000.

[2] Eldredge, John, *Wild at Heart*, Nelson Books, 2001, 197

[3] Eldredge, John, *Wild at Heart*, Nelson Books, 2001, 200

[4] A grocery store chain found in South Florida

[5] *Simplified Swahili* by P.M. Wilson

[6] Water filters known as *katadyn* filters do not require water to be boiled; they are, by far, superior to these traditional water filters but are far more expensive!

[7] Coffee

[8] Sometimes we were fortunate enough to find sugar from Malawi which would, 20 years later, be the place in which God would call us to plant a church.

[9] Pentecostal Assemblies of Canada

[10] Babysitter or nanny

[11] Carmichael, Amy, *Whispers of His Power*, Fleming H. Revell Company, 1982, 99

[12] 1 Timothy 6:12

[13] Cell phones and Internet in 1987 were not available in Zaire (DRC) but in recent times have become available.

[14] Shibley, David, *Heaven's Heroes*, New Leaf Press, 1994, 33

[15] We also had mail delivered to us via a post box the Hagemeiers maintained in Nairobi, Kenya. The Kenya mail was delivered whenever someone passed through Nairobi and was able to pick up the post.

[16] Swahili for *Europeans* or *white people*

[17] Swahili for *entrails*

[18] In Zaire gauging what new regulations the officials would set from day to day was impossible. Living there was a real walk of faith, because new regulations at the spur of the moment apparently could be made up.

[19] 1 Corinthians 12:7-11

[20] An old Ford truck that was in a poor state of repair was there; most of the time it was unusable.

[21] The approximate distance by road between Kalemie and Bukavu is 450 km or 281 miles. Because the roads are nearly unnavigable, traveling between the two cities by road takes days instead of hours.

[22] The hospital was run by American missionaries and, as such, would celebrate the American holiday of Thanksgiving.

[23] The fight of faith is the only fight that the Scriptures call *good*: 1 Timothy 6:12 *Fight the good fight of faith, lay hold on eternal life, to which you were also called and have confessed the good confession in the presence of many witnesses.*

[24] Psalm 118:17

[25] Carl Johnson since has passed away to his eternal reward.

[26] Those first few weeks we were in Bujumbura, Lea's system of hand-washing the clothes she used in Bukavu became very handy.

[27] NGO—Non-Government Organization

[28] At that time approximately $20 USD

[29] Zaire—now the Democratic Republic of the Congo, or DRC

[30] The Zaireans (now Congolese) are some of the most hospitable people we ever have had the honor of serving.

[31] Zaire—now the Democratic Republic of the Congo, or, the DRC

[32] Missionaries serving with the Hagemeiers at that time once were held in their home at gunpoint; only by God's grace and protection were they not killed. When such violence hits, those holding the weapons seem to be possessed by an unexplainable need to kill and pillage.

[33] As of this writing 5,400,000 deaths have occurred in the Democratic Republic of Congo (formerly Zaire). Every month 45,000 deaths occur that are either directly or indirectly related to the civil unrest and war that has gripped the region (International Rescue Committee *www.theirc.org*). The conflict in the DRC, swiftly approaching the death toll of the Holocaust in World War II, goes largely unreported in the world media. It is Africa's forgotten, ongoing war.

[34] We had purchased these radios in the event that telephones were cut off, as they were during the initial coup attempt in 1993.

[35] Shibley, David, *Heaven's Heroes*, New Leaf Press, 1994, 31

[36] Zachary, Rick, *The Master of Relationships*, Keepsafe, Inc., 78

[37] Ibid., 7

[38] Sometimes we use the simple word *Dar* to refer to Dar es Salaam.

[39] The couch worked just fine and looked better once the cushions were covered and the broken parts were glued together.

[40] For a little more than a year the Wells served us faithfully. They were wonderful assets to the work; we appreciate them so very much!

[41] Audrey returned to the US shortly after our move to Zambia. She was a great help in our initiation of the work in Lusaka. Thank you, Audrey!

[42] While we have since left Tanzania, we all believe TCI is only gone for a season. There will come a day when TCI will return, somehow, to the country, and we will see the church born.

[43] As of this writing the church has grown to 4,000.

[44] Philippians 1:12

[45] The Principle of 12 is a disciple-making strategy that utilizes cells.

[46] *The Evidence Bible*, 1471

[47] *http://ipsnews.net/news.asp?idnews=50665*

[48] *http://www.un.org/ecosocdev/geninfo/afrec/vol15no3/153chil5.htm*

[49] Malawian law requires any adoptive parents to foster the child for a minimum of 18 months in the country before the adoption can become final.

[50] Andreya had been prescribed low-dose antibiotics to take daily to help prevent infection.

[51] While she finished her high school in Malawi, TCI's academy in Florida allowed Mandy to participate in its graduation ceremony the year she finished school.

[52] James 5:14-15

[53] With this type of test, when a result is negative after a previous positive result already has occurred, the usual course is to take two more tests to confirm the negative result.

[54] Romans 12:1

[55] Hebrews 11:10

To contact the Peters family
or to order additional copies of this book,
visit http://web.me.com/tciafrica/tciafrica